D0906628

A PSALM IN MY HEART

A PSALM IN MY HEART

Brownlow Publishing Company,
6309 Airport Freeway,
Fort Worth, TX 76117

Printed in the United States of America.

Gift Edition: ISBN 0-915720-32-9
Trade Edition: ISBN 0-915720-33-7
Leather Edition: ISBN 0-915720-34-5

10 9 8 7 6 5 4 3 2 1

This Book Belongs To:

19

A Psalm in My Heart

Daily Devotionals from the Book of Psalms

LEROY BROWNLOW

Brownlow Publishing Company, Inc.

Other Brownlow Gift Books

A Father's World
A Few Hallelujahs for Your Ho-Hums
As a Man Thinketh
Better Than Medicine—A Merry Heart
Children Won't Wait
Flowers for Mother
Flowers for You
Flowers of Friendship
Flowers That Never Fade
For All My Special Days
For Mom With Love
Give Us This Day
Grandpa Was a Preacher
Great Verses of the Bible
It's a One-derful Life!
Jesus Wept
Just Between Friends
Leaves of Gold
Living On the Plus Side
Making the Most of Life
The Fruit of the Spirit
The Greatest Thing in the World
The Other Wise Man—A Christmas Classic
Thoughts of Gold—Wisdom for Living
Today and Forever
Today Is Mine
University of Hard Knocks

Foreword

A Psalm in My Heart is a day-to-day guide containing 365 original essays — devotionals — based on Psalms, which is the world's most popular book.

The Psalms continue to live and grip the attention of needy humanity. Fads blossom and wilt, generations come and go, civilizations rise and fall, but the Psalms continue to survive the ages. No other book has been so fondly read and so freely commented on. The inescapable conclusion is — it has something helpful for man in every circumstance of life.

Psalms is a stupendous and marvelous book, enormous in teaching, amazing in faith, astonishing in trust and astounding in relevancy. It is something! It covers the whole scope of living: everything that accompanies the farflung and eventful life of man. Its extensive, up-to-date thoughts testify that man has ever had to face the same problems. How little man changes through the ages! And as we read them, we realize that — with slight variations of circumstances — the author could be speaking of us this very hour.

The Psalms are our common heritage, filling common needs. They contain guidance for the errant, power for the weak, courage for the trembling, rest for the weary, cheer for the despondent, hope for the faint-hearted and comfort for the afflicted. By lifting high the rulership and interposition of God to aid man, they encourage him to live a victorious life, marked with optimism and jubilation. "For all's well that ends well."

FOREWORD

In this volume, *A Psalm in My Heart,* at least one devotional is based in numerical order on everyone of the 150 Psalms — no Psalm is omitted. To have one for each day (365), we took more than one from some of them.

It was the aim of the author to give each topic and text a relevant treatment and a suggestive application to assist man in gaining instruction, inspiration and power for a wiser, fuller and nobler life. Additional thoughts could have been given, but for the sake of brevity each treatise was limited to one page.

This volume is by no means a book to be read at a sitting. Its nourishment and stimulation are too concentrated for such reading. It can be used to greatest profit a little at a time. It is what it was meant to be — a daily meditation. However, in addition to the daily thought, a person can read and think on the particular devotional best adapted to his particular mood and circumstance that calls for help.

Believing in the power of daily meditation, convinced that men's thoughts constitute the army that conquers the world, we present this volume from the voice of yesterday with the hope that it will be a helpful voice today and the herald of tomorrow.

LEROY BROWNLOW

Blessed is the man that walketh not in the counsel of the ungodly, nor standeth in the way of sinners, nor sitteth in the seat of the scornful. But his delight is in the law of the Lord; and in his law doth he meditate day and night. —1:1,2

We Are Blessed

IN A PREFACE TO THE ENTIRE BOOK of Psalms, David appropriately begins by describing the blessed or happy man. Happiness is largely due to our own making. For there are conditions to meet, both negative and positive.

Negatively: The person described as blessed refuses to be guided by the counsels of the ungodly. This is vital, for we cannot become better than the principles or plans by which we walk.

He does not stand in the way of or closely associate himself with confirmed sinners. Neither does he sit with scorners: jokers of good, mockers of morals and ridiculers of religion. We must be careful of those with whom we sit. In choosing our friends we go a long way in choosing our future faith, conduct and destiny.

Positively: His delight, pleasure or happiness is in the Lord's law. His heart, out of tune with the world, is in tune with Divinity.

For us to be blessed, the Written Word must be precious to us, so highly esteemed that we read it and meditate on it. In our homes it is no dust-catcher, but a practical, usable Book. Through usage it becomes a faith-builder and hope-maker. It is the source of life, and those who feed on its pages live.

Why do the heathen rage, and the people imagine a vain thing? The kings of the earth set themselves, and the rulers take counsel together, against the Lord, and against his Anointed, saying, Let us break their bands asunder, and cast away their cords from us. —2:1-3

The Futility of Opposing God

THE WICKED OF THE WORLD have always felt that God's rules were too restrictive, too confining, too narrow for truly intelligent people. As they chafed in their ill-fated desire for uninhibited living, they cried, "Let us break God's cords from us!" No cords. No bands. No controls. What a deplorable and calamitous but accurate picture of so many.

However, their evil imaginations are vain. They imagine they will be really happy without God, that they will be in a world of peace and love with no one to spoil their fun. But they are left defeated and crushed. Not only have they broken God's rules, they have broken their lives and shattered their dreams by their own stubbornness and refusal to acknowledge God as God.

How silly for us to think we can win in opposing God. God's rule cannot be overthrown. Every attack against Him rebounds against the attacker. Against Him, we face defeat. With Him, we are sure winners.

He always wins who sides with God,
To him no chance is lost;
God's will is sweetest to him when
It triumphs at his cost.

—FREDERICK WILLIAM FABER

Lord, how are they increased that trouble me! many are they that rise up against me. Many there be which say of my soul, There is no help for him in God. Selah. But thou, O Lord, art a shield for me; my glory, and the lifter up of mine head. I cried unto the Lord with my voice, and he heard me out of his holy hill.—3:1-4

Peril and Prayer

HERE IS THE PERIL, STRUGGLE, PRAYER and victory of God's beloved David. It gives the experience of the *him* and the *then*—and hope to the *us* and the *now*. For we are all brothers in trial, the difference being only in time and degrees.

David's own son Absalom led a revolt against him. Trouble in the family. Trouble in the kingdom. When our family does not stand with us, it multiplies our hardships.

The scoffers got busy. They always do. They said, "There is no help for him in God." A common joy of sinners is to taunt the people of God in their trials with the ridicule that they are God-forsaken.

But David never lost faith. In the face of peril, he turned to prayer: "I cried unto the Lord with my voice." His enemies used their voice to defy God. But David used his to praise God. What a difference! And enough to always make a difference. For God heard him. He won. They lost.

As a result, David could sleep. While prayer is stimulative and therapeutic, its greatest power is in the answer that God grants it.

Hear me when I call, O God of my righteousness: thou hast enlarged me when I was in distress; have mercy upon me, and hear my prayer. O ye sons of men, how long will ye turn my glory into shame? how long will ye love vanity, and seek after leasing? Selah. But know that the Lord hath set apart him that is godly for himself: the Lord will hear when I call unto him. —4:1-3

When in Distress

"HEAR ME WHEN I CALL, O GOD," was the constant plea of David. "Have mercy," he begged—not justice; for justice would doom him and all of us.

"I was in distress," he acknowledged. Actually, this is the plight of the whole race, and fortunate are those who know it.

In his anguish, caused by humanity, David found consolation in Divinity, in two assuring thoughts: First, God sets apart for Himself the godly. This means to be made holy, committed by loving obedience to God. Second, God answers prayer. How strengthening: hope to lift our sinking hearts and faith to energize our lagging steps.

Let us, therefore, bravely face the world's blows, for we can bear them. David could. We can. With God's help, no tribulation can overwhelm us. As David concluded, let us stand in awe of God, stick with Him, sin not, be still, sacrifice and trust Him forever.

This thought shall cheer me:
That thou art near me,
Whose ear to hear me,
Is still inclined.

There be many that say, Who will show us any good? Lord, lift thou up the light of thy countenance upon us. Thou hast put gladness in my heart, more than in the time that their corn and their wine increased. I will both lay me down in peace and sleep: for thou, Lord, only makest me dwell in safety.—4:6-8

Who Will Give Us Good?

AMONG DAVID'S SUPPORTERS there were pessimists. Nothing new. They have always been numerous and vocal. In this instance, they asked, "Who will show us any good?" In these hard times who will give us good? Who will give us satisfaction? Who will give us peace? The pessimists could not see any source of good; they saw only the visible aspects of life.

For a true answer, however, David looked beyond the gloomy circumstances and prayerfully appealed to the source of all good, saying: "Lord, lift thou the light of thy countenance upon us." Somewhere there must be an answer to man's cry in the night for light, peace and rest. David knew that the somewhere is with God.

In contrast with worldly views, the psalmist knew that the fulfillment of man's greatest needs is not in materialism, and in our case: clothes and cars, boats and businesses. It is in devotion to the Lord, in seeing the invisible with the eye of faith and doing the impossible with the power of God. All other answers are no answers—only vain echoes in empty hearts.

If I him but have,
Glad I fall asleep;
Aye the peace His heart gave
My poor heart I shall keep.

—ADAPTED, GEORGE MACDONALD

Give ear to my words, O Lord.—5:1

A Plan for Living

THE FIFTH PSALM CONTAINS AN EXCELLENT PLAN FOR LIVING:

Meditation: "Consider my meditation" (verse 1). One of the grievous errors of this age is our fast pace which leaves no time to think and meditate. Meditating on the majesty of God will make a difference in our lives.

Morning prayer: "In the morning will I direct my prayer unto thee (verse 3). A good way to start the day. God's help is needed every day, all day.

Acceptance of mercy: "I will come into thy house in the multitude of thy mercy" (verse 7). We are imperfect. Mercy is needed. And if we accept God's mercy which forgives us, then we should forgive ourselves and put our mistakes behind us.

Worship: "And in thy fear will I worship" (verse 7). Approach God with reverential fear. He is God. We are human. Never try to humanize Him. Keep the distinction. Let God be God. Worship Him. The need is as old as man.

A straight way: "Make thy way straight before my face" (verse 8)—not smooth, not easy. Just let the way be Thine and show me clearly.

Rejoice: "But let all those that put their trust in thee rejoice" (verse 11). Our days should be lived joyfully—not in serving a rigorous sentence. And where does it come from? From trusting the One who created us for joyful living. This puts *A Psalm in My Heart.*

Destroy thou them, O God; let them fall by their own counsels; cast them out in the multitude of their transgressions; for they have rebelled against thee.—5:10

Self-destruction

SOME PEOPLE RISE, OTHERS FALL. And a determining factor is counsel. In wise counsel there is success, but in foolish counsel there is failure.

The ill-advised suffer bitter defeat because they do not "with good advice make war" (Proverbs 20:18). Poor counsel! Multitudes land at the wrong place when misdirected. Legions see their houses collapse because they listen to the grasshopper philosophy that says it is too strenuous to dig deep enough to build on the rock.

Rejoicing in humanism, glorying in defiance of righteousness, the wicked miss the good life. It is their own doing, or rather their own undoing. They fall for they have no internal strength.

God does not help the rebellious in their sins. The transgressors are doomed to perish. It is God's appointment that they be destroyed by their own devices. And on they go to their self-made woes. It is as Isaiah recorded:

> *Woe to the rebellious children, saith the Lord,*
> *that take counsel, but not of me.*
> —ISAIAH 30:1

They get lots of advice, but from the wrong ones. It's a case of human destruction, resulting from human misdirection.

O Lord, rebuke me not in thine anger, neither chasten me in thy hot displeasure. Have mercy upon me, O Lord; for I am weak: O Lord, heal me; for my bones are vexed. My soul is also sore vexed: but thou, O Lord, how long?
—6:1-3

O Lord, How Long?

HERE IS A MAN WHO WAS BEING TESTED to the limit. He was exhausted. Vexed in body and soul, could he survive?

He was conscious of some grievous sin in his life; and though he deserved rebuke, he asked that the chastisement be applied in love rather than anger.

His health failed him. "My bones are vexed." Additionally, his soul was vexed. The mental suffering was more agonizing than the physical. It always is.

In his affliction he had groaned until he was weary. He had cried and cried. "All the night make I my bed to swim; I water my couch with my tears" (verse 7).

As his enemies continued to torment him, he asked, "O Lord, how long?" How long can I endure? How long can I suffer? How long must I wait for relief? In the depths of despair, this has ever been the question on the lips of man—how long?

The writer was conscious of his weakness—"I am weak"—but this was the beginning of strength. The weakest are those who are not aware of it and never seek help. Though he was weak, he was strong enough to pray. His supplication was heard and that sufficed. There was strength enough in God, but not in himself alone. This is our lesson, and blessed are we if we learn it.

O Lord my God, if I have done this; if there be iniquity in my hands.—7:3

Hurt by Rumor

THE SEVENTH PSALM APPARENTLY was written during the earlier part of David's public life. As is true of all public men, he had persecutors. And King Saul, encouraged by the detractors, sought his life. But David returned good for evil and spared the king (I Samuel 26:1-25).

In referring to the charges against him, David said, "If I have done this." Done what? If I "sought the king's hurt" (I Samuel 24:9). "If there be iniquity in my hands" (verse 3). "If I have rewarded evil unto him that was at peace with me" (verse 4).

The charges were false. In his denial, David stated that if he were guilty, he would be willing to pay the penalty: "Let the enemy persecute my soul…tread down my life…lay mine honor in the dust" (verse 5).

Now, in his innocence, David lays his burden on God and makes a fivefold petition, verses 1-9.

- Save me.
- Arise, O Lord, do something.
- Judge me, vindicate me.
- End their wickedness.
- Establish the just.

Have you ever been falsely accused? Take heart and find comfort in God's hands. God is able to defend, vindicate and establish you.

God judgeth the righteous, and God is angry with the wicked every day. If he turn not, he will whet his sword; he hath bent his bow, and made it ready. He hath also prepared for him the instruments of death; he ordaineth his arrows against the persecutors.—7:11-13

If We Turn Not From Evil

GOD, IN A JUST JUDGMENT, will vindicate the righteous. When they are assailed by their enemies, He will interpose to lift them up.

Concerning the wicked—God is angry with them every day. His love for righteousness necessitates strong feelings against wickedness and consistency requires Him to feel the same way every day. Being God, His feelings do not vary as the sentiments of fickle, temperamental humans. If sin is wrong today, it is wrong tomorrow; and, accordingly, God's view of it remains constant.

If justice requires God to bless the righteous, it also compels Him to punish the wicked. The whole world recognizes the equity of this principle; and by following it civilization is maintained.

However, God tempers justice with a mercy that civil magistrates do not follow (they cannot look into the heart); and thus Divine execution of punishment is against only him who refuses to repent—"if he turn not." All who turn may escape. Mercy like this is found nowhere else—only in God. But if the sinner doesn't turn, justice prescribes punishment. The decision is his. No person can repent too soon because he doesn't know how soon it may be too late.

He made a pit and digged it, and is fallen into the ditch which he made. His mischief shall return upon his own head, and his violent dealing shall come down upon his own pate.

—7:15,16

Trapped in One's Own Pit

DOING MISCHIEF TO HURT ANOTHER returns to harm the mischief-maker. The pit he digs to entrap another becomes his own pitfall.

In hunting wild beasts during ancient times, a pit would be dug and covered over with brush and leaves. As unsuspecting animals were driven over it they would fall through and be trapped.

The lesson is that the person who lays a deceptive plan for the destruction of others will be ensnared by his own devices. Such retribution is not uncommon among the crafty who are caught in the consequences of their own devilment. They become entangled in the recoils of their own cunning. They are trapped in self-dug pits. They are caught in self-made nets.

History is replete with examples. Many a Haman has been hanged on the gallows he prepared for another (Esther 7:10). Many a Judas has sold himself with his own kiss.

With what measure ye mete,
it shall be measured to you again.
—MATTHEW 7:2

We can never overestimate the danger of a crooked and mischievous policy. Neither can we overvalue the worth of an open and straightforward course in dealing with others—both friends and foes.

What is man, that thou art mindful of him? and the son of man, that thou visitest him? For thou has made him a little lower than the angels, and hast crowned him with glory and honor.—8:4,5

What Is Man?

THE GOD WHO CREATED THE HEAVENS, the vastness and complexity of the celestial bodies, was mindful of man and visited him with a position and destiny just a little lower than the angels, crowning him with glory and honor.

That such a powerful God would regard man so highly should inspire us to praise and thank our Creator. Though we are made of clay, we bear the image of our Maker.

Endowed with the capacities that distinguish man from all other creatures, he was made to rule. We have been given dominion over the works of our Designer's hands. All things were put under our feet. Our nature gives us the advantage over the lower creatures who tend no flocks, sow no harvests, plant no forests, build no hospitals and entertain no hope of immortality. Man is really something! Too bad we sometimes drop beneath our greatness.

That God is mindful of us is perhaps the most moving and inspiring thought ever to pass through the mind of man. It will not let us settle for a lower existence. It should rouse in us the exclamation, "O Lord our Lord, how excellent is thy name in all the earth!"

I will praise thee, O Lord, with my whole heart;
I will show forth all thy marvelous works. I will be glad and rejoice in thee: I will sing praise to thy name, O thou Most High. —9:1,2

With My Whole Heart

DAVID STATED THAT HE WOULD praise the Lord with all his heart. This is essential. God will not accept a divided service.

A half a heart never finds him—

And ye shall seek me, and find me, when ye shall search for me with all your heart.—JEREMIAH 29:13

Laudations from a forked tongue are no praise at all—

Out of the same mouth proceedeth blessing and cursing. My brethren, these things ought not so to be. Doth a fountain send forth at the same place sweet water and bitter? Can the fig tree, my brethren, bear olive berries? either a vine figs? so can no fountain both yield salt water and fresh.—JAMES 3:10-12

A double eye (one for Him and one for the world) never sees Him—

If therefore thine eye be single, thy whole body shall be full of light. But if thine eye be evil, thy whole body shall be full of darkness.
—MATTHEW 7:22,23

So with a whole heart, a straight tongue and a single eye, let us lift up our praises to the Most High. For the First and Great Commandment is: "Thou shalt love the Lord thy God with all thy heart, and with all thy soul, and with all thy mind" (Matthew 22:37). Anything less than this is unacceptable.

Put them in fear, O Lord: that the nations may know themselves to be but men.—9:20

Only Men

WHAT A NEEDED LESSON! The poet understood this—his humanity and God's Divinity. The ninth Psalm makes plain the distinctions. While the psalmist knew and extolled the exalted place of man (8:5), he still realized that men are only men. But how often man has forgotten his true identity and deluded himself into believing in his own divinity.

We confuse right and wrong and support evil and call it "good." Our definitions of good and bad are often faulty; but in contrast, God is always right in his judgments (verse 4).

We see men and women mushroom and flourish awhile. They strut in their short-lived place in the sun and then soon perish. In time, our monuments to them crumble and our memory of them fades; but in contradistinction, God lives on forever (verses 5-7).

We are limited in abilities and resources to help the oppressed, capable of doing little more than treating symptoms; but God is an unlimited "refuge in times of trouble" (verse 9).

Because of unconcern or fickleness, we sometimes forsake those in need—even among our own family. But God is constant, never wavering in His care and concern. He forsakes not them who trust in Him (verse 10).

In our humanity we are sometimes tempted to be more attentive to the rich and powerful than to the poor and needy. We want to know and be known by the influential and glamorous. But God is different—He gives ear to the humble, the lowly, the outcast and the unglorified (verse 12).

Oh, that men may always know the distinction that *they are only men!*

Why standest thou afar off, O Lord?
why hidest thou thyself in times of trouble?—10:1

Why Doesn't God Do Something?

ONE THING ABOUT THIS LIFE—it is filled with trouble. While it comes in degrees, it comes to all.

Man is born unto trouble.—JOB 5:7

But it seems the psalmist had more than his share: envious enemies, callous calumniators and family feuds, plus the ordinary distresses we all experience.

When trouble comes, it is natural for us to ask, "Why? Why me? Why do I have to suffer? Why doesn't God come to my rescue? Why does God permit the wicked to continue in their blackguard ways? Is God going to let them get away with it? Why doesn't He lift up His hand against them? Doesn't God require anything of them? Why doesn't He break their power? Why? Why? Why?"

Such questions indicate that we are too impatient, that our ways are not God's ways. God will take care of the trouble in His own time and in His own way. Vengeance belongs to Him. Fret not. Furthermore, some suffering on the part of His children can be chastening and rewarding.

After asking *Why?* as humans do, David extols his Maker as the God who answers prayer and helps "the oppressed." And that is good enough for any of us.

The wicked, through the pride of his countenance, will not seek after God: God is not in all his thoughts.
—10:4

Portrait of the Proud

IN THIS TENTH PSALM THE WRITER PAINTS a portrait of the proud and wicked and gives us insights into their thinking. What are their assumptions, their thoughts? This is fundamental and basic. For our behavior always begins with our attitudes toward God. The wicked delude themselves into accepting one of two mistaken views of God:

1. ***That God is dead*** (verse 4). There is no God, so live for yourself, live for the pleasure of the moment. Sage after sage has attempted to bury our God, but they lie in infamous graves and God continues to walk the face of the earth in fame.

2. ***That God—if there is a God—will never know what we are doing*** (verse 11). He cannot see us. Such people are like little boys playing in the backyard. They presume their plans and schemes go unnoticed by a watchful mom or dad.

What are the results of such faulty thinking? It misdirects their conduct. David says the proud and wicked pounce upon the poor; they lie in wait as lions to murder the innocent; and brag of their evil ways. They are proud of their own supposed strength and are confident in their own resources. They think they will be happy forever, but they are set up for disappointment. See them a few years later—spectacles of forlornness.

And to think it all began with a false attitude toward God. Indeed, what we think of God determines our destiny.

In the Lord put I my trust: how say ye to my soul, Flee as a bird to your mountain? For, lo, the wicked bend their bow, they make ready their arrow upon the string, that they may privily shoot at the upright in heart. If the foundations be destroyed, what can the righteous do?

—11:1-3

A Time to Stand

WHEN DAVID WAS SUFFERING from traitorous accusations, his friends advised him to flee to the mountain. They reasoned: The enemy is after you; and if the foundations be destroyed, there is no hope left for the righteous. There are always reasons for running, but ordinarily there are better reasons for remaining. Because often—

Who flees the wolf meets with the bear.

However, there are circumstances in which it is right to take flight. But this was not the time. We should never walk away from duty or unpopularity or peril just for the sake of safety. And David didn't.

The Psalm contains the only sure answer to the question of fear—faith. The writer's faith was not in the mountain but in the Lord who made the mountain. The One higher than the mountain "is in his holy temple," reigning and ruling, declared David. Thus there was no need to fear Saul.

David believed the Lord's scrutinizing eyes give the Just Judge the knowledge to try the wicked and the righteous, to rain punishment on the wicked and bestow favor on the righteous. Such a faith kept David from running away and will keep us from running. There is a time to stand.

If the foundations be destroyed, what can the righteous do?
—11:3

If the Foundations Be Destroyed

DAVID'S FEARFUL FRIENDS WERE WRONG in suggesting that he flee, but they were right in suggesting that society must have its pillars or fall.

If the past has any lesson at all for the present, it is that we can build no stronger than our foundation. History's pages are marked with individuals and nations that tragically fell because their supports were too weak.

If the foundations of society are destroyed, humanity sinks lower and lower. When the people replace religion with irreligion, morality with immorality, justice with injustice, industry with indolence, and service to man with exploitation of man, that league of people is already declining.

Laws alone will not prop up a society. We must have more than a community of puppets on legal strings. The strongest control of the citizen is from within the heart by moral and religious principles. Almost every downfall of men and nations has been an inside job—weakness within.

David was a pillar in society, but some others were burdens. Every person belongs to one category or the other, a support or a burden. Quite a sobering thought.

The Lord trieth the righteous: but the wicked and him that loveth violence his soul hateth. Upon the wicked he shall rain snares, fire and brimstone, and a horrible tempest: this shall be the portion of their cup.—11:5,6

This Is Their Cup

WE HAVE HEARD, "THIS IS YOUR CUP," and the negative, "This is not your cup." However, only a few people are aware that the metaphor is in the Bible, found a few times in Psalms and in other places.

David's enemies had filled their cup with the bitter dregs of hate and violence. It was their making and they had to drink it. For as we brew, so must we drink.

God does not tolerate a lawless world but does respect man's volition. Man was not made to be a pushbutton mechanism but rather a self-determining creature who must make the decisions and live his life.

However, in the interest of motivating man, God reproves to improve and punishes to reward. The God of Justice permits man to brew his cup, but he must drink it.

In this particular case, the cup consisted of: ***Snares***—difficulties in which they would be entangled. ***Fire and brimstone***—God's punishment. —literally, a breath of horrors.

What can we learn for today? Our cup is good or bad to the last drop, depending on how we prepare it; and when it is made, we must drink it.

Help, Lord; for the godly man ceaseth; for the faithful fail from among the children of men. They speak vanity every one with his neighbor: with flattering lips and with a double heart do they speak.—12:1,2

Lord, Help Us

HELP! THIS IS THE CRY OF MILLIONS around the globe. We hear the anguish in divorce courts, in bankruptcy courts, in unemployment lines, in sick rooms, and around the flower-decked mounds in the silent cities of the dead.

Help! This is the cry of our distress. It is proof of our inadequacy. If we were big enough, strong enough and smart enough to solve our problems, why beg for assistance? Thus a million cries for help are audible proof of our weak humanity, that it is not within frail and ailing man to supply all his needs.

But why did David cry for help in this instance? Godly men were disappearing; the faithful were failing; and in their place, people with lying lips and double hearts were prevailing. Enough to frighten anybody!

Whatever the cause, the forlorn feeling comes to all. When it does, let's say more than, "Help!" Let's say, "Help, Lord." May we address the powerless feeling to Him who is the ablest to help, as David did; for humans can go only so far and do only so much. And now let us remember:

God helps them that help themselves.

—BENJAMIN FRANKLIN

Who have said, With our tongue will we prevail; our lips are our own: who is Lord over us?—12:4

Who Is Lord Over Us?

REBELLIOUS PEOPLE ARE REALLY STUBBORN. No one, not even God, is allowed to tell them what to believe and how to live. They are determined to be the sole masters over themselves. Mighty big talk! How brave are some people in fair weather; but, oh, how pale they turn at the clap of thunder.

The rebellious spirit is often the main cause for some people's turning to atheism. They drive themselves into infidelity by their desire to be free of any restrictions or rules. The proposition that the Lord exists implies that He is over man. This means rules for man, and rules are sure to be broken occasionally. Man's falling short of the precept may produce guilt feelings and fear; but instead of overcoming the discomfort with faith and resolution, some seek relief in no faith and no pattern. By deciding that God is a farce and the Bible is a fable, they find consolation in becoming freethinkers. Believing there are no Divine requirements to meet, they feel they can never commit any divine violations to distress them.

Playing god by deciding there is no God is a self-deception that brings self-destruction.

Blind unbelief is sure to err,
And scan his work in vain;
God is his own interpreter,
And he will make it plain.

—WILLIAM COWPER

How long wilt thou forget me, O Lord? for ever? how long wilt thou hide thy face from me?—13:1

Despondency Turns to Assurance

ONE THING SURE—DAVID WAS VERY HUMAN. His emotions sometimes varied widely between despair and hope. As we behold his depression, we sorrow with him. We have been through some of it, too. No one can stay on top of the world all the time.

David complained that God had forgotten him, but He hadn't. It just seemed that way.

Have you ever felt like God had just simply forgotten you? When was it? Was it the time you lost your job and the bills continued to pile up? They just wouldn't stop. Was it the time your marriage hit the rocks and it seemed that all hope had vanished for a Christian home? Was it the time your kids rebelled and left home? You thought you were going to die.

But remember, God really never forgot you—or any of us. Our problems blurred our vision for a time; our tears blinded us to the God who was always there. In the midst of a storm, we cannot see very far, but the unseen objects are still there. It is only our eyes that fail us, not God.

David took his questions and doubts and laid them at the feet of God and waited. How admirable. How noble. What do we do with our nagging doubts and gnawing fears? Too often we are tempted to tell everyone else—except God. We parade them and publish them for all to see. How much better it would be if we with reverence and prayer presented our questions to God and searched His Word. Then we could get answers and rejoice.

The fool hath said in his heart, There is no God. They are corrupt, they have done abominable works, there is none that doeth good.—14:1

The Blindest Foolishness

IN THIS CASE, the fool is not the blundering idiot we typically imagine. He could be a Ph.d. or the president of a major corporation. He is simply one who says *There is no God.* Denying God is the most foolish foolishness. It leaves too many unanswered questions to be smart and scientific:

• ***How could there be creation without a creator?*** Spontaneous generation has never been proved.

• ***How could there be life that never came from life?*** Science says that life can only come from life.

• ***How could there be design without a designer?*** There is too much to assume everything is an accident.

• ***How could there be law (law of gravity, law of production, etc.) without a law-giver?*** We have many laws. If God didn't give them, who did?

The only way to explain our world is to start with a self-existent First Cause from which everything else has come. Note this syllogism:

Something cannot come from nothing (admitted fact).
But something is (does exist).
Therefore, something always was.

This proves it. And that something that always was is God. Isn't it much more sensible to start with a living, powerful Being as the First Cause than to start with lifeless, powerless matter?

The Lord looked down from heaven upon the children of men, to see if there were any that did understand, and seek God. They are all gone aside, they are all together become filthy: there is none that doeth good, no, not one.—14:2,3

A World Without God

JUST THINK FOR A MOMENT what it would be like in a world without God. For depravity is a natural consequence of disbelief: no God, no ruler; no ruler, no law; and no law, no restraint. And apart from a regenerating influence, man's steps are always downward. Paul emphasizes this in the Roman epistle:

> *Because that, when they knew God, they glorified him not as God, neither were thankful; but became vain in their imaginations, and their foolish heart was darkened.*—ROMANS 1:21
>
> *Being filled with all unrighteousness, fornication, wickedness, covetousness, maliciousness; full of envy, murder, debate, deceit, malignity; whisperers, backbiters, haters of God, despiteful, proud, boasters, inventors of evil things, disobedient to parents, without understanding, covenant breakers, without natural affection, implacable, unmerciful....* —ROMANS 1:29-31

What a terrible world! Is this what the atheist wants? I think not. Moreover, it strips the race of a common unity, a common purpose and a common goal. It leaves the pricking conscience with no healing balm, the briny tears with no blessed comfort, and the weary steps with no assuring direction. What a void! And that is atheism!

May God use us to show the rest of the world what it is like to live in God's world under His direction and in His peace and comfort.

Have all the workers of iniquity no knowledge? who eat up my people as they eat bread, and call not upon the Lord.—14:4

Have They No Knowledge?

THE QUESTION EXPRESSES WONDER at the folly of evildoers. Their witless shortsightedness bewilders thinking people. Don't they know better? Do they think they can escape the reaping?

> *For they have sown the wind, and they shall reap the whirlwind.*
> —HOSEA 8:7

The ignorance of atheism is incredible. Workers of iniquity should learn from observation and experience. As they endure pain, suffer sorrow, surrender in defeat, and fret with frustration, they should perceive that an Eternal Refuge to which man may fly is too necessary not to be true.

As seen in the text, those who reject God reject His people—attack them, eat them up. They try to confirm themselves by condemning the godly. They point to good people's inconsistencies, mock at their shortcomings and make fun of their weaker moments.

This is unfair, for example is harder than precept. We can preach a perfect gospel, but we cannot live a sinlessly perfect life. The spirit of man is willing, but the flesh is weak. This was true of Abraham, David, Peter and Paul.

And it is true of us.

Lord, who shall abide in thy tabernacle? who shall dwell in thy holy hill?—15:1

Questions of Divine Acceptance

THIS IS LIFE'S MOST BASIC QUESTION. Who is acceptable to God? Who is permitted to abide in God's tabernacle? Who can have fellowship with Him? The answer is found not in census but in character, not in rhetoric but in right, not in mere profession but in many proofs. The answer—a classic on real religion—embraces ten practical particulars, as follows:

1. ***The upright:*** "He that walketh upright" (verse 2).
2. ***He who is right with God and man:*** "And worketh righteousness" (verse 2).
3. ***The truthful:*** "And speaketh the truth" (verse 2).
4. ***One who guards his tongue:*** "He that backbiteth not with his tongue" (verse 3).
5. ***The person who treats his neighbor properly:*** "Nor doeth evil to his neighbor…" (verse 3).
6. ***The individual who regards men according to a moral standard:*** "In whose eyes a vile person is contemned" (verse 4).
7. ***He who honors the righteous for what they are:*** "But he honoreth them that fear the Lord" (verse 4).
8. ***The one who keeps his word or contract, despite its pain:*** "He that sweareth to his own hurt, and changeth not" (verse 4).
9. ***The man who does not oppress others in his greed:*** "He that putteth not out his money to usury" (verse 5).
10. ***And he who cannot be bribed:*** "...nor taketh reward against the innocent" (verse 5).

Preserve me, O God: for in thee do I put my trust.—16:1

A Plea for Preservation

THIS PETITION EXPRESSES a keenly felt need of man, ever present through the ages. This urgency was heavy on the heart of David when he went forth to meet the champion warrior Goliath. Likewise, it was self-preservation that prompted Naaman to make a trip to a foreign country in search of recovery from his leprosy. And, wishing to escape the wrath of Herod, Joseph took Mary and Jesus down into Egypt. And it was this ever-abiding feeling to be preserved that prompted Peter to draw the sword in Gethsemane.

In the text we hear the pleadings of a man who put his trust in God. He was sure his own wisdom, unaided by Divinity, was too faulty to cope with life's blows. He knew his own hands, unsupported by the hand of God, were too feeble to triumph over the world's constant opposition.

Likewise, each of us in need of God's preservation should freely plead:

• ***Protect me from my enemies:*** Enemies I have caused who refused to be reconciled. Enemies without cause who have picked me as the object of their tormenting anger.

• ***Keep me from my friends*** who mean well but whose careless words can be so hurtful.

• ***Spare me from myself*** (Romans 7:15), for there is no destruction so tragic as that which is self-inflicted, and no darkness like one's putting out his own light.

O my soul, thou hast said unto the Lord,
Thou art my Lord: my goodness extendeth not to thee
[I have no good beyond thee, *ASV*];
but to the saints that are in the earth,
and to the excellent, in whom is all my delight.—16:2,3

Two Attachments

After pleading for his preservation, David stated his closeness to God and his affinity to God's people. The two go together. When we truly love the Father, we shall also love His children.

Concerning God, he said, "I have no good beyond thee." He was saying, "My good is not independent or separate from thee. I have no source of good of any kind—salvation, safety, happiness or hope—but in thee." He found in Jehovah all that the concept of deity implies.

Relative to God's people, David declared, "…in whom is all my delight." He cited this as evidence of his feelings toward the Heavenly Father—since he delighted in God's children he evidently delighted in God. In the fellowship of God's people he enjoyed the sweetest bond and the easiest living. Among them he found kindred hearts with whom he shared mutual beliefs and common aspirations.

If like appeals to like—and it does—then our fondness for godly people shows that we belong with them. For where our affection is, there we gravitate.

Remember—our attachments are telling on us.

Their sorrows shall be multiplied that hasten after another god: their drink offerings of blood will I not offer, nor take up their names into my lips.—16:4

Chasing Other Gods

COMPOUNDED HEARTACHES—and they all began by chasing after another god. If our god is false, our life can hardly be true.

In this case, the sufferer brings the agony on himself, causes the grief that envelopes his life, creates the very fountain that feeds his tears. The way of the transgressor is hard. This is why sin is forbidden.

Sin is not hurtful
Because it is forbidden,
But it is forbidden
Because it is hurtful.
—BENJAMIN FRANKLIN

Whatever joy sin offers, it must be viewed as fleeting. The transgressors may appear to have the whole world in their hands—glory, honor, wealth and speed. But just over the hill are widening pitfalls, boulders, blinding darkness and multiplying sorrows. This is the unimpeachable witness of experience, observation and history. Remember—all's bad that ends bad.

In view of this danger, David resolved to shun the peril of idolatry: not even to mention the names of false gods, which was forbidden (Exodus 23:13), for familiarity has a tendency to take away the repugnance and horror of that which is wrong.

The lines are fallen unto me in pleasant places; yea, I have a goodly heritage.—16:6

Pleasant Places

THE "LINES" MENTIONED IN THE TEXT were employed to measure or survey land, to denote one's possession. David's portion had fallen into pleasant places. He had a "goodly heritage." But more than the land, he had the Creator of the land. He had the Possessor as well as the possession. He declared in verse 5, "The Lord is the portion of mine inheritance."

May we, too, reflect upon the advantageous circumstances into which we have fallen. Born free, we have:

- ***Free politics.*** We can vote as we please.
- ***Free education.*** A poor child can become a scholar.
- ***Free religion.*** We can worship according to our own interpretation.
- ***Free opportunity.*** A peasant can become a principal in the endeavor of his choice. The country is wide and the only limit is the sky. There is nothing wrong with it that man has not caused and that man cannot cure.

Truly, God has filled our cup with blessings. But our most precious blessing is not to be found in the above-mentioned benedictions. Our greatest blessing is *God,* not the *gifts* of God.

Therefore my heart is glad, and my glory rejoiceth: my flesh also shall rest in hope. For thou wilt not leave my soul in hell; neither wilt thou suffer thine Holy One to see corruption.—16:9,10

Hope Beckons

MY FLESH SHALL REST IN HOPE. Here we see David's confidence in a bodily resurrection. The Old Testament writers did teach the resurrection of the body. They did believe the dead would come forth incorruptible. As Isaiah said, "Thy dead men shall live, together with my dead body shall they arise" (Isaiah 26:19).

Thou wilt not leave my soul in hell. The original word is *Sheol,* meaning the abode of the dead, symbolized by the grave. Thus the word "hell," as used here, does not mean a place of punishment but rather a resting place for the dead.

The Savior is "the resurrection and the life" (John 11:25) and the victor over the grave for the redeemed.

> *Then shall be brought to pass the saying that is written, Death is swallowed up in victory.*—I Corinthians 15:54

The resurrection is a necessary part of religion. As the journey gets shorter, there must be at the end a new beginning. For humanity will not settle for obliteration. Hence, let us be so sure of our salvation that we look forward to the resurrection rather than cringe at the thought of it. Hope beckons.

Concerning the works of men, by the word of thy lips I have kept me from the paths of the destroyer.—17:4

Kept by the Word

THE *WORKS* SPOKEN OF IN THE PASSAGE are the doings of men. In this instance, their conduct was evil and hurtful. The author had kept himself from their sinful paths: not through an all-sufficiency of his own but rather through the word of the Great Keeper.

What a sublime tribute to the power of the Word. He gave a similar ovation in 119:11: "Thy word have I hid in mine heart, that I might not sin against thee."

From the Word he received direction, and wise living necessitates wise instruction. Without guidance it is easy for us to lose our way. It is important that we keep an eye on the road signs, and it is as equally important that we remember the destroyer changes the signs. He erects guideposts that point the wrong way. We must be wary. We need to examine the signs in the light of the whole counsel of God, remembering—

The devil can cite Scripture for his purpose.
—William Shakespeare

The Word strengthened David in times of peril. It is vital that there be a protective power in our hearts to guard us in times of temptation so that we shall not be tempted above that we are able to bear (I Corinthians 10:13). If we keep the Word, we shall be kept by the Word.

Keep me as the apple of the eye; hide me under the shadow of thy wings—17:8

The Apple of His Eye

GOD AND DAVID KNEW EACH OTHER on a level most of us have never known. David knew he was *the apple of God's eye.* This is one of the most encouraging and hopeful thoughts ever held by man, that he is *the apple of God's eye.* A child of God is not a nobody that attracts no attention; he is a special somebody in the eye of God. What is the significance?

It means that God sees and hears us when we pray. He responds gently to our every need. No, He doesn't give us the answer we always want. He is too kind for that. He gives us the answer we need.

Furthermore, it means that we are under the providential care of God who makes things work for our betterment. He does so much! More than we are aware!

Indeed, it means that God is not an abstraction withdrawn from man's everyday living and need—not just a God who sees us for an hour on Sunday morning at church but one who beholds us the whole week. Our God is not just a God of words; He is the God of action. And think of it—we are *the apple of His eye.* Never doubt it!

From men which are thy hand, O Lord, from men of the world, which have their portion in this life, and whose belly thou fillest with thy hid treasure: they are full of (satisfied with, *ASV*) *children, and leave the rest of their substance to their babes.*—17:14

A Pitiful Portion

THESE MEN SOUGHT THEIR REWARD strictly in this fleeting life, while David sought his in God. Observation confirms they were wrong. All along the shores of time the live-for-the-moment people are wrecked and scattered on the cruel rocks of "eat, drink and be merry, for tomorrow you die." This is all they sought, and this is all they got—a pitiful portion.

Those give-me-my-portion-now people centered their lives around the prosperity and pleasures of this world and thus were aptly described as "men of the world."

In the affairs of the world, they were successful. They prospered in their purpose. Their stomachs were filled. They had all the stuff and pleasure that money could buy. And after all their worldly needs were taken care of, there was left an inheritance for their children.

But this was their only reward. They had nothing! absolutely nothing to look forward to beyond this life! Since their plans and purposes were solely connected to this world, it was only natural that their lot consist in only what this world has to offer—vanity.

Solomon summed up for us the materialistic life—

Vanity of vanities; all is vanity.

—ECCLESIASTES 1:2

*As for me, I will behold thy face in righteousness:
I shall be satisfied, when I awake, with thy likeness.*—17:15

Satisfied Then

IN THE REALM OF MATERIAL THINGS the heart of man keeps saying, "It is not enough." "He that loveth silver shall not be satisfied with silver; nor he that loveth abundance with increase: this is also vanity" (Ecclesiastes 4:10). Every material thing turns to "vanity and vexation of spirit" (Ecclesiastes 1:14). The whole human family testifies that the longings of man are satisfied in only that which rises above materialism. Yet—

How often do we labor for that which satisfieth not.
—JOHN LUBBOCK

David realized that the deepest cravings and sweetest joys would be fulfilled in perfect satisfaction when he awoke in the incorruptible and immortal likeness of his Creator. He evidently believed that he would be given a glorious body like that of his Lord, a body suited to an everlasting habitation; and that over there he would dwell forever in a state where service is never blemished, where peace is never disturbed and where happiness is never marred.

Accordingly, then, the only real satisfaction we can enjoy in this world is in pursuing the course that leads to the resurrected, blissful state. Like David, we want to be released from this faulty, frail form. We want to be like You, O God, and we shall be satisfied then.

I will love thee, O Lord, my strength. The Lord is my rock, and my fortress, and my deliverer; my God, my strength, in whom I will trust; my buckler, and the horn of my salvation, and my high tower. —18:1,2

God in Seven Tributes

IN AN UNRIVALED HEART FULL OF PRAISE, David used seven tributes in describing and lauding God:

• ***My strength.*** The psalmist knew where his strength lay—in God. Without God he would have succumbed; with Him he had been victorious.

• ***My rock.*** My cliff. When the storms beat the hardest, he found God a rock, a solid rock, a cliff of shelter.

• ***My fortress.*** A place of defense and protection. There is no safety like Fort Divine.

• ***My deliverer.*** The original word is often translated shield, a shield buckled to the arm. Life is a warfare, and to win we need God on our arm when we raise it in defense.

• ***The horn of my salvation.*** Jehovah was to the writer what the horn is to an animal, the means of defense.

• ***My high tower.*** Or refuge, that being the translation of the word in 9:9. Truly, "The name of the Lord is a strong tower: the righteous runneth into it, and is safe" (Proverbs 18:10).

How great God is!

I will call upon the Lord, who is worthy to be praised: so shall I be saved from mine enemies.—18:3

Worthy of Praise

GOD IS WORTHY OF EXALTATION beyond human expression. No language is adequate to fully express the praises due Him. But in our feeble way we unreservedly say: *To Thee, O God, belongs all the praise, for in Thee is all the merit.*

For God is merciful.

Sinlessly perfect.

Completely just.

Longsuffering to all.

The giver of every good and perfect gift, seen and unseen, thousands upon thousands.

No respecter of persons though He does respect faith and character.

Loves the world, the whole world, everybody in it.

He extends His grace to all. No exceptions.

His ability and power are so unlimited that with Him on your side you have the majority.

And so we, too, extol His name and sing:

Worthy of praise is God our Redeemer;
Worthy of glory, honor and pow'r!
Worthy of all our soul's adoration,
Worthy art Thou! Worthy art Thou!

—TILLIT S. TEDDLIE

He brought me forth also into a large place;
he delivered me, because he delighted in me.—18:19

He Delighted in Me

Why does God Help One and doesn't help another? We shall never know all the answers until we see Him face to face. But we do know that God is fair. His justice and mercy are not subject to question, so there must be some reasons. The eighteenth Psalm helps to explain some of the reasons for God's help:

1. David asked for help: "In my distress I called upon the Lord, and cried unto my God" (verse 6). This proves his faith and humility, that he believed in God and that he was not too proud to ask Him for assistance.

2. The writer was rewarded "according to his righteousness" (verse 20). God is always on the side of right, and this is where David was.

3. He had "kept the ways of the Lord" and had "not wickedly departed from" Him (verse 21). David could say, "I did not put away his statutes from me" (verse 22). He had not substituted human commandments for the Divine ones. Neither had he followed opinion instead of faith, nor convenience in preference to conviction. He was a stickler for the Word. He had faults, but supplanting Scripture with a make-believe religion of convenient views was not one of them.

This is why. While God "no respecter of persons,"He is a respecter of righteousness. Can we claim that God delights in us? *Yes!* if we will but delight in Him.

Thou hast also given me the shield of thy salvation: and thy right hand hath holden me up, and thy gentleness hath made me great.—18:35

True Greatness

DAVID KNEW A LOT ABOUT GREATNESS. He knew what true greatness was and where it came from. He knew it was not found in armies or gold or intellect or beauty. None of these fleeting, temporary qualities of life can make us great. True greatness comes from God and is comprised of a life with God.

We live in a world desperately seeking greatness. We see the arrogant try to inflate their gross egos with pompous claims. We see the fearful look for eminence in trying to dominate and crush all those around them. We see the inwardly poor try to buy greatness with money and extravagance. But it is not found in such veneer.

As David said, God condescends Himself and stoops down to make us great. He sacrificed to lift us. Christ became poor that we in our poverty might become rich. Hopefully, we shall never strive to be "self-made men," but strive to be "God-made men." Our God is our stay, support or prop; and even more, He made us invincible. Indeed, it is God who lights our candle and gives us power to shine. And then we are great. For we are the light that reflects His light and the clay that bears the Potter's image.

The heavens declare the glory of God; and the firmament showeth his handiwork. Day unto day uttereth speech, and night unto night showeth knowledge. There is no speech nor language, where their voice is not heard. Their line is gone out through all the earth, and their words to the end of the world.—19:1-4

The Heavens Attest to God

HUNDREDS OF MILLIONS OF STARS hang in the heavens, but they are not stuck up there in some haphazard, irregular manner. They are grouped together in universes like our own, and operate on a perfect timetable. To say this is an accident is as ridiculous as to say that the telephone directory is the result of an explosion in a printing plant.

The firmament goes on and on. No end has been found to it. And if space can go on and on, so can the next life, so can eternity.

Since every effect must have a cause, those heavenly bodies lift a voice to man, testifying to a cause which says, "God exists." The message goes "to the end of the world." Consequently, no tribe has ever been found that does not believe in super-human power.

Years ago a French infidel strutted and bragged that infidels would tear down the churches and destroy everything that reminded the people of God. A poor peasant replied, "But you will leave us the sun, the moon, and the stars; and as long as they shine, we shall have a reminder of God."

Though time may dig the grave of creeds,
and dogmas wither in the sod,
My soul will keep the thought it needs—
Its swerveless faith in God.

The law of the Lord is.... —19:7-11

More Precious Than Gold

WHILE THE WORKS OF NATURE TESTIFY TO GOD (verses 1-4), they do not tell us how to live, how to worship and what to expect in destiny. In meeting these needs, God has given His inspired word, called in this Psalm "the law of the Lord."

In singing its praises, the writer declares it is:

• "Perfect, converting the soul." Complete. Adequate to accomplish the purpose intended.

• "Sure." Fixed and definite in contrast with the shifting and uncertain precepts of men.

• Capable of "making wise the simple." Enlightens.

• "Right." Correct, conforming to duty and justice.

• Proficient in "rejoicing the heart." Its gracious instruction lends beauty, faith, hope and joy to man.

• "Pure." Holy. Faultless.

• "Enduring for ever." Heaven and earth shall pass away, but not God's word (Matthew 24:35).

• "True and righteous." Nothing false in it.

• "More to be desired are they than gold." Priceless.

• "By them is thy servant warned." They caution us.

• "In keeping of them there is great reward." The keeper of the Scriptures shall be blessed.

What a Book! Vast and wide as the world, rooted in the abyss of creation, and towering up behind the blue secrets of heaven. Sunrise and sunset, promise and fulfillment, birth and death, the whole drama of humanity all in this Book.

—HEINRICH HEIN

The law of the Lord is perfect, converting the soul: the testimony of the Lord is sure, making wise the simple.
—19:7

Power to Convert

THE WORD "CONVERSION" is one we freely use in everyday conversation. We speak of converting water into ice, and we know what that means. We talk of converting a forest into a field, and a log into lumber, and in each case we know there is a changing or making-over process.

Conversion simply means a changed or new life. It is an essential part of religion. Unless our religion makes some changes in us, then it has failed us—or we have failed it. One hundred percent conversion requires a threefold change:

1. ***A change of heart.*** That part of us with which we understand, believe, love and obey must be changed from a lack of knowledge to understanding, from unbelief to belief, from hate to love and from rebellion to obedience.

2. ***A change of life.*** We must start living differently.

3. ***A change of state.*** We must be changed from a child of the world to a child of God. This is accomplished by the new birth.

The power to bring about the conversion of the soul is the law of the Lord. In a similar wording, Peter said: "Being born again…by the word of God, which liveth and abideth for ever" (I Peter 1:23). May we let it rule our hearts.

Who can understand his errors? cleanse thou me from secret faults. Keep back thy servant also from presumptuous sins; let them not have dominion over me: then shall I be upright, and I shall be innocent from the great transgression.—19:12,13

Secret Sins

TO OMIT GOD'S LAW OR GO BEYOND IT is an error. So, after discussing the statutes of God, it was natural that David would turn his attention to this soul-searching question: *Who can understand his errors?* And error necessitates forgiveness.

So David first asked forgiveness of his secret sins. All of us have committed those sins in private that we thought were secret, that we thought were hidden from the world. And maybe they were. But this was not what David was talking about. He was referring to the sins that even he himself was unaware. He was asking for forgiveness of the sins he didn't even know he had committed. How thoughtful! What concern!

Next, David asked for forgiveness of the willful, arrogant sins which he had committed boldly in the very face of God. All of us have sinned boldly at times when we wanted the pleasure of sin strongly enough to break the heart of God.

Do we hate sin as much as David did? If so, we shall today pray for God to forgive our sins—our secret sins as well as our bold sins.

Let the words of my mouth, and the meditation of my heart, be acceptable in thy sight, O Lord, my strength, and my redeemer.—19:14

Words and Meditations

DAVID'S PLEA FOR ACCEPTANCE suggests that he was well aware that man's thoughts, words, deeds and acts of worship may be accepted or rejected by Him before whom we live. Man who was given the volition to do right must of necessity be endowed with the freedom to do wrong; therefore, he ever faces the matter of heaven's approval or disapproval.

The converted soul longs for Divine acceptance. He is anxious to please God, not man, not self. His constant prayer is, "Not my will, but Thine be done."

Our thoughts and words are indicative of the real people we are. For as we think in the heart, so are we. "Out of the abundance of the heart the mouth speaketh." Our premeditated thoughts and unguarded words tell our biography a day at a time.

The text surely lends purpose to this volume—a year of daily meditations. For we are lifted by pondering the higher and nobler things of life. May our meditations this year be lofty, productive of good, and acceptable to God, our strength and our redeemer.

The Lord. . . . —20:1-9

A Prayer for the King

THE TWENTIETH PSALM WAS COMPOSED for the occasion of David's going to war. It was designed to be used by the people in expressing their feeling toward their king and the impending military action.

Believing in prayer and feeling the need of Divine assistance, the people prayed for David their king and their ruler. They prayed for God to protect him in his time of trouble, and that was one thing he had—trouble! trouble! trouble! They prayed for God to defend David and to remember his faithfulness. Finally they asked God to simply save their king.

What lessons can we learn for ourselves and our own rulers? We should be as prayerful for those who rule over us as were the people of Israel. Whether our presidents, senators, congressmen and governors are God fearing or not, they need our prayers and God's help; and we need to be able to lead quiet and peaceable lives. They are fulfilling the God ordained function of civil rule and authority. They can, like the godly or godless kings of old, be used by God to accomplish His will. They may or may not have our votes, but they certainly should have our prayers.

Fear God. Honor the king.
—I PETER 2:17

Some trust in chariots, and some in horses: but we will remember the name of the Lord our God. They are brought down and fallen: but we are risen, and stand upright.—20:7,8

Trust in God or Weapons

IN THIS MILITARY PRAYER, prayed by David's loyal subjects, they showed their trust in God.

With hope in God, they would set up their banners in His name (verse 5). In going to war, all nations have their standards or banners. And David's army would unfurl one in the name of God. Under it they would rally.

Their confidence was *greater* in the saving strength of God's right arm than in military equipment. They felt a greater urgency to have God with them in battle than to be well armed with armaments though they did use weapons. In what must have been an unpopular view among fearful doubters, they mentioned in the prayer the mistaken view of some nations' exclusive trust in chariots and horses. And the Psalm continues by voicing the hard truth of disappointment for those who trust only in weapons: "They are brought down and fallen; but we are risen, and stand upright."

While man uses weapons in warfare, it is God who has the power to schedule the timing, stage the events, and multiply their effectiveness. No one knew this better than David; for he had gone forth to meet the giant Goliath, taking only a sling and some stones.

Effective arms require good hands, smart minds and strong hearts—and God on your side.

The king shall joy in thy strength, O Lord; and in thy salvation how greatly shall he rejoice! Thou hast given him.... —21:1,2

A Victory Prayer

THIS PSALM, BEING A COMPANION to the previous, is one of thanksgiving and rejoicing, following the victory. One is a military prayer, the other a victory prayer. It proves God answers the supplications of His children. That God answers prayer is one of the most basic and heartening promises repeated in the Scriptures. If He doesn't, why do we pray?

Their petitions had been granted. In their thanksgiving they mentioned that the Most High had given their king "his heart's desire"; had not withheld "the requests of his lips"; had given him a golden crown; that the blessings were good; had granted him life and "length of days for ever and ever" (referring perhaps to a continuance in his posterity, and in the full sense especially to Christ); that his glory was great; and that honor and majesty had been laid upon him.

It is easy to pray before a battle, but what is our attitude after it is won? These people rejoiced. They were grateful. Victory did not ruin them. Some people are wasted in defeat, while others are wasted in victory. Some can stand failure easier than they can stand success. But these people who remembered God in crisis did not forget Him when it passed. Victory comes too hard not to be grateful.

For they intended evil against thee: they imagined a mischievous device, which they are not able to perform.—21:11

They Intended Evil

THE SECOND PORTION OF THIS PSALM is addressed by a victorious people to their triumphant king, assuring him of future successes.

It sings of the "intended evil" against David by his enemies who concocted a mischievous scheme which they were not able to accomplish. It wasn't an incident of unintentional harm, but rather a case of deliberate evil which they were not big enough to execute. Heaven found ways to frustrate their evil purposes and laid an awesome paralysis upon their wicked hate.

They were put to flight. Indeed, they were destined to fail before they started. For the best-laid plans are doomed to miscarry when God wills they fail. And if they had won, they still would have lost. For no one wins, in the long run, in his intention to harm another.

Though they failed in their mischief, they were still guilty. In measuring guilt, the intent is equivalent to the act. St. Bernard said, "Hell is full of good intentions," but remember—hell has its share of bad intentions, too.

My God, my God, why hast thou forsaken me?—22:1

The Passion in Prophecy

IT APPEARS THAT IN THE TWENTY-SECOND PSALM David was not only describing his own perils, sufferings and fate but also those of the Messiah. For portions of it are expressly fulfilled and applied to Jesus in the New Testament.

Note these accurate and singular descriptions: *Suffered loneliness*—"why hast thou forsaken me?" *Rejected*—"despised of the people." *Mocked*—"they that see me laugh…shoot out the lip…saying, he trusted in the Lord…let him deliver him." *Completely exhausted*—"I am poured out like water." *Nailed to the cross*—"they pierced my hands and my feet." *Made a gazing-stock*—"they look and stare upon me." *Gambled for His clothes*—"they part my garments among them, and cast lots upon my vesture."

Surely the fulfillment of these plain predictions in Jesus add credibility to David's inspiration and to Christ's divinity.

Jesus was no fraud—He was real; no fake—He was actual. Even secular history supports the Biblical record. Josephus, an eminent historian who lived at that time, stated: "He was the Christ. And when Pilate, at the suggestion of the principal men amongst us, had condemned him to the cross…he appeared to them alive again the third day, as the divine prophets had foretold" (Book 18, Chapter 3).

Though infidels continue to mock, yet they cannot date a letter without acknowledging Christ's birth—A.D., in the year of our Lord. Let's keep the emphasis on *our*—make Him *OUR LORD.*

My God, my God, why hast thou forsaken me?—22:1

Cry of Anguish

WE IMMEDIATELY RECOGNIZE THESE WORDS as the same ones spoken by Jesus on the cross. The "why" requires an answer. Why did Jesus feel a lonely abandonment? Though He was not really abandoned, He felt the sense of it. Why? Jesus—a representative of the human family, the Son of God born of a woman—had shouldered the guilt of the race. "The Lord hath laid on him the iniquities of us all."

Sin had separated the family of man from God; Jesus bore our sins; therefore, He suffered a sense of separation. He took our place and became a sin-offering to draw us near to God.

But God never abandoned His Holy Son. As evidence, the earth shook and trembled, the sun hid its face and refused to shine on Christ's death. This left the people with only one conclusion, which they immediately voiced, "Truly this was the Son of God." No! Jesus was not forsaken; He was in a forsaken role for us.

Now when the going gets extremely rough—we have to live through bitter anguish that defies explanation—remember that the disciple is not above his Master. And above all, let's hold on to the faith that cries out, "My God, my God."

Be not far from me; for trouble is near; for there is none to help.—22:11

When Trouble Comes

HERE ARE SOME TIME-PROVEN REMEDIES for handling trouble when it comes:

Pray to God, "Be not far from us." If we want Him close, pray and draw near to Him; then He will draw near to us. He has promised.

Do no enlarge the troubles. They are big enough without making them bigger.

Let us accept the misfortune as a proving period from which we emerge bigger and stronger than ever.

Take our mind off our distresses by giving thanks to God. Tell of His wondrous works. It will surprise us to see what God has done.

Hold to the blessed promise that God can hide us in time of trouble and can set our feet on a rock.

Never lose confidence in the eventual winning of integrity and righteousness, which—with God's help—can preserve us. Troubles may force a detour and a delay, but they make the destination all the sweeter when we arrive.

Sometimes we reach the point where all human answers fail and all our resources collapse. Then the only thing left is to turn the misfortune over to God, say to Him, "My times are in Thy hand." And this is victory!

The Lord is my shepherd, I shall not want. He maketh me to lie down in green pastures: he leadeth me beside the still waters. He restoreth my soul: he leadeth me in the paths of righteousness for his name's sake. Yea, though I walk through the valley of the shadow of death, I will fear no evil: for thou art with me; thy rod and thy staff they comfort me. Thou preparest a table before me in the presence of mine enemies: thou anointest my head with oil; my cup runneth over. Surely goodness and mercy shall follow me all the days of my life; and I will dwell in the house of the Lord for ever.

—Psalm 23

The Lord Is My Shepherd

THIS IS THE BEST KNOWN and most often quoted Psalm. In all literature its popularity has no equal. Its beauty is unmatched. Its comfort has no rival. This Psalm has been on the lips of countless numbers as they confidently walked through the valley of the shadow of death. Its precious words stand engraved today on a million marble shafts in the peaceful cities of the dead.

This beautiful, metaphorical hymn embraces the complete needs of man: The Lord's leadership. A life free from want where the pastures are green and the waters are still. A restored soul. Paths of righteousness. No fear of death. Comfort. The Shepherd's constant presence. Protection from enemies. The Shepherd's approbation. Goodness. Mercy. A glorious certainty. And the hope of immortality.

Nothing could be dearer in life or death!

The Lord Is My Shepherd

A continuance of the Shepherd Hymn:

Picture ourselves in the Orient where the sun is hot and the earth is scorched. There life is a struggle with the elements.

We see hungry sheep that need help. The shepherd calls and the sheep muster their last ounce of strength to follow. They know not the path ahead, but they know the shepherd.

The journey commences amidst choking dust. As they go, the shepherd avoids the treacherous rocks that cause stumbling and the hidden holes that entrap spindling legs. He bypasses the thorns that reach out to cut. At last they arrive in the valley of plenty where the grass is green and the waters are still.

The wild animals are kept at a distance. They only howl. They dare not come any closer. For the good shepherd is present.

Now the day is far spent, and the sheep are in need of more mercy. He beckons. Together they head toward the fold provided by his grace. When they arrive he anoints every head with oil and gives to each a cup of cold water. As the night closes in he bars the door. The sheep sleep in peace. Blessed sheep.

David who had been a shepherd boy sums up the pastoral scene by ascribing to himself this poetic hope: "And I will dwell in the house of the Lord for ever." Blessed man.

The earth is the Lord's, and the fullness thereof;
the world, and they that dwell therein.
For he hath founded it upon the seas,
and established it upon the floods.—24:1,2

The Rightful Owner

GOD IS THE CREATOR AND PROPRIETOR of the whole world. All creation is vested in Him. He has the right to use it and dispose of it as He pleases. He can sweep it away by flood or fire. It is His.

The ground of ownership is given in the test: *He hath founded it…and established it*. His by right of creation. This is the first thought presented in the Bible—and the most basic: "God created the heaven and the earth" (Genesis 1:1). Accept this and we are ready for more lessons and broader horizons.

How deceived we are in our attachment to materials. We call them ours when they are not. The wealthiest and most powerful holder is but a tenant who may at any moment receive notice to vacate. And with the notice comes the revealing question in Luke 12:20: "Whose shall those things be, which thou hast provided?" In our extreme pursuit of possessions, this appropriate question can give our lives a new meaning by causing us to relax some of the grip on that which must be given up sooner or later anyway.

One generation passeth away, and another generation cometh:
but the earth abideth for ever.—ECCLESIASTES 1:4

Who shall ascend into the hill of the Lord?
or who shall stand in his holy place?
He that hath clean hands, and a pure heart;
who hath not lifted up his soul unto vanity,
nor sworn deceitfully.—24:3,4

Who Shall Stand in His Holy Place?

THROUGH THE AGES HUMANITY HAS ASKED the question in the title. The hill of the Lord was Mount Zion, for it was a place of worship. Who can stand there? Who can worship acceptably?

The answer is simple. A more beautiful and comprehensive outline of terms could not be crowded into such few words. A higher standard of practical religion cannot be found:

Clean hands. Kept clean by the power of God. For if our hands are not cleansed by Him, no soap will wash away the stain.

A pure heart. The worth of service and worship depends on the motives. Worship from a wicked mind is vain (Proverbs 21:27).

Has not lifted up his soul to vanity or falsehood. Not carried away by false standards and erroneous appeals.

Not sworn deceitfully. True. Sincere. No falsehood-spinner. No shadow-chaser.

Faithfully faithful to every trust,
Honestly honest in every deed,
Righteously righteous and justly just,
Religiously religious—'tis his creed.

Such a person is acceptable in God's holy place.

Lift up your hands, O ye gates; and be ye lifted up, ye everlasting doors; and the King of glory shall come in. Who is this King of glory? The Lord strong and mighty, the Lord mighty in battle.—24:7,8

Who Is This King of Glory?

AS MENTIONED THREE DAYS AGO, He is our Shepherd; as such, we should never hesitate to follow. His steps lead to still waters and green pastures.

Then two days ago we reflected on God's ownership of the earth and all therein. We own nothing. It was His before we were born, and it shall be His when we are gone. The knowledge that we are stewards accentuates responsibility and quickens gratitude.

The next day it was pointed out that our God maintains a holy place, and only those with clean hands and a pure heart can ascend its heights. Thank God for this. For it would weaken and cheapen us for Him to make no demands of us. To do this would reduce Him to the role of an over-indulgent grandfather who hurts his offspring by spoiling them.

Now in today's text, there is an exhortation that the gates be lifted, that the doors be opened. Why? That the King of glory might enter in. He does not go where He is not welcome. He rather says, "I stand at the door and knock: if any man hear my voice, and open the door, I will come in to him" (Revelation 3:20). The lock on that door is on the inside of our heart and must be opened from within. Let's let Him in. He is described in the text as *mighty.* We need His might that victory may be ours.

O my God, I trust in thee; let me not be ashamed, let not my enemies triumph over me.—25:2

Let Me Not Be Ashamed

MAY I HAVE NO OCCASION FOR SHAME, that's the prayer. May my trust hold that shame does not ensue. May I be spared the painful emotion of guilt, shortcoming, impropriety or failure. This is practical religion.

When one starts to build and is unable to finish, he feels ashamed. Others will say, "This man began to build, and was not able to finish" (Luke 14:30). So, Lord, help me to plan wisely and to work diligently.

When one trips and falls, he feels ashamed. Falling is humiliating. Therefore, Lord, give me a good footing (26:12), and may I watch my step.

When one loses control of himself, he is later sheepish. Indeed, Lord, help me to keep myself in subjection (I Corinthians 9:27).

Begging is shameful (Luke 16:3). Lord, may there be no occasion for it. Give me health and opportunity that I may make a living.

May I not be ashamed of my religion. "If any man suffer as a Christian, let him not be ashamed" (I Peter 4:16).

May I never be "ashamed of the gospel of Christ" (Romans 1:16). When it is derided, may I waver not.

Lord, though I'm asking not to be ashamed, may I ever be ashamed when shame sits on my brow.

Yea, let none that wait on thee be ashamed:
let them be ashamed which transgress without cause.—25:3

Sin Without Cause

ONE THING SURE, DAVID WAS A MAN OF PRAYER. His yearnings were ever heavenward. There was much to hold him back, but he pressed onward. "Nearer my God, nearer to Thee," was the cry of his heart and the focus of his life. And what David desired for himself, he desired for others—that they be not ashamed (verses 2,3). But he could not pray this for those who "transgress without cause."

Surely there is no cause for sin that makes sin righteous. But there are extenuating circumstances that cry out for understanding and mercy. One of which is a lack of knowledge. Ignorance of the law does not change a violation to compliance, but it does attest that the infraction was of the mind and not of the heart.

Here is a Biblical example: "Whom therefore ye ignorantly worship…" (Acts 17:23). The worship was wrong, but there was a cause—ignorance; not a cause that turned idolatry into truth, but a cause for their doing it.

But to sin without any extenuating cause is to sin willfully and without regard for God's laws. Whatever the sin and whatever prompted it or didn't prompt it, let us draw near to the heart of God by walking in the light that the blood of Jesus may wash away every stain.

Lead me in thy truth, and teach me: for thou art the God of my salvation; on thee do I wait all the day.—25:5

Lead Me

ONE OF OUR GREATEST NEEDS is capable leadership. We need to be led—not misled. However, the one and only unerring direction is found in God and His unerring truth.

David recognized his need of guidance, its true source, and sang of it. And so do we, as expressed in this popular hymn:

Lead kindly Light, amid the encircling gloom,
Lead thou me on:
The night is dark, and I am far from home;
Lead thou me on.
Keep thou my feet; I do not ask to see
The distant scene—one step enough for me.

—J. H. NEWMAN

Unless we are led by the light of truth, we are left to grope and stumble in darkness. Being well aware of this, the psalmist pleaded for leadership in truth, effected by teaching.

"The paths of the Lord are mercy and truth" (verse 10)—where mercy is extended and truth is kept. Those who walk the higher paths are those who "keep his covenant and his testimonies." Every person who follows Him does it by virtue of heeding Him. So if we want Divine leadership, we have a responsibility to move at His command.

Remember, O Lord, thy tender mercies
and thy loving kindnesses; for they have been ever of old.
Remember not the sins of my youth,
nor my transgressions: according to thy mercy
remember thou me for thy goodness' sake, O Lord.—25:6,7

The Sins of My Youth

THIS WAS THE PRAYER OF THE WRITER: Forget! forget! O Lord, the sins of my youth. And God will; for when He forgives sin, He remembers it no more forever (Hebrews 10:17).

David asked God *to remember* and *to forget*—remember His own Divine mercies and kindnesses, but forget David's youthful sins. And what about our own sins? How foolish we have been in youth, and perchance in middle age, and possibly in old age. Fortunate for us, God's willingness to forgive is never strained. If it were not for His affectionate and merciful spirit, we would be doomed to live apart from God and bear our guilt forever.

This prayer was very human. And how very human was the man who prayed it. And we, too, bear the stamp of the same clay. Who among us would be willing to dig up the follies of our youth, breathe life into those skeletons and parade them for all to see? We rather beg: Let them lie. Forget them. Don't deal with me according to what I have been but rather according to what I have become, and especially according to what Thou art: the God of mercy and kindness, goodness and righteousness. This is our prayer.

What man is he that feareth the Lord? him shall he teach in the way that he shall choose. His soul shall dwell at ease [lodge in goodness]; *and his seed shall inherit the earth.*
—25:12,13

At Ease

THE PERSON SPOKEN OF IN THE TEXT finds a resting place in contrast with the restlessness of the one who has lost his way. In the school of the human heart he does well in the following courses:

- Fear of God and trust in Him. The psalmist stipulates this as a condition of ease (verses 12,13). This is a protector against worry and tension.
- The unashamed life (verse 2). Wrong may grant a temporary satisfaction, but right gives us a permanent peace.
- The leadership of God (verse 3). Many are disturbed because of the pull of many ways. They shall never find peace until they obtain unity of direction.
- Meekness (verse 9). No one smarts so much as the proud. Pride knows no rest.
- Eyes that see the Lord (verse 15). The self-centered eye has no ease, only frustration gone mad.
- Forgiveness (verse 18). Only the person feels free in the life where pardon has broken the shackles of guilt, granting a freedom freer than the birds, as expressed by Thomas Parnell:

My days have been so wondrous free,
The little birds that fly
With careless ease from tree to tree,
Were but as bless'd as I.

Judge me, O Lord; for I have walked in mine integrity: I have trusted also in the Lord; therefore I shall not slide.
—26:1

Safeguards Against Slipping

IT IS OUR AMBITION TO ADVANCE—not slide back. And thanks to David, he has given us in this Psalm the simple but sublime conditions to hold our balance and go forward. Let us ponder them:

• ***Integrity:*** "I have walked in mine integrity" (verse 1). Integrity is truly the basis of all stability. When we walk in the path of uprightness, we encounter fewer slippery places. Being true in word and deed, our footing is good.

• ***Trust:*** "I have trusted also in the Lord" (verse 1). Trust in Him energizes our steps and keeps us moving.

• ***Truth:*** "I have walked in thy truth" (verse 3). The truth needs no shift, thus those who imbibe it have no need to change positions. Only truth marches with the future.

• ***Association:*** "Will not sit with the wicked" (verse 3). Wrong company has been the undoing of many people.

• ***Worship:*** "So will I compass thine altar" (verse 6). We become like the object we worship.

• ***Even places:*** "My foot standeth in an even place" (verse 12). On level ground we are less apt to lose our balance. We should watch where we stand, which is determined by what we stand for.

That I may publish with the voice of thanksgiving, and tell of all thy wondrous works.—26:7

Tell the Whole World

WHAT WAS IT HE WANTED TO TELL? "All thy wondrous works." They are many. Creation is God's handiwork. Providence is His control of matters for the good of his people. Love is His gift to all, to even those who hate Him. His word is a guide to a people who without it would not know which way to go. The sunshine and the rain are but two of a thousand earthly blessings. How great they are.

Why did David want to tell it? He said it was because of thanksgiving. His telling the story was an expression of gratitude.

What man tells,
Tells on him.

It told on Paul. He stated that God had done so much for him that he owed something in return, that he was a debtor to make known the gospel (Romans 1:14).

To whom was David thankful? To God. The works were wondrous, but the worker was greater than the works.

Tell it, but to whom? The people. David's concern for them was a factor. He loved them enough to share the good news with them.

How grateful are we? Are we willing for it to be measured by what we declare?

Lord, I have loved the habitation of thy house, and the place where thine honor dwelleth.—26:8

I Love to Go to Church

IN MODERN LANGUAGE, DAVID'S SENTIMENT WAS, "I love to go to church." This is the sentiment of millions today, expressed by regular attendance. Millions more are in regular absence, evidencing they don't like to go.

It was a delightful experience for David, of which he said, "How amiable are thy tabernacles, O Lord of hosts!" (84:1). It was so enjoyable and profitable that he sang: "For a day in thy courts is better than a thousand" (84:10). It was no irksome ritual.

The psalmist was committed to worship. His mind was made up. He knew what he was going to do. The pain that some people go through each week, not knowing whether to go or not go, is tortuous. A once-for-all, irrevocable decision to attend worship would save them from a weekly, tormenting experience of indecision.

A telephone caller inquired of the minister of a church in Washington where the President attended: "Do you expect the President to be in church Sunday?" "That," replied the minister, "I cannot promise, but I do expect the Lord to be there, and that should be incentive enough for a reasonably large attendance."

For where two or three are gathered together in my name, there am I in the midst of them.

—MATTHEW 18:20

*The Lord is my light and my salvation:
whom shall I fear? the Lord is the strength of my life;
of whom shall I be afraid?*—27:1

Whom Shall I Fear?

THE WRITER'S FEARLESS LIFE was an extraordinary accomplishment due to his belief that God was with him. "For thou art with me" is his previous explanation (23:4).

He did not fear darkness, for he believed the Lord was his light. Many of our problems are due to a lack of enlightenment.

Neither was he afraid of condemnation, because he was assured his salvation was in the Lord.

Nor did he fear weakness. He believed that with the Lord's help he would be strong enough to meet every eventuality.

Neither did he flinch before his enemies, for his experience had been that when they came upon him the Great Protector caused them to stumble and fall (verse 2).

Nor did he fear trouble of any kind, because he felt that when it came God would hide him in His own dwelling place, shelter and protect him (verse 5).

This glorious valor was strengthened and fed by the promise that God "shall strengthen thine hand" (verse 14). So there is hope for all of us to become braver. In the same way, our courage should increase as we see God's promises fulfilled and feel His presence more closely.

One thing have I desired of the Lord, that will I seek after; that I may dwell in the house of the Lord all the days of my life, to behold the beauty of the Lord, and to inquire in his temple.—27:4

One Thing I Desire

IT WAS AN INTENSE DESIRE. A gripping aspiration. So major and singular was this longing that David called it the "one thing have I desired of the Lord." With an overwhelming yearning he said he would seek after it. He knew that a person seldom gets what he doesn't seek.

What was it that meant so much to him? The one thought that overpowered all others? The one desire that gave the greatest purpose to living? Was it eating? No. Health? No. Entertainment? No. Recreation? No. Yet all of these are worthwhile. *It was worship, dwelling in the Lord's house and beholding His beauty, inquiring of Him*. That was it. What the poet placed first, some place last. An absence from worship was to him an insufferable privation. He longed to be there, to offer sacrifices of joy and thanksgiving (verse 6). It was a privilege he loved.

There is no association like that of being by the Lord's side. There our eyes easier see "the King in his beauty." There the musings on the glories of Jehovah freely and fully pace the soul. There we nourish our spiritual hunger.

O why do we feed on husks when there is
bread in the Father's house?

I had fainted, unless I had believed to see the goodness of the Lord in the land of the living.—27:13

Saved From Fainting

THE PSALMIST ADMITS that he has had a rough time of it. He had some close calls. Life hadn't been a bed of roses. He had been tested and tried, subjected to fiery ordeals, but he had gotten through.

What was it that protected him, that gave him strength to endure when otherwise he would have fainted? It was faith. His own heart condition of unrelenting confidence supported him. This quality is called "the good fight of faith." It keeps us from turning and running in battle. Where the faith is great, the trials are less. If he had quit believing, the good life of persevering, meeting all adversities and overcoming them, would have been over.

So it is absolutely necessary that we protect ourselves from fainting, that we guard ourselves from a powerless existence. One day at church a man in the pew fainted. There was no need to pass him a hymnal, he couldn't sing; nor call him to pray, he couldn't pray; nor to speak to him, he couldn't listen. In this state, life was no more than breathing.

We must avoid fainting; and the way to do this is to increase our faith, which is accomplished by giving the Word a chance in our hearts.

Faith cometh by hearing, and hearing by the word of God.
—ROMANS 10:17

Draw me not away with the wicked, and with the workers of iniquity, which speak peace to their neighbors, but mischief is in their hearts.—28:3

Smooth Words

LATER DAVID ADDED THIS THOUGHT concerning the deceiver: "The words of his mouth were smoother than butter, but war was in his heart: his words were softer than oil, yet were they drawn swords" (55:21).

And Jeremiah had this to say: "One speaketh peaceably to his neighbor with his mouth, but in heart he layeth his wait" (Jeremiah 9:8).

And Samuel gave this example:

> *And Joab took Amasa by the beard with the right hand to kiss him. But Amasa took no heed to the sword that was in Joab's hand: so he smote him therewith....*—II SAMUEL 20:9,10

The possibility of being taken by smooth-talking deceivers has ever been a danger. Their words hide their intents. Behind the kindest words, soft as butter, sweet as sugar, the hand clutches a concealed dagger. Deceitful lips press a kiss on our cheek, but a circling hand rams a dagger in our back—or slips a hand into our pocket. Thus until we know a person, it is wise to insist that he only throw the kisses at us, that we may stay beyond the reach of the dagger or the lift of the wallet.

Give them according to their deeds,
and according to the wickedness of their endeavors:
give them after the work of their hands;
render to them their desert.—28:4

According to Their Deeds

THIS IS A PRAYER that the people be rewarded according to their deeds. *Render to them their desert.* This is in keeping with the will of God, which means that it was not improper. However, if the motive had been wrong—prayed out of malice and vindictiveness—it would have been evil in spirit, though it was correct in content. It seems that righteous indignation entered into the prayer, which is not wicked. If the time comes when we cease to become indignant at evil, we have lost our concern for the outcome of the struggle between right and wrong.

The concept of justice in all civilization is that men must account for their deeds. Responsibility requires it. Fairness says this is the way to play the game. If we could sow idleness and reap plenty, or scatter gossip and harvest goodwill, or disseminate hate and gather love, it would be extremely unfair. It is an equitable and just law of nature and of human behavior that everything and everybody be rewarded in kind. The three laws of sowing and reaping are: we reap what we sow; we reap later than we sow; and we reap more than we sow.

The tissue of the life to be
We weave with colors all our own,
And in the field of destiny
We reap as we have sown.
—JOHN GREENLEAF WHITTIER

Give unto the Lord the glory due unto his name; worship the Lord in the beauty of holiness.—29:2

The Beauty of Holiness

WE APPRECIATE THE BEAUTIFUL, the elegant, the graceful, the adorable: the majestic mountain, the blue ocean, the singing tree, the green grass, the red rose, the flying bird, the good looking child, and the handsome adult.

But the most adorable beauty is *the beauty of holiness,* which is the most accurate description of good looks. And what is that? Human character copied after the character of God. It is the likeness of God thriving in the human heart, beaming from our eyes, and breathing from our lips. A beauty unexcelled! Too bad that beauty contests have to omit this standard.

This personal quality is more charming and refined than any other beauty because it is human and inward. Holiness is truly a masterpiece of beauty within the individual, developed by the individual with the help of God. A major achievement.

This attractiveness is more genuine. It does not fade with years but rather blossoms with time. It does not improve with a new cream, or face-lift, or a change of wardrobe. Indeed, it is too untouchable by materials to be affected by a handful of credit cards in a shopping mall. Hence, let us seek the beauty and handsomeness that are from above that grow from here to eternity.

The voice of the Lord is upon the waters:
the God of glory thundereth:
the Lord is upon many waters.—29:3

Like a Thunderstorm

INDEED, GOD SPEAKS in the quiet, running brook; in the soft, sparkling dew; in the gentle, refreshing rain; in the cloudless, peaceful sky; but also in the flashing, roaring thunderstorm. In the symbol of a thunderstorm, we are reminded of His voice of power. It is expressive of His might. May we never doubt the power of His word.

This Psalm contains one of the grandest and most awe-inspiring descriptions of a thunderstorm. It was given to praise the glory and strength of God and to encourage and comfort the people. The hymn ascribes glory to God seven times in the expression, "The voice of the Lord." God's voice was powerful, forceful and supreme enough to give us a world, and the same might now sustains it. It is majestic, grand and magnificent, filled with splendor. His every utterance flashes with brilliance and lights the world like a flash of lightning. And just as the storm shakes our world, God's voice is adequate for every occasion. He has stated,

> *"So shall my word...accomplish that which I please, and it shall prosper in the thing where to I sent it.*—ISAIAH 55:11

As we ascribe to God the same praise mentioned in the Psalm, it quiets our nerves and gives us peace.

O Lord my God, I cried unto thee, and thou hast healed me. O Lord, thou hast brought up my soul from the grave: thou hast kept me alive, that I should not go down to the pit.—30:2,3

Kept Alive

DAVID HAD BEEN ILL, CRITICALLY ILL. While on the brink of the grave he prayed unto God. The prayer was heard: "Thou hast healed me." He attributed his recovery to God: "Thou hast kept me alive."

David's experience has been the experience of countless numbers. Some of us have walked down the slippery path and stood lingering at death's door. Yet we were pulled back when it seemed but natural for us to go on. A power stronger than medicine did it. Up from the grave, as it were, we sang praises unto God and exclaimed that we would give thanks unto Him forever, as David did (verse 12).

Illness has its compensations. It can open deaf ears and unlock closed eyes. It teaches us that the thread of life is brittle. Health is no longer presumed. Friends are more highly esteemed than ever, for they stood by with sympathy and kindness. Having a more accurate view of what really counts in life, we resolve to better use whatever days may lie ahead for us. We are thoroughly convinced that we had been caught up in too much ado with unimportant things. We realize that God kept us alive for some worthwhile purpose. The suffering was not in vain.

Weeping may endure for a night,
but joy cometh in the morning.—30:5

Joy in the Morning

THE PASSAGE REFERS TO THE TROUBLES and heartaches which the psalmist had suffered. He was so human. And he suffered so humanly.

No pain or trial seems short at the time. Weeping endures for the night, and it seems it will never pass. But every night has its ending. Every spell of darkness is finally scattered by the light of a new day. This we need to remember in the gloom of the night. And at the dawning there is joy, jubilation, singing—*joy cometh in the morning.* A morning free from sorrow. Our tears have dried. Our eyes see a new, unblurred outlook. Our ears hear a new call or an order back to old responsibilities. Our heart now beats with a new hope. Our steps once again march with certainty. The world keeps turning, and we have climbed back on.

Life has its night and day, uphill and downhill; so whatever comes, whenever it comes, we must search our soul to find strength to live through it.

Let us take courage in the blessed fact that the affliction, whether short or long, is but for a moment in comparison with eternity, and that it has its compensation:

> *For our light affliction, which is but for a moment, worketh for us a far more exceeding and eternal weight of glory.*
>
> —II CORINTHIANS 4:17

And in my prosperity I said, I shall never be moved. Lord, by thy favor thou hast made my mountain to stand strong: thou didst hide thy face, and I was troubled.
—30:6,7

My Mountain Stands

THERE HAD BEEN A TIME in David's life when he felt too self-secure. It was at an interval of prosperity in which he experienced comparative peace and ease. Looking around him, David said in substance, "Nothing can happen to me. I have everything under control." He just took it for granted that his prosperity would last, as most of us do. When we enjoy good health, grand success, many friends and what appear to be safe investments, it is easy for us to suffer the illusion that tomorrow will be the same as today.

Poor David. He saw his mountain come tumbling down. The reason—it had been resting too much on self and not enough on God. If our mountain stands, it must have a stronger base than human tact, skill and industry—it must rely on God. And when it doesn't and when it tumbles, we see the folly in counting on materialism. Then as we pick up the pieces, we put our dependence where it belongs—in God. Then—and only then—is our mountain strong enough to stand when trouble comes and danger strikes. David later acknowledged this: "…thy favor has made my mountain to stand strong."

God, help us to build our mountain not upon the sands of self but upon the rock of You. There it can tower toward the heavens and stand tumble-proof.

I cried to thee, O Lord; and unto the Lord
I made supplication. What profit is there in my blood
when I go down to the pit? Shall the dust praise thee?
shall it declare thy truth? Hear, O Lord,
and have mercy upon me: Lord, be thou my helper.—30:8-10

Why Me?

DAVID WAS NOT AFRAID TO TALK HONESTLY with God. During his afflictions he pointedly asked God, "Why is this happening to me? What profit is there in my going down to the pit of defeat? Shall the dust of defeat praise You? Shall my downfall raise You up?"

Have we not all asked the same questions in the midst of our miseries and sufferings? Why me? Why, God, is this happening? Surely it will only cause the unrighteous to rejoice when they see me, a servant of Yours, go down in ruin? What profit is it? However, sometimes our falling flat on our back provides a posture that gives us an upward view of God we never see while standing erect. Indeed, setbacks, defeats, sufferings and afflictions can be realistic eye-openers and disciplinary friends that give us gratitude, will, muscle and perspective never obtained in easy living.

This great but fallible man pleaded for mercy. And that, too, expresses our feelings: Have mercy upon us. In view of all our shortcomings, which ordinarily are the cause of our problems and troubles, we don't want justice—we want mercy. And it is most heartening to know that God will grant it. So, let us hold His hand and walk with Him. If the going gets too rough, He will pick us up and carry us in His arms.

Into thine hand I commit my spirit:
thou hast redeemed me, O Lord God of truth.—31:5

Total Commitment

THESE WORDS WERE EXCEEDINGLY IMPORTANT at the time David sang them, but they increased in distinction and popularity when Jesus repeated them on the cross (Luke 23:46). That pinpointed them with a special significance. Perhaps David was not thinking—as Jesus thought—of a final entrustment of his spirit into the hands of God, but rather of a solemn placement here on the earth of his whole self, body and soul, into the keeping of God.

Additionally, David said:

My times are in thy hand.—VERSE 15

The passage recognizes the sovereignty of God: His prerogative to rule and bless, man's to trust and obey.

This commitment is appropriate at all times:

- In life, for David pledged it.
- In death, for Jesus uttered it.

We, too, must be involved in this total dedication. To cope with a world of troubles and dangers, we need a faith in God that expresses itself in a living commitment and in a resigning trust. Then we can work in the day without fear, sleep in the night without worry, and wake up in the morning without dread. Every night is a beautiful dream. And every dawn is a pleasant awakening.

Thou hast set my feet in a large room.—31:8

Opportunity

THE AUTHOR SANG that God had given him a large room, plenty of space for movement and action—opportunity. He was not confined. He was not shackled or hindered in any way. He was given what we all need—opportunity.

When God gives us a large room, that implies an obligation to use it. For every right carries a responsibility.

Those who try to get the most for the least are not in the room of opportunity; they have already stepped into the hall of disaster.

The world does not owe us a living. It was founded to give us room. It is up to us to work it. Remember—the ant and the grasshopper had the same opportunity.

Life is full of possibilities. But to take advantage of them, most of us have to begin in a small way. Though the job is humble, it is a good place to begin to apply our industry, skill and honesty. These approaches are the best training and preparation for advancement.

Grab the opportunity; for such a chance, when taken seriously, leads to fortune.

There is a tide in the affairs of men,
Which, taken at the flood, leads on to fortune.
—WILLIAM SHAKESPEARE

Have mercy upon me, O Lord, for I am in trouble: mine eye is consumed with grief, yea, my soul and my belly.
—31:9

Hasty Decisions

DAVID DECLARED, "I am in trouble."

His enemies sought to ruin his reputation. They caused his neighbors and his friends to forsake him (verse 11). It was as if David had become a dead man or a useless, broken pot—unnoticed and unwanted (verse 12).

And, of course, David's enemies made sure there were plenty of lies floating around about him (verse 13). His enemies relentlessly defamed his character and recklessly plotted to kill him. As a result, David's health failed, and he grew weaker and weaker. Indeed, a sad state!

But, the worst was yet to come. Really? What could be worse than to be in this poor man's condition? The greatest impairment was that David gave up on God: "I said in my haste, I am cut off from before thine eyes." A hasty decision and a bad one. This was David's most defeating problem—his haste in deciding that God had given up on him.

When things in our lives get about as bad as we think they can, do we write off God? Do we give up on Him because we think He has already given up on us? "O thou of little faith." So, a practical lesson in the Psalm is: *Learn patience in trouble.* Just because God does not act as fast we desire does not mean that He is not watching over us.

Blessed is he whose transgression is forgiven, whose sin is covered. Blessed is the man unto whom the Lord imputeth not iniquity, and in whose spirit there is no guile.—32:1,2

Covered Sin

THE SIN REFERRED TO IN THE TEXT is sin that has been covered with forgiveness and is no longer imputed to the sinner. It is past sin—iniquity no longer active in the heart of the offender.

There are many wrong ways to try to cover sin:

• ***Hide.*** Adam and Eve tried this (Genesis 3:1-8).

• ***Shift the blame to another.*** Adam blamed Eve. And Eve blamed the serpent.

• ***Run away.*** Jonah took a ship and went to sea (Jonah 1:1-4), but God kept up.

• ***Criticize the righteous.*** "And why beholdest thou the mote that is in thy brother's eye, but considerest not the beam that is in thine own eye?" (Matthew 7:3).

• ***Persecute the reprover.*** The sinners Stephen rebuked sought relief by killing him (Acts 7:54-60).

• ***Bring in false witnesses.*** If one is guilty, all the witnesses in the world cannot swear him innocent.

• ***Measure self by a weaker person.*** Say, "I am not as bad as they are." Maybe not. But it doesn't cover sin. It is unwise: "They measuring themselves by themselves, and comparing themselves among themselves, are not wise" (II Corinthians 10:12).

There is only one right way to cover sins—get forgiveness!

When I kept silence, my bones waxed old
through my roaring [groaning, *ASV*] *all the day long. For*
day and night thy hand was heavy upon me:
my moisture is turned into the drought of summer.
I acknowledged my sin unto thee, and mine iniquity
have I not hid. I said, I will confess my transgressions
unto the Lord; and thou forgavest the iniquity of my sin.
—32:3-5

Peace Through Confession

IN DAVID'S SILENCE HE FOUND NO REST. Conscience-smitten, troubled, agonizing in soul, his "bones waxed old"; that is, his strength failed and it seemed that the weakness of old age was upon him.

There was conviction of sin but no confession. Trying to hide sin in his life, unwilling to confess it, refusing to seek pardon, life became hard for him. While his mouth kept silent on sin, David's heart groaned with anguish. Pressure built up within him, but he refused to open the valve of confession. As it wore on, he felt more distressed. His remembrance of guilt seemed to be the pressing hand of God upon him. Finally, when it became intolerable he confessed his sins. Forgiveness lifted the weight. Peace came.

What the psalmist suffered is the experience of millions. In an effort to obtain ease from a painful guilt, yet unwilling to seek pardon, we become amusement worshippers, bar flies, business pushers, honor chasers, or big givers. After suffering futility and disappointment, some of us will go on to seek release in the Divine way—as David did—and peace shall come.

For this shall every one that is godly pray unto thee in a time when thou mayest be found.—32:6

When Do I Approach God?

AS CHILDREN, ALL OF US SOON LEARNED when to ask for favors or special privileges. We knew how to gauge just the right time to hit Dad up for money. We knew Mom was more willing at certain times than others to bend the rules—"just this once." We learned to play the game and have seen our children, and perhaps grandchildren, learn it too.

But is God like a parent in this respect? Is our Heavenly Father occasionally more disposed to listen and grant favors to us while at other times He is too busy or unconcerned to be approached? *No, not at all!*

The truth is God may be found when we turn to Him. The time of mercy with our Father is when the sinner submits himself to the Father's will.

> *For he saith, I have heard thee in a time accepted, and in the day of salvation have I succored thee: behold, now is the accepted time; behold, now is the day of salvation.*—II CORINTHIANS 6:2

The time is *now* with God, if the time is *now* with us. We shall find God when we seek Him with all our heart (Jeremiah 29:13).

It is most heartening that we don't have to tip-toe around behind God and wait for Him to get in a good mood. It is unrealistic to wait for God to be approachable; He is ready if we are ready.

Be ye not as the horse, or as the mule,
which have no understanding: whose mouth
must be held in with bit and bridle,
lest they come near unto thee.—32:9

Just Like a Mule

ISRAEL HAD ALWAYS BEEN STIFF-NECKED, obstinate and stubborn, like an unruly mule or horse. It is acceptable for a mule to act like a mule and a horse to behave like a horse, but it is highly unacceptable for us to conduct ourselves like either. The ways of a mule are normal for a mule because he has no understanding, but for us it is indefensible.

> *God made him, and therefore let*
> *him pass for a man.*
> —WILLIAM SHAKESPEARE

A mule is controlled by reins, but our higher nature requires that our obedience be free and cheerful. It must come from the heart—not bit and bridle.

A mule has no conscience, and we cannot appeal to it with moral and spiritual law or reason. And when our conscience becomes completely seared over, then we lose this faculty or restraint—this human distinction—and we take on the image of a brute. Mules bray. People pray. I prefer to be classified with the latter.

God fashioned us to live like men. Our place is exalted and privileged: "a little lower than the angels." Let us not exchange it.

For the word of the Lord is right;
and all his works are done in truth.—33:4

God's Word Is Right

THIS IS A GLORIOUS TRIBUTE to the infallible Word of God. It is right! Of course, it has been accused of being wrong, but the wrong was in the eyes that beheld it and the ears that heard it and the heart that considered it—not in the Word itself. "The law is holy, and the commandment holy, and just, and good" (Romans 7:12).

God's Word is in exact agreement with right. His nature would not allow Him to give one word that is wrong. This is good enough reason for accepting the Word—it came from God.

He gave it not to inform, guide or comfort Himself. He needs none of these. He gave it to help humanity, and the one who sins against it wrongs his own soul (Proverbs 8:36).

And the person who thinks the Bible is dry on the inside should at least withhold the criticism until he gets the dust off the outside.

The Bible has been here too long to become outmoded. The things that are right and practical are here to stay, like the Bible and the multiplication table—they are not in danger of becoming obsolete.

Our fathers needed the Word. We need it. Our children need it. And feeling this essential want, we sing:

Give me the Bible,
Write on my heart every word.

By the word of the Lord were the heavens made;
and all the host of them by the breath of his mouth.
He gathereth the waters of the sea together as a heap:
he layeth up the depth in storehouses.—33:6,7

Made by the Lord

ALL OF US HAVE SEEN ARTICLES with such stampings on them: "Made by Toys, Inc." "Made by Artificial Flowers Co." But when we look at creation we see the inerasable stamping—

Made by the Lord.

This label is written all over the heavens (19:1). It is stamped everywhere on earth.

Moses ascribed creation to God (Genesis 1,2).

Paul attributed the universe to Divine power: "…by whom he also made the worlds" (Hebrews 1:2).

Thus *creation by the Creator* is a primary and fundamental teaching of the Bible. This is rational. For there had to be a beginning point sometime and somewhere by a self-existent First Cause.

One evening Napoleon with a group of French officers was on the deck of a ship in the Mediterranean, returning from an expedition to Egypt. In a discussion of God, the officers were unanimous in their atheistic expressions that God does not exist. They then turned to Napoleon who stood alone in deep thought and asked him, "Is there a God?" Raising his hand and pointing to the starry firmament, he simply replied, "Gentlemen, who made all that?"

Blessed is the nation whose God is the Lord; and the people whom he hath chosen for his own inheritance.—33:12

The Blessed Nation

THE BLESSED NATION IS A GODLY NATION; hence religion is indirectly a form of patriotism. Some don't see it this way, but civil lawmakers have thought that religion added stability and greatness to a nation and for this reason have given it tax-exempt status.

Religion has the leavening influence of spreading truth, purity and virtue, which strengthen the nation.

The Bible teaches work, sacrifice, thrift and self-restraint, all of which are essential in lifting up a society.

Godliness is the guardian influence which has protected many from criminality. It is the rescuing power which has broken crime's grip on many others.

One thing history is sure of:

Righteousness exalteth a nation: but sin is a reproach to any people.

—PROVERBS 14:34

A nation never falls but by suicide.

—RALPH WALDO EMERSON

National history is but the history of many individuals. So after all is said and done, we determine the nation's rise or fall. Each day we furnish the material for the history books.

I will bless the Lord at all times:
his praise shall continually be in my mouth.—34:1

At All Times

AT ALL TIMES! And they do come. But no circumstances should cause us to withhold our praise to the Lord. If our extolment of Him continues regardless of what happens, it proves that the praise is no surface whim but rather a deep-seated conviction of the heart, a faith that refuses to be shaken.

We should bless Jehovah at all times: When we are glad and when we are sad. When little ones are born and when old ones die. When our purse is full and when it is empty. When fortune smiles and when it frowns. When victory awards us and when defeat floors us. When health radiates us and when illness racks us. When we are applauded and when we are condemned. When friends stand by and when they walk away. In youth and in old age. In public worship and in private meditation. Praise Him. All of us. *At all times.*

We have been in contact with thousands of people in all circumstances, but we have never seen the time when praise to God was inappropriate.

Whatever the time is, it is essential that we keep our reasoning and our perspective. A closeness with God will safeguard this.

By all means, praise to Jehovah is for such a time as this! Bless the Lord today!

O magnify the Lord with me,
and let us exalt his name together.—34:3

Together

THE TEXT SUGGESTS THAT BELIEVERS EXALT the Lord's name together. If we are born-again children of the same God, why shouldn't we magnify His name together?

Since believers have a common cause and a mutual goal, it is only natural that we worship and work together. The Scriptures teach it:

Not forsaking the assembling of ourselves together.—HEBREWS 10:25

We then as workers together with him....—II CORINTHIANS 6:1

Togetherness lends strength to each. "Two are better than one" (Ecclesiastes 4:9).

Unity generates warmth for all. "How can one be warm alone?" (Ecclesiastes 4:11). Fellowship among the children of God is like several sticks laid together on a fire, whereby one kindles another. It is easy, however, for the fire in one stick, separated from the others, to go out.

The hermit has fewer provocations to do wrong, but he also has fewer urges to do right.

We need God, but we also need each other.

This poor man cried, and the Lord heard him, and saved him out of all his troubles.—34:6

Poor Rich People

WEALTHY, BUT POOR. There are lots of poor rich people. They have lands that stretch beyond the eyes, stocks that bulge bank boxes, bonds that bind cities and states, oil wells that flow and skyscrapers that mark the concrete jungles—but they are poor. Riches are not always what people think they are; neither is poverty. Being without money can be a problem, but being with money can be a bigger problem.

Powerful, but poor. David was king, but he had enough responsibilities to make him the object of pity—poor king.

There is but one measuring rod to determine whether one is rich—is he rich in joy and hope? The Master Teacher said the rule of measurement is not in earthly possessions: "For a man's life consisteth not in the abundance of the things which he possesseth" (Luke 12:15).

David, suffering persecutions and reverses, was poor because he felt desolate, forsaken and crushed. Any man who thinks he's poor is poor.

Additionally, one is poor if he: 1) Cannot enjoy what he has. 2) Is not content. 3) Is short on good works. 4) Has no self-respect. 5) Has no real friends. 6) Has lost the zest for living. 7) Has little joy. 8) Has lost his health. 9) Has no Divine comfort. 10) Has no eternal hope.

What man is he that desireth life, and loveth many days, that he may see good? Keep thy tongue from evil, and thy lips from speaking guile. Depart from evil, and do good; seek peace, and pursue it.—34:12-14

A Quest for Good Days

GOOD DAYS! And David gave us a plan to find them, a program which calls for both positive and negative living:

• "Keep thy tongue from evil." This is negative: avoid all falsehood, deceit, slander, gossip and vituperation. Refrain from hasty words. Never speak without knowledge.

• "Depart from evil." Another negative approach: do no wrong; engage in no vice; follow no evil. Don't is a necessary word in the field of happiness.

• "Do good." Just refraining from evil is not enough. Everyone must actively and positively do good to others for his life to be blessed with good days.

Life is a mirror, if you smile upon it,
it smiles back again on you.
—JAMES T. FIELD

• "Seek peace and pursue it." Peace is not a passive matter—we have to work for it. Do something ourselves to be at peace with our neighbor and the world.

Hundreds of years after David gave this outline for peace, Peter quoted it (I Peter 3:10,11). It works. Summed up, well spent days are good days.

For without cause have they hid for me their net in a pit, which without cause they have digged for my soul.—35:7

For No Cause

THE COMPLAINT IN THE TEXT is one David sang repeatedly in Psalms: "Hate me without a cause." "Fought against me without a cause." "Persecuted me without a cause." He had not wronged them. Envy and hate, however, need no cause to harm another. They are cause enough to incite the evil.

The injurer always hates his victim.
Whom they have injured they also hate.
—SENECA

This was what caused some to hate David—not what he had done to them but what they had done to him. Solomon stated the same principle of evil behavior: "A lying tongue hateth those that are afflicted by it" (Proverbs 26:28). The person who lies about us feels compelled to do more lying to make us look like what he says about us—persecution without provocation.

Envious people never like the ones they envy. The begrudging *have-nots* hate the prosperous *haves.* They resent us not for what we are but for what we have—dislike without cause.

There are those who try to equalize their position by knocking down those above them—injury without cause. When this happens to us, remember the lives of David, Jesus and Paul. We are in good company.

False witnesses did rise up; they laid to my charge things that I knew not. They rewarded me evil for good to the spoiling of my soul.—35:11,12

Falsely Accused

IN SUFFERING FROM FABRICATED CHARGES David met a fate that is not uncommon to good people.

Be thou as chaste as ice,
as pure as snow,
thou shalt not escape calumny.
—WILLIAM SHAKESPEARE

The lie peddlers went before King Saul and privately accused David of seeking the king's hurt (I Samuel 24:9). For his own safety, he had to flee. He became a fugitive and wanderer, which separated him from friends and desolated his soul.

The detractors had rewarded David evil for good. Even Saul admitted this guilt: "Thou hast rewarded me good, whereas I have rewarded thee evil" (I Samuel 24:17). Helping undeserving people is like casting pearls before swine that later turn and rend us.

The false witnesses committed a sin God especially hates (Proverbs 6:19). And why shouldn't He? For it is mean, heartless and devoid of conscience.

No wonder one of the Ten Commandments reads: "Thou shalt not bear false witness" (Exodus 20:16). It is an essential ethic in society. Centuries have passed, but its need has not lessened.

But as for me, when they were sick,
my clothing was sackcloth: I humbled my soul with fasting;
and my prayer returned into mine own bosom.
I behaved myself as though he had been my friend or brother.
—35:13,14

But As for Me

AS SEEN IN THE PREVIOUS ESSAY, the psalmist experienced the sharp darts of lying tongues. Now he contrasts his conduct with theirs. "But as for me," he declares. And this is the only life any person can live—his own.

His kindness was especially shown when it was needed most—in their illness. This is always the time for the good man to come through—when he's needed. When they were sick he showed the deepest distress by donning sackcloth, a customary emblem of mourning. Furthermore he fasted, which was a common custom associated with prayer. Fortunate is the person who has anybody in all the world who cares enough to pray for him.

David had treated the traitor as though he had been his friend or brother. Extra-special! For friends or brothers extend to each other more than ordinary considerations. Then the supposed friend turned on him.

Though occasionally our former favors are rewarded with evil, let us take comfort in that a greater reward cannot be denied us—the conscience of doing right.

A good deed has a witness in the heart.

*With hypocritical mockers in feasts,
they gnashed upon me with their teeth.*—35:16

Unmoved by Mockery

MOCKERS. MORE THAN MOCKERS. Hypocritical mockers. The people that David had formerly aided drew around them at the feasts the buffoons and clowns—artists in jest and ribaldry—who made David the object of their salty ridicule and coarse derision.

Mockery is the fume of little hearts.
—ALFRED TENNYSON

When reason is against a man he resorts to ridicule. It gives joy to little minds that need no evidence of truth. It was a low, backhanded stroke to turn public opinion against David. They intended to incite the rabble, which is not difficult; for they, without thinking, are ever ready to join in a cry and a march.

The mockers did friendly joking in an atmosphere of goodwill. They gnashed upon him with their teeth, which is a Biblical expression of an angry desire to harm. It was low and cheap.

Lest we be dismayed, may we keep in mind that mockery in the end mocks the sport it feeds on. All of us have work to do and are obligated to do the best we can; so let us not be deterred by the sneers of those who grovel in ridicule.

For he flattereth himself in his own eyes,
until his iniquity be found to be hateful.—36:2

Obnoxiousness of Self-flattery

ALL OF US NEED TO BE REALISTIC in assessing self. No person should underrate himself. It is self-defeating to assign yourself to a role beneath your ability. Neither should one think more highly of himself than the facts permit (Romans 12:3).

The egotist in the text made the grievous blunder of overrating his judgment of what is right. It set him on a course of conduct that became hateful and odious. This is what happens when a man disregards the standards of God and civilization to follow his own rules. Yes, it's his life, but it's not his society, and what he does affects the whole.

The basic error of the man who makes his own rules is his exalted confidence in himself to map a course without any assistance from God or anyone else. Like a little god he sits on a creaky throne he's not qualified to occupy and wears a shaky crown with this inscription, "Nobody tells me anything." By supposing whatever he wants to do is right he gives himself the latitude of an outrageous conduct as wide as any whim he possesses. With this creed his sins compound and become more obnoxious.

Who venerates himself, the world despises.

The words of his mouth are iniquity and deceit:
he hath left off to be wise, and to do good.
He deviseth mischief upon his bed; he setteth himself
in a way that is not good; he abhorreth not evil.—36:3,4

Set the Wrong Way

HE HATH LEFT OFF to be wise and to do good. This is one of the saddest statements in all the Bible. Here is a man who once followed the way of wisdom and goodness and then left it off. He can't plead ignorance, for he once knew to do right. Neither can he argue that he can't do better, for he has. He is without excuse.

Perhaps his word was once good, but now it is deceitful.

Probably he once prayed in bed, but now in bed he meditates on mischief.

There was a time when he abhorred evil, but now he abhors nothing.

Banish wisdom, discard honor, and
man sinks lower and lower.

But it doesn't occur suddenly. It is gradual.

The lesson is for us to guard against the things which cause us to drift from right. But if we already have drifted, remember it was not due to the wind but to the set of the sails; and now we can reset the sails and be brought back again.

How excellent is thy loving-kindness, O God! therefore the children of men put their trust under the shadow of thy wings.—36:7

Wings of Protection

THE PSALMIST FREQUENTLY USED the impressive metaphor of wings: "Hide me under the shadow of thy wings" (17:8). "Yea, in the shadow of thy wings will I make my refuge" (57:1). "Because thou hast been my help, therefore in the shadow of thy wings will I rejoice" (63:7).

Wings—a very expressive word. It indicates a place of care and safety. The analogy is striking. Just as little birds seek safety under the wings of the mother-bird, poor helpless man finds refuge under the care of his Creator. The only sure place for assistance is under those wings.

Refuge! From the plots of men. From the strife of enemies. From the bitterness of tongues. From the baseness of exploiters. And from the ill advice of friends.

There are so many opposing powers to crush and defeat. Had we not been protected by those invisible wings we would have been trampled many times. Thus humanity continues to cry out:

Oh that I had wings like a dove!—55:6

Cheer up, God has some: wings stronger than the wings of a dove; the only wings we dare to trust; the only sure wings of the future. Use them. Use them for protection. Use them for flight.

Fret not thyself because of evildoers,
neither be thou envious against the workers of iniquity.
—37:1

Envy Not the Evildoer

ENVY IS DISCONTENT AND PAIN at the comparative prosperity or excellence of another. Some people compare themselves with more successful or gifted people and, lo, the feeling begins to build up—especially when we behold the wealth of the wicked. However, there are many reasons why this is sheer folly, as stated in the Psalm.

In verse two it says, "They shall soon be cut down." This is understandable, for there is nothing to sustain them. They flourish for a while and pass away (verses 35 and 36). Actually, they destroy themselves, fall on their own sword (verse 15). We should no more envy them than we do the people on death row.

May we ever remember that ill-gotten money is no cause for envy and "a little that a righteous man hath is better than the riches of the wicked."

If we could, we wouldn't alter nature's law which sends rain on the just and on the unjust, whereby the wicked is allowed to prosper.

Think what envy does: it stirs up evil passions; agitates a sense of inferiority; wastes time; embitters life; and questions the justice of God. It remedies no ill; only aggravates an internal malady, causing us to rot on the inside until it destroys us (Proverbs 14:30).

*But the meek shall inherit the earth;
and shall delight themselves in the abundance of peace.*
—37:11

The Heritage of the Meek

JESUS USED THIS PASSAGE in giving the beatitudes: "Blessed are the meek: for they shall inherit the earth" (Matthew 5:5). Others have also taught it. The smartest and wisest have seen its value.

The meek are humble, gentle and mild, in contrast with the wicked who are proud, haughty and arrogant.

Contrary to public opinion, meekness is not weakness. Moses was the meakest man of his day (Numbers 12:3), but he was not weak. He had the courage to go against Pharaoh and the valor to lead the children of Israel.

Just common sense tells us which group is more apt to inherit the earth—the good things it has to offer, like goodwill, friendship, love and peace. The meek can occupy the earth in quietness and tranquility whereas the proud are caught up in the disturbances of jealousies, contentions and strifes. The meek "shall delight themselves in the abundance of peace"—peace with God, peace with themselves and peace with others. Their disposition does not excite vengeance nor stir up wrath but rather makes for harmony by holding out the olive branch. Truly—

It's wiser being good than bad;
It's safer being meek than fierce;
It's fitter being sane than mad.

—ROBERT BROWNING

The wicked borroweth, and payeth not again: but the righteous showeth mercy, and giveth.—37:21

Pay Your Debts

THE TEXT SUGGESTS THE ESTABLISHED VIEW of economics that the righteous, following a way of life which makes for prosperity, are more apt to be in a position to lend and to give.

Some borrow with no intention of repaying—and this is wicked. Others borrow with no prospect of repaying—and this is also wicked, for willingness alone settles nothing. Others borrow with the idea they are honest, and that if the time should ever come when they have more than they need and do not have to sacrifice or put themselves out any, they will repay—and this, too, is wicked. So here are some *don'ts* in borrowing:

- Don't be reckless about borrowing.
- Don't be careless about paying.
- Don't hold yourself flawless if the debt pinches.
- Don't think that words pay debts.
- Don't let your creditor have a better memory than you.
- Don't let it be habit forming.
- Don't think that if you owe someone a hundred dollars and God forgives you that it pays your debt.

Remember—it is better to live in less comfort than to live in more debt than you can pay.

I have been young, and now am old;
yet have I not seen the righteous forsaken,
nor his seed begging bread.—37:25

Taught by the Years

I HAVE BEEN YOUNG, AND NOW AM OLD. This is a solemn place in life. The journey on earth is almost ended. Here is an old man who through the years has seen the plan of God bless man. Experience has taught him much. In fact, he had to live a long time just to learn how to live—to live in more trust, peace and expectation. This is one of the good things about age—experience. The years teach what we could never master in youth from books.

He knows best who has experienced it.

Now what was the specific lesson the psalmist had learned from the passing years? That religion is an advantage to man; that God's wings of protection are not withdrawn from His children; that even in material matters the people of God are more consistently blessed than aliens; and that he had not seen the children of the godly begging bread.

It is an economic fact that the religion of God blesses materially as well as spiritually. It teaches industry, prudence and thrift, and promises the care of God for His own. Begging is usually the result of a course contrary to the Scriptures. It is ordinarily brought on by extreme misconduct. Religion teaches man to depend on God and himself while beggary teaches him to depend on the handouts of others.

There is no soundness in my flesh. . . . —38:3

Faith in Sickness

HOW DOES A FAITHFUL BELIEVER RESPOND to illness? David's conduct in time of severe illness and torturing pain tells us. When the body is wracked by pain and friends forsake and enemies threaten, this Psalm is exceedingly relevant and especially helpful.

Note the condition of the sufferer as stated in this chapter, a great source of help: His flesh was without soundness, no vigor, no strength. There was a burning inflammation in his loins, which was loathsome. Feebleness gripped him, and his condition produced "roarings" or groanings. He experienced palpitation as strength waned. And his sight was failing.

To make it worse, his condition was aggravated by friends and kinsmen who turned away from him and by enemies who took advantage of his sickness to bring false charges against him.

His sickness sharpened his memory and caused him to suppose that it was the result of his sin and foolishness, an effect not uncommon among sufferers.

Yet the writer never despaired of faith. He freely confessed his sins, asked God for help and found greater faith in time of sickness.

I said, I will take heed to my ways that I sin not with my tongue: I will keep my mouth with a bridle, while the wicked is before me.—39:1

Bridle My Tongue

I WILL. This was a resolution on the poet's part. A necessary one. For we improve ourselves only through concerted effort. He resolved not to sin with his tongue. This was truly a mouthful—a mouth he would keep full rather than unload on others.

The tongue offends and the ears get the cuffing.
—ANONYMOUS

This is the biggest job any of us have ever had. But don't blame the tongue, blame the heart that controls it (Matthew 12:34).

However, he expected to keep the resolution through two efforts: First, he would take heed to his ways. Second, he would bridle his tongue. He was determined to say nothing. This was a big order to give himself.

Does this mean it is as bad to think a thing as it is to say it? No! It is worse to give expression to the sentiment. A wise man holds in his words for the proper time (Proverbs 29:11).

David's resolution to hold his tongue was a noble intent and one that we should imitate today.

My heart was hot within me;
while I was musing the fire burned:
then spake I with my tongue.—39:3

A Burning Heart

THOUGH THE PSALMIST HAD RESOLVED to remain totally silent in his affliction, refusing even to speak good, he found it an impossible restriction. The silence was like a fire that burned within him. When the fire became too hot he had to speak. Not to man who wouldn't understand or who might misrepresent him, but rather to God who is intellectually wise and mercifully kind.

The deeper view of life makes surface hurts more bearable. For the glorious life beyond makes every earthly thing pale into insignificance by comparison. Knowing the real source of help, he declared that he expected relief from God alone. Sometimes our problems are so big they defy the help of helpless humanity.

And in this commendable relationship of man and deity, he implored God to hear his prayer (that is always proper), to deliver him from his transgressions (a human need), to protect him from the reproaches of the foolish (how they hurt), and to spare him that he might have time to recover his strength. Time to recover! O precious time!

When we can open our mouths this way and to this One, it is good to speak. David broke his silence but not his resolution: "that I sin not with my tongue."

Lord, make me to know mine end
and the measure of my days, what it is;
that I may know how frail I am.—39:4

Make Me to Know

THE THIRTY-NINTH PSALM IS OFTEN READ at funerals. It offers some timely and needful lessons on:

• ***The frailty of man.*** "Thou hast made my days as a handbreadth; and my age is as nothing before thee" (verse 5). In measurement of time, life is just a breath—and often a gasping one. But it is hard for us to learn this lesson. While we know others are passing, we think we are here to stay. But to stay—we can't; for we are only walking shadows.

Out, out, brief candle,
Life's but a walking shadow, a poor player
That struts and frets his long hour upon the stage,
And then is heard no more.
—WILLIAM SHAKESPEARE

• ***The vanity of man.*** "Verily every man at his best state is altogether vanity" (verse 5). Life is burdened with allusive attainments, useless trifles and worthless wonders. Our days are crowded with the hustle and bustle of cares that don't care for us, that have no real meaning and no lasting purpose. Edmund Burke, the eloquent statesman, gave this memorable comment on the passage: "What shadows we are, and what shadows we pursue."

• ***The separation of man from all earthly treasures.*** "He heapeth up riches and knoweth not who shall gather them" (verse 6). This gives much to ponder.

Before I go hence.—39:13

More Lessons From Man's Frailty

FROM WHAT IS CALLED a funeral Psalm, we continue:

• ***The hope of man.*** "My hope is in thee" (verse 7). Not in self, for man is too powerless. Not in riches, for they can do only so much and go only so far. Not in friends, for they often turn fickle. But cheer up. God is alive! In Him there is hope. In Him we rise in this material sphere until we break the mortal barrier and then it's—immortality.

• ***The deliverance of man.*** "Deliver me from all my transgressions" (verse 8). From sin. From its slavery. From the discontent it produces within us. From the reproaches it brings on us. From the forebodings it hangs over us. And from the guilt it presses on our brow.

• ***The sojourn of man.*** "I am a stranger with thee, and a sojourner" (verse 12). Every critical illness is a reminder that we are strangers and sojourners swiftly moving to our permanent home. And every bereavement reemphasizes the thought.

• ***The plea of man.*** "O spare me that I may recover strength, before I go hence, and be no more" (verse 13). He asked to be spared for a better time to go. This is a common plea—"spare me." But why? To correct errors? To retrieve follies? To do more for God? Maybe we have already been spared. If so, let us use the spare time in the noblest manner.

And he hath put a new song in my mouth, even praise unto our God.—40:3

A New Song

THE SWEET SINGER OF ISRAEL was given a new song, one that came forth freely and naturally from an internal compulsion that felt the need to express itself.

It was a song of deliverance. "Out of a horrible pit." "Out of the miry clay." Deeper and deeper he had sunk in the pit of misery and the mire of sin until he reached the frightful state of "innumerable evils…more than the hairs of mine head" (verse 12). But up from the pit he came, out of the mire he ascended, with an appreciation of his deliverance that inspired him to sing.

He sang of personal progress, which is an uplift all of us need. He had been "in the pit," then on his knees and then "on the rock." When weighed down by sin, he was lifted up by prayer and firmly established on the Rock of Ages.

It was a song of praise, which should be on the lips of all of us. Recognizing the inexpressible wonders of God, David burst forth in a new song.

He sang of obedience, which should be humanity's song. The compliance was cheerful and from the heart, which are essential requisites of true obedience.

If our relationship with God while here on earth gives rise to a new song, it is only a little foretaste of the song of Moses and the Lamb we shall sing together in the great forever.

I delight to do thy will, O my God;
yea, thy law is within my heart.—40:8

Acceptable Obedience

WHAT IS TRUE OBEDIENCE? It is not robot service that ritualistically gives gifts and offers sacrifices. We are told in the sixth verse that this is not what God wants: "Sacrifice and offering thou didst not desire." However, God commands sacrifice; but apart from a spirit of free and loving obedience, it is not desired at all. Good deeds from wrong motives are in vain.

Acceptable obedience begins with open ears: "Mine ears hast thou opened." Let's keep our ears open to God's every command. "Stopped ears" stop us.

Additionally, cheerful submission is required. "I delight to do thy will" describes it. For obeying the letter without the spirit does not meet the Divine standard.

And lastly, approvable obedience must be from the heart, as the text states. Otherwise its only reward is the applause of men. But when the heart is in our profession we go the full distance, we accept the whole package rather than pick out the commands we want to obey, rejecting all others. For when the heart is in it, no command is slavish. All are delightful!

The Lord will strengthen him upon the bed of languishing: thou wilt make all his bed in his sickness.—41:3

Making Our Bed Soft

WHICHEVER WAY WE MAKE OUR BED we have to lie on it. But with God's help it can be made soft. *Thou wilt make all his bed in his sickness:* literally, thou will turn it, turn its cushions and make it comfortable. God does it, but conditionally. The condition is that one considers the poor, regards and assists those in poverty, sickness, humiliation, defeat and all others in any other affliction (verse 1).

We cannot do good without being made better by it. Every act of pity raises us in self-respect and power. Furthermore, there is the blessing which comes from the needy, many of whom will never forget us. Their confidence, gratitude and prayers might prove to be the figurative bed upon which we may someday lie. Besides this, we do have the promise of God to soften our bed.

> *He that hath pity upon the poor lendeth unto the Lord; and that which he hath given will he pay him back again.*
> —PROVERBS 19:17

The great basis of religion is compassion. And God is asking us: "Shouldest not thou also have had compassion on thy fellow servant, even as I had pity on thee?" (Matthew 18:33).

I said, Lord, be merciful unto me: heal my soul; for I have sinned against thee.—41:4

I Have Sinned

DAVID'S CONFESSION OF SIN has been the admission of many. Some were sincere, others pretentious.

Pharaoh said, "I have sinned this time" (Exodus 9:27). But he didn't mean it. Under the temporary shock of a plague, he confessed his guilt; but when the plague was removed, he returned to his true self.

Balaam confessed, "I have sinned" (Numbers 22:34), and subsequently changed his course.

Achan admitted, "Indeed I have sinned" (Joshua 7:20). He took forbidden spoils when Jericho fell. When confronted by Joshua, he owned up to it.

Job confessed, "I have sinned" (Job 7:20)—the humble admission of a bankrupt, afflicted man who was deeply religious.

Judas stated, "I have sinned" (Matthew 27:4). Unable to live with his sin, he committed suicide. All of us have to deal with sin, but this is not the answer. How tragic!

The Prodigal Son confessed, "I have sinned against heaven, and in thy sight" (Luke 15:21). He saw his mistake and penitently corrected it, returning home to his father.

May we be sincere in confessing our shortcomings—to ourselves and to others. It is essential to the reformation of life and the restoration of the soul.

Yea, mine own familiar friend, in whom I trusted, which did eat of my bread, hath lifted up his heel against me.—41:9

The Betrayal

THIS QUOTATION FROM THE PSALM had a fulfillment in the betrayal of Christ by Judas. Jesus said that it did:

> *I speak not of you all: I know whom I have chosen: but that the Scripture may be fulfilled, he that eateth bread with me hath lifted up his heel against me.*—JOHN 13:18

Even if the text in Psalms refers to an official counselor of David who defected from him and joined a conspiracy, it undoubtedly has a fuller and truer application in the treachery of Judas and was used accordingly.

After the betrayal of Christ, despair possessed Judas and he chose to die at the end of a rope rather than to live with his guilt. So he hanged himself. He didn't sell Christ, he sold himself. Now Jesus lives in glory, Judas in infamy.

With a kiss of treason, Judas made a mockery of loyalty and rent the apostleship with the unkindest cut of all. To think upon it stirs our blood and renews our determination to make ourselves of sterner stuff.

Let us be loyal for there are those who trust us. And above all, let us be true for it is right.

As the hart panteth after the water brooks, so panteth my soul after thee, O God.—42:1

A Thirst for God

THE POETIC SINGER BEGINS THIS PSALM with an analogy: As the deer pants after the water in the brook, so pants his soul, he declares, after God. The panting of the deer is indicative of its thirst for water, and the panting of the soul is expressive of its thirst for God. The soul craves its Creator.

The thirst that from the soul doth rise
Doth ask a drink divine.
—BEN JOHNSON

David uses similar language in chapter 63:1: "My soul thirsteth for thee in a dry and thirsty land, where no water is." Often we feel that our world is struck with drought and there is nothing on earth to quench our thirst. True! But beyond the earth of materials there is a Quenching Power, a Living Fountain, God! And every soul that drinks of Him is satisfied.

Isn't it strange that so many are dying of thirst when they have free access to the Ever-flowing Fountain of Life?

Thank God for the intense panting of the soul. It is inborn in our nature. Now let us quench the profound longing by drinking! Today! And forever!

My soul thirsteth for God, for the living God: when shall I come and appear before God? My tears have been my meat.... —42:2,3

A Diet of Tears

TEARS ARE A MEAT THAT FEEDS THE SOUL in various circumstances. In sorrow. In ecstasy. In pain. In fear. In helplessness. They can ease a hunger that bread never satisfies.

All tears, however, are not the same in every person's eyes. With David—they were related to his absence from worship services and to the taunting he took from vilifiers who asked, "Where is thy God?" As the deer pants for water, his soul panted for God. But his adverse circumstances made it impossible for him to attend the house of God. As he looked back on former days when he freely went with the multitude to public worship, the privation of the privilege pierced his heart and the tears flowed. They were the tears of a spiritual desire. He hungered to be in the house of God; and when he could not, his soul was fed by his tears.

A little rain blesses man, and so do tears.

Would we know the meaning of happiness,
Would we feel that the day was bright,
If we'd never known what it was to grieve,
Nor gazed on the dark of night?

Here is a man who had the heart to go to worship, but not the opportunity. How different from many today who have the opportunity but not the heart.

Why art thou cast down, O my soul?
and why art thou disquieted in me?—42:5

Overcoming Despair

AT TIMES ALL OF US HAVE our disquieting moments in which we lose heart and feel that fate has cast us into a losing role. From John Dryden's extreme melancholy we have this dismal view:

When I consider life, 'tis all a cheat;
Yet, fool'd with hope, men favor the deceit;
Trust on, and think tomorrow will repay.
Tomorrow's falser than the former day;
Lies worse, and while it says we shall be blest
With some new joys, cuts off what we possest.

I hasten to say: life is not that gloomy. However, a strong man like David felt the pain of despair. So what he did to cure it is most helpful to us. In the remedy we find such words as *God, hope, praise, remember* (verses 5-9). He knew that God was the rock on which he could stand and be safe. His hope was in Him, that he "will command his loving-kindness in the daytime, and in the night his song shall be with me." Praising God changed his thought process from earthly woes to heavenly wonders. A remembrance of what his Lord had done at various places lifted David's soul. For what God had done, God would do.

To be practical, when we feel depression coming on, seize these words: *God, hope, praise, remember.* As we dwell on them, they will fill our hearts with optimism.

O send out thy light and thy truth:
let them lead me; let them bring me unto thy holy hill,
and to thy tabernacles.—43:3

Plea for Deliverance

THE AUTHOR APPEALS TO GOD to plead his "cause against an ungodly nation" and to deliver him "from the deceitful and unjust man" (verse 1)—perhaps Absalom.

In recognition of the source of unfailing help, he prayed to God: "Send out thy light and thy truth: let them lead me." Exiled and cast into the darkness of trouble, he invoked God's grace and faithfulness to lead him back to his former privileges. As an exile banished from the holy hill and the tabernacles, David's heart cried out to be led back to Jerusalem and to the altar of God and there, he said, "will I praise thee, O God, my God."

O worship the King, all glorious above,
And gratefully sing His wonderful love;
Our Shield and Defender, the Ancient of Days,
Pavilioned in splendor and girded with praise.
—ROBERT GRANT

All of us need deliverance of some sort, of some kind, at least to some extent. As earth's pilgrims, we desperately need to be led by light, to ascend the holy hill, and to worship the God of our being. This lets our souls breathe a new celestial air and get a little foretaste of what it will be like in that land where no chains shall bind, no enemies pursue, and no burdens press down.

*We have heard with our ears, O God,
our fathers have told us, what work thou didst
in their days, in the times of old.*—44:1

Heritage of Faith

THE FATHERS FROM generation to generation had told their children of God: God's mercy, God's power, God's deliverance, how that He had driven out the heathen (or the idolaters) and given Israel the land of Canaan. The children were taught that their forefathers did not get the land "by their own sword," nor that they were saved by their own arm, but that the possession came through the favor of God (verse 3). May we never forget the source of our blessings.

The Law required the fathers to teach their children the history of the nation and especially what God had done for them: "that thou mayest tell in the ears of thy son, and of thy son's son, what things I have wrought in Egypt..." (Exodus 10:2). The command recognizes the molding power of teaching and the duty of godly fathers.

What are we teaching our children and grandchildren about God? Are we shaping their faith in a God of power, love, compassion, holiness and purity?

Faith cannot be taken for granted. Will our children have faith? As the child is influenced, so lives the adult.

All this is come upon us; yet have we not forgotten thee, neither have we dealt falsely in thy covenant.—44:17

Yet Not Forgotten

MANY REVERSES CAME UPON THEM. As seen in verses 10-22, they were:

- Defeated.
- Plundered.
- Scattered.
- Reproached.
- Derided.
- Martyred.

Yet they did not forget God. With a strong assertion they sang, "Our heart is not turned back, neither have our steps declined from thy way" (verse 18). Pressured by the biddings of idolatry and afflicted by dreadful tortures for refusing to comply, yet they generally remained true to their religion. We can learn much from this. For God uses the past to teach the present. We should learn that apostasy does not come so often from privation and persecution as it does from affluence and popularity. Faithfulness is not dependent on wealth, popularity or affiliation with a prestigious group, but rather on faith and hope, which are begotten and strengthened by teaching.

By persevering we obtain the promised crown. God help us to overcome.

It matters not how the battle goes,
The day how long;
Faint not! Fight on!
Tomorrow comes the song.

*Shall not God search this out?
for he knoweth the secrets of the heart.*—44:21

Secrets of the Heart

IN THE CONTEXT the sacred writer made the point that if there had been any alienation from God in the hearts of the people, God would have known it. This is repeatedly affirmed in the Scriptures.

The heart of each has its wall of concealment and veil of privacy. Every heart has its own secrets. And this is good. It would be bad, terribly bad! if every person could look into the heart of every other person and behold the privileged facts. Curious, intolerant and gossipy people would misuse the information.

But there is one who searches the heart and knows its secrets—God. No thought lies buried too deep in the heart of man for Him to see, nor flashes through too fast for Him to behold. But it is classified information, belonging only to Him and the person.

He searches the heart for the *intent* and sees the extenuating circumstances, which often put the deed in a more tolerable perspective, though cold and self-righteous critics come running with hammer and nails to crucify the person on what they call a cross of justice.

What goes on in the heart is often a mystery to the person himself, but God understands its workings better than man. I am glad He sees inside us! I am glad others don't!

My heart is inditing [overfloweth with] *a good matter: I speak of the things which I have made touching the King.*
—45:1

A Bubbling Heart

MY HEART IS INDITING A GOOD MATTER: literally, it means *bubbles with a good matter.* His heart was bubbling over with things pertaining to the King of Kings.

The world is drawn to the person with the bubbly heart. We like to be in the presence of an exciting life.

When the heart starts bubbling, something is going to happen: praise, propagation, outreach and achievement. Enthusiasm puts the sparkle in living, provides the drive for accomplishment. Without zealous hearts no battles have been won, no wilderness conquered, no frontiers extended and no religion propagated. The men and women with bubbly hearts have kept the fires of progress burning when others would have allowed the flames to fade into the cold, gray ashes of despair.

Every great achievement is the story
of a flaming heart.
—A. B. ZU TAVERN

Hence, one of the greatest needs in the church is enthusiasm. The religion of God is not cold, dull, lifeless. As an example: The minister brought out a great truth and a visitor said, "Praise the Lord." Immediately an usher touched his arm and whispered, "You can't praise the Lord in this church." Why? It might disturb the corpses sitting in the pews.

My tongue is the pen of a ready writer.—45:1

A Ready Writer

THE PSALMIST'S HEART WAS FULL of his subject—bubbling over—and he desired to express his thoughts in the warm, overflowing emotion of a ready writer. Because he wrote, the world has this lovely and romantic Psalm.

God places extraordinary value on writing. He said: "I will write upon these tables" (Exodus 34:1). "Write thee all the words that I have spoken unto thee in a book" (Jeremiah 30:2). "But these are written that ye might believe" (John 20:31). The Bible itself is irrefutable proof that God greatly favors writing—and consequently reading.

Books give men great dreams to dream,
Sun-lit ways that glint and gleam,
Where the sages
Tramp the ages.
—WILLIAM L. STRIDGER

Many noble causes have died for the lack of a writer. *The pen is mightier than the sword.* Our society is maintained by a war of ideas.

For our own self-preservation we must not allow a nation of readers to become solely a nation of watchers. The trend is already having adverse effects. If the church would encourage its members to read something worthwhile everyday, the leavening results would exceed our fondest dreams.

Upon thy right hand did stand the queen in gold of Ophir.
—45:9

The Bride and the Groom

THIS PSALM PROPHETICALLY AND FORCEFULLY portrays Christ and His church in the meaningful figure of a marriage: bridegroom and bride. To have used this symbol is proof that the church means much more to the Lord than many people realize. The Psalm contains two main divisions which shed light on both:

First, an address to the bridegroom: A man fairer than the sons of men; blessed with gracious speech; dressed as a warrior, for He has enemies; goes forth in majesty; wields His right hand with power; has the power to chastise enemies; His throne is forever; loves righteousness and hates wickedness; and anointed with gladness above his fellows.

Second, an address to the bride, the church: Bidden to hearken; to break with relationships that interfere; to worship the Lord; shall attract heathen nations; is glorious within; a virgin train shall follow the bride—probably symbolizes the Gentiles' following the Hebrews into the church; her fame shall not come from predecessors but from her own sons; and her name shall be remembered in all generations.

We need both. If we appreciate the groom (the Lord), we should appreciate the bride (His church).

God is our refuge and strength,
a very present help in trouble.—**Psalm 46:1**

God Our Help

WE ARE NOT THE FIRST TO LIVE in a threatening, chaotic world. The people of Israel were delivered mightily by the hand of God from an oppressing evil. This Psalm throbs with their gratitude, thanksgiving and praise.

The story of God's unfailing deliverances must be repeated and requoted and remembered. Though the earth gets bumped out of orbit and spins endlessly through space, though the mountains be carried and dumped into the seas, we will not fear.

When everything is stripped from us (mate, child, career, health), when life gets as bad as it can be, when times are as tough as they can get—we have a refuge, a strength. We have a God!

While we must never forget that God is *our* refuge, we must firmly believe that he is *my* God, *my* strength, *my* help. Unless the promises of God become personal to me, they lose their power for me.

With these assurances, maybe we can stop relying so heavily on earth-made tranquilizers and trust more on heaven-made tranquility.

Be still and know that I am God.—46:10

The God Who Stills Us

THE FORTY-SIXTH PSALM WAS COMPOSED at a time when Israel was in great peril. Just what it was we are not certain, but we are certain it is one of the most beautiful and reassuring of all the Psalms. It was the favorite of Martin Luther who often quoted it when troubles threatened. Its contents of blessed assurance will lift our sinking spirits:

• "God is our refuge" (verse 1).

Should storms of sevenfold thunder roll,
And shake the globe from pole to pole,
No flaming bolt shall daunt my face,
For my God is my hiding place.

• "Therefore will not we fear" (verse 2). With God as our refuge, nothing should scare us.

• "God shall help" (verse 5). Though troubled waters rise and mountains tumble, there is the life-sustaining river of God that flows into the heart of man.

• "The Lord of hosts is with us" (verse 7). Though the heathen rage and kingdoms fall, there is one immovable power that remains with us—the Lord.

• "He maketh wars to cease" (verse 9). God's righteousness expels from the hearts of men the very things that produce war. For wars are first inward.

Be still! This command was not just for country folk who lived in a slow time and a passive pace. Even today it is necessary to "be still" to make progress.

Clap your hands, all ye people;
shout unto God with the voice of triumph.—47:1

Clap Your Hands

THIS PSALM IS A TRIUMPHAL ONE, probably composed to celebrate some victory.

We are constantly engaged in conflicts, some we win, some we lose. When we win, it's time to clap hands and sing. Clapping the hands is no cold gesture, but rather the spontaneous coming together of the heart's ready servants—the hands. And singing is no senseless emotion, but the echo of the heart.

In an adaptation of the Psalm, let us also clap our hands and sing, for the reasons are the same:

• The same God who was called *terrible* has not changed. The avenger of all wrongs! So let us turn the injustices we have suffered over to Him.

• God still has the prerogative to choose His people's inheritance (verse 4). If Israel would praise Him for giving them an earthly land of death and sorrow, how much more we should praise Him for offering us the deathless land of endless joy.

• He still sits "upon the throne of his holiness" (verse 8). His government is not oppressive. He has no unjust demands. Every regulation is for the good of man.

Truly, we have cause to clap our hands and sing. This puts *A Psalm in My Heart.*

As we have heard, so have we seen in the city of the Lord of hosts, in the city of our God: God will establish it for ever.—48:8

We Have Seen

THEY HAD HEARD OF GOD'S DELIVERANCE of Jerusalem. Now they had seen it with their own eyes. They had listened with pride to the stories of how God had put the heathen to flight for Israel's sake. Now it has been confirmed in their own sight.

This assurance lifts the soul heavenward, bends the knees to pray, tunes the lips to sing and strengthens the heart to continue. This we know, He cares for us. So, in all trials and sorrows, let us to His bosom fly.

We, too, can say, "As we have heard, so have we seen." We were told that God answers prayer; now we know it: our prayers have been answered. We heard of the providence of God; moreover we have seen it actually work. We heard that the right way to treat enemies is to return good for evil; after trying it, we know it is best. We heard that God would provide for His children; the years have passed and now we say with David, "We have seen."

What we "heard" and what we have "seen," now let us "tell." Let us tell the wondrous story of God's redeeming love and power in our lives.

Mark ye well her bulwarks, consider her palaces; that ye may tell it to the generation following.—48:13

Mark Well Her Bulwarks

THE ADMONITION WAS to pay close attention to the fortifications and breastworks protecting Jerusalem. Behold its safety.

That ye may tell it to the generation following. The object is to give the next generation a correct account that they may be inspired to believe the city cannot be vanquished, that within the city there is safety.

Our fortress today is the New Jerusalem, the church, which has bulwarks of safety and protection. The church was established on solid rock, founded by God, headed by Christ, and is guided by Scripture.

Thus, the church is distinguished with Divine defenses which make it safe: impregnable bulwarks, everlasting fortifications. Its only human aspect is its membership (human beings, but saved ones); and this also is to the glory of God: a divine church for people, just as Jerusalem was the city of God for people.

The church is not another option for people looking to fill out the empty spaces of their lives. It is the body of Christ. It is essential. Mark well her bulwarks.

For this God is our God for ever and ever:
he will be our guide even unto death.—48:14

Choosing a Guide

THEIR CHOICE WAS DEFINITE. It was final—"unto death." Happiness requires some basic, once-for-all-time decisions that may be spared the worry and fret of wondering what to do. Those ancients made the most basic one of all—to follow God. A smart choice!

They didn't know where the Guide would lead them, but they knew the Guide. So on they went. Such confidence was needed for the completion of the journey. Wagon trains that once rolled across the West moved only because those who followed put trust in their guide.

When all is considered, the lifetime resolution of Israel should be the natural and easy one for all of us.

> *When confronted with two courses of action, I jot down on a piece of paper all the arguments in favor of one—then on the opposite side I write the arguments against each one. Then by weighing the arguments pro and con and cancelling them out, one against the other, I take the course by what remains.*
>
> —BENJAMIN FRANKLIN

If we, in selecting a guide to the promised land, will do as Franklin suggested, there is no question about the choice. And then when the journey has ended, how comforting it will be to have picked the Guide who knew the way.

This their way is their folly;
yet their posterity approve their sayings.—49:13

Their Wealth Is Their Folly

THE AUTHOR PRESENTED some irrefutable arguments in this Psalm, which show the folly of trusting in wealth and boasting in riches.

First, riches won't buy the redemption of a soul. Salvation cannot be bought in the market.

Second, the rich "perish, and leave their wealth to others." It's only a temporary possession.

Third, their deception "is, that their houses shall continue forever" and that their lands are in their names—theirs. But they are only tenants.

Fourth, man abides not. Both the rich and the poor have appointments with death.

Fifth, and "when he dieth he shall carry nothing away." Nothing! Absolutely nothing!

But to be factual and practical, let us remember: while money cannot buy redemption, it can aid the church; cannot fully support a family, yet it can feed, clothe and house them; cannot give an education, but can pay school tuition; cannot purchase health, but can pay the hospital bills; and cannot give life in the next world, but can pay the cost of leaving this one. Beyond this, wealth is not needed; and to chase it needlessly is labeled *folly.* For to be wealthy, unhealthy, unhappy, unsaved and dead is unwise.

Though while he lived he blessed his soul,
and men will praise thee, when thou doest well to thyself.
—49:18

Double Praise for a Single Error

THE RICH MAN IN THE TEXT PRAISED HIMSELF. So did others. All because he became rich. Double praise for a single error. The fault, however, was not in amassing riches but in overestimating their value.

The wealthy man "blessed his soul," blessed himself, praised himself. He regarded his affluence as an accomplishment to be admired and envied. He thought his standing on a pile of gold made him taller than others and that they should look up to him. Of course, the accumulation of wealth does require thought, sagacity, hard work, sacrifice, thrift and wise investments. It doesn't come easily; if so, everybody would be rich. But to make it the chief aim in life and an end within itself is not praiseworthy. To allow the big purse to give one the big head shrinks nature.

Wealth turns the heads of a lot of people—especially the ones who don't have it to the ones who do. The *have-nots* applaud the *haves.* It is a sad commentary on our society that other accomplishments more important go unnoticed. But our society uses a ruler of gold to measure a man's success. Many a person is blinded by the luster of that gold ruler until finally it becomes cankered, and then he sees that he misread it.

For when he dieth he shall carry nothing away.—VERSE 17

I will not reprove thee for thy sacrifices or thy burnt offerings, to have been continually before me.
—50:8

The Gift Without the Giver

"THE GIFT WITHOUT THE GIVER IS BARE," wrote James Russell Lowell. He also stated:

He gives only the worthless gold
Who gives from a sense of duty.

This was a common fault of many worshippers. For the Israelites to think the ritual of giving, irrespective of the spirit, met Divine approval was most appalling, and the Lord rebuked them for it: not for neglecting ceremonial sacrifices because they hadn't (as seen in the text) but because their spirit was wrong.

The Lord would not accept any sacrifice offered amiss. For "every beast of the forest...and the cattle upon a thousand hills...the fowls of the mountains, and the wild beasts of the field" were already His. He needed nothing. He even asked if they thought He needed material nurture (verse 13).

Next, the Psalm gives the basic instruction for acceptable worship: "offer unto God thanksgiving." Material gifts could be given from the hands out, but thanksgiving and praise (which are to accompany giving) could come only from the heart.

In this materialistic age when the size of a gift is emphasized more than the spirit, we need to reread the Scriptures which teach that the giver should give *himself,* give *willingly,* not *grudgingly,* or of *necessity* (II Corinthians 8:5,12; 9:7).

But unto the wicked God saith,
What hast thou to do to declare my statutes,
or that thou shouldest take my covenant in thy mouth?
—50:16

Teacher, Teach Thyself

THE FIFTIETH PSALM IS ONE of the most instructive in setting forth the necessity of a spiritual religion in contrast with the mere observance of religious forms.

Those religionists claimed the privileges of the Divine covenant but ignored its duties. However, they did not have the privilege to declare the statutes to others until those ordinances meant something to them, no right to open their mouth to men until they first opened their heart to God.

While performing religious ceremonies with scrupulous regularity, they committed the basest crimes: They hated instruction which disqualified them as instructors, for the best teacher is willing to be taught. They cast their lot with thieves and became partakers with adulterers. Their tongues were used to propagate deception and detraction. Moreover, they slandered their brothers, which is a form of spiritual cannibalism.

Centuries later Paul put the inconsistency in focus by asking:

Thou therefore which teachest another, teachest thou not thyself?
thou that preachest a man should not steal, dost thou steal?
—ROMANS 2:21,22

The ever relevant lesson is: *Teacher, teach thyself.*

These things hast thou done, and I kept silence; thou thoughtest that I was altogether such a one as thyself: but I will reprove thee, and set them in order before thine eyes.—50:21

Thinking That God Is Like Man

SINCE THE PEOPLE IN THE TEXT did not regard sincerity, justice, purity and morality as essential, they supposed God felt this way, too, and that He would be satisfied with the mere rites of religion. It met their approval, so they thought it met His.

Thinking that God is like man is one of the most common errors and one of the greatest menaces to religion. Men and women make their images of God—not metal but mental—to conform to their own views. They make God in the likeness of themselves, corresponding to their likes and dislikes, beliefs and disbeliefs, with all their prejudices, limitations, weaknesses and follies.

Men can hide from men, therefore they suppose they can hide from God. Humans can be bribed, hence they imagine God also can be bought. Since men feel that they do not have to obey the laws of God, they think He feels the same way. The masses are impressed with pomp and ostentation, thus they assume it appeals to God. Whatever teaching they espouse, they presume God favors the same.

The most common idolatry is the Specter of the mirror in which one sees God as a colossal, shadowy figure of himself, of course, with human frailties, passions and scanty virtues.

For I acknowledge my transgressions: and my sin is ever before me.—51:3

Real Repentance

THREE STEPS ARE ESSENTIAL IN REPENTANCE: First, a broken and bruised spirit caused by sorrow for sin. David experienced this heart feeling and offered it to God as a sacrifice: "The sacrifices of God are a broken spirit: a broken and contrite heart" (verse 17). God delighted in this rather than in burnt offerings and was pleased with the latter only after the former was offered to Him. The emphasis is placed on what goes on in the inward man:

Behold, thou desirest truth in the inward parts.—VERSE 6

No outward acts of religion will satisfy the Father unless they emanate from inward purity.

Second, confession. "For I acknowledge my transgressions" (verse 3). This was David's free and open confession. It is very similar to his admission of guilt in 32:5: "I acknowledged my sin unto thee, and mine iniquity have I not hid." He did not try to conceal the fact that he was a sinner. Nor did he try to exonerate himself.

Third, reformation in life. This is the test of repentance, provided the amendments are prompted by grief for sin rather than for economic, social or political gains. The changed heart produces a change in living, as stipulated by John the Baptist: "Bring forth therefore fruits meet for repentance" (Matthew 3:8).

Against thee, thee only, have I sinned,
and done this evil in thy sight:
that thou mightest be justified when thou speakest,
and be clear when thou judgest.—51:4

God's Judgment Is Justified

DAVID'S SIN, WHICH IS TRUE OF ALL SINS, was primarily against God. Of course, David knew that he had wronged some humans and had hurt society. His sin against Uriah and his family was low, treacherous and violent (II Samuel 11), but still the offense derived its greatest shame from the fact the Divine law had been transgressed. God gave the law that David sinned against, and God—not Uriah—would judge him. The chief heinousness of sin is not in its devastating power to disgrace, or to bankrupt, or to sadden, but in its disregard for the law of God. Even the sins of David, adultery and murder, faded into insignificance as wrongs against humans when viewed as offenses against God. This is why David said, "Against thee, thee only, have I sinned."

To his credit, David did not try to excuse himself. He could have blamed Bathsheba—"She shouldn't have paraded herself in full view." Oh! how we blame others for our own mistakes!

But no! David blamed no one else, not even God. He accepted full responsibility for his sin. He even wanted the world to know that God was just in the punishment of his sin. In a world of sinners, this attitude is hard to find. May the same spirit be yours. And may it be mine.

Then will I teach transgressors thy ways;
and sinners shall be converted unto thee.—51:13

Life After Failure

IN THIS CHAPTER DAVID PENITENTLY PLEADED for forgiveness, that he be purged and made clean, whiter than snow. In his appeal for pardon, he promised to use his restored life to the conversion of man and to the praise of God.

First, he pledged to teach others: "Then will I teach transgressors…sinners shall be converted." Jesus enunciated the same principle of soul-winning in the Great Commission: He commanded the apostles to go teach and baptize and then teach the new converts to observe all things He commanded the apostles, one of which was to go teach (Matthew 28:19,20). This is a most obsessive and lovely pursuit.

How beautiful are the feet of them that preach the gospel of peace, and bring glad tidings of good things!—ROMANS 10:15

Second, he promised to praise God: "My mouth shall show forth thy praise" (verse 15). His awareness of guilt had closed his lips too long. But with sins forgiven and conscience cleared, his mouth would open and his heart would flow with praise. A condemning conscience interferes with devotion and worship. It dries our hearts and seals our lips, shutting off praise of God and teaching of sinners. But when we are washed in the mercy of God and made whiter than snow, we can preach and pray and sing with a full heart.

Why boastest thou thyself in mischief, O mighty man? the goodness of God endureth continually.—52:1

Nothing to Brag About

WHEN PEOPLE APPLAUD THEMSELVES for being evil, they have much to brag about—if it were a laudable matter. For they must be mighty wicked to commend themselves for it.

Boasting is never good, and it is all the worse when it is for being bad. But some are determined to have something to brag about, even if it's their depravity. They feel the need to excel, though it's in immorality and criminality. Thus the world has its champions in corruption: the boldest bank robber, the slickest confidence man, the shrewdest forger, the sharpest shoplifter, the filthiest mouth, the thirstiest drinker and the cruelest heart.

Also, there are other braggarts of their shortcomings.

Did you ever hear a person boast about missing church? And have you heard a person brag about paying no attention to a sermon?

Likewise, there is the man who pats himself on the back for cheating somebody.

And there is the person who extols himself for telling somebody off.

Furthermore, there is the employee who blows his trumpet about how little he works on the job.

On and on its goes, but not to one's glory.

An empty barrel makes the loudest noise.

*Thou lovest evil more than good;
and lying rather than to speak righteousness.*—52:3

More Love for Evil Than Good

It is thought that Doeg was the low character spoken of in the text. He loved the mischief of devouring words, preferring to use his tongue like a razor, slashing the innocent (verse 2). Doeg lent support to the ungrounded suspicions of Saul that David was a traitor.

The explanation of this vilifier's meanness is given in the seventh verse: "Lo, this is the man that made not God his strength; but trusted in the abundance of his riches, and strengthened himself in his wickedness." The key to the whole problem is Doeg's lack of trust in God and consequently his opposition to Him. This led to a trust in riches; and to obtain it, he became Saul's bought tool of brutality, for no doubt he was rewarded. His crimes sprang from his love of evil, which is the lowest form of degradation, described by Milton:

Evil, be thou my good.

How depraved! But what people love most leads them through life. There is always before us the conflicting loves—love of evil versus love of good—and one must prevail over the other.

The fool hath said in his heart, There is no God. Corrupt are they, and have done abominable iniquity: there is none that doeth good.—53:1

The Root of Atheism

THE PSALM DESCRIBES ATHEISM AS FOOLISH: "The fool hath said in his heart, There is no God." It is contended, however, that this is only a mere assertion and that to assert a proposition proves nothing. True. But neither do mere denials prove anything. However, this particular negative—no God—infers some unreal positives: No God—the world is an accident. No God—life sprang from lifeless matter. No God—man is strictly a fleshly being. No God—the Bible is a fraud. No God—heaven is a fable. No God—man's fulfillment is found in materialism.

As seen in the text, the thing that encourages atheism is personal corruption and iniquity: "Corrupt are they…there is none that doeth good." If they were doing good, God with His restrictions would not seem odious to them. Thus the Biblical explanation of infidelity is that it is rooted in man's moral nature, grounded in a defect of the heart. Not wanting to submit to God's will, a person finds the rejection easier if he assumes there is no God—and especially if he calls it intellectual or scientific.

The fool says, "There is no God"; but the wise man says, "There is." Label yourself.

There were they in great fear, where no fear was: for God had scattered the bones of him that encampeth against thee; thou hast put them to shame, because God hath despised them.—53:5

Farewell to Fear

THE PEOPLE OF GOD BECAME FEARFUL where there was no fear. They were filled with consternation because they felt the threat of being overthrown by the wicked. It was a cycle of decreasing faith and increasing fears. Hence, the Great Protector reminded them that He had scattered the bones of an adversary and had put the enemy to shame. He refreshed their memory to abate their misgivings.

The passage addresses a common woe of man: fear, which often exists for no cause other than fear. Man's major fear is fear.

A wild, fearful imagination sees a storm in every cloud, a falling limb on every tree, a snake behind every log, and a death in every illness. The scared person sees more dangers than the world could possibly hold.

O anxious people! O blind hearts! In what uncalled-for fear we spend these few fleeting years! Where is our faith? If we are living in the promises of God, we have nothing to fear. For—

God tempers the wind to the shorn lamb.
—HENRI ESTIENNE

So with renewed faith we say, Farewell to fear.

Hear my prayer, O God;
give ear to the words of my mouth.—54:2

Praying in Troublesome Times

IN THIS SHORT PSALM we have a most earnest prayer in time of dreadful trouble.

First, there is a plea for deliverance:

• "Save me, O God." From the oppressors.

• "Judge me." Vindicate me.

• "Oppressors seek after my soul." Seek my life.

• "They have not set God before them." Having no regard for God, they follow no rules but their own.

Second, there is an expression of confidence in the forthcoming help and a vein of gratitude for it:

• "God is mine helper." The only sure help.

• "The Lord is with them that uphold my soul." The Lord works with the helpers.

• "He shall reward evil unto mine enemies." They shall reap their wrongs.

• "I will freely sacrifice unto thee." He vowed a thanksgiving offering.

• "I will praise thy Name…for he hath delivered me." In his assurance and praise he treats the future as if it were the past.

Begin the day with God!
He is thy Sun and Day!
—HORATIUS BONAR

And I said, Oh that I had wings like a dove!
for then would I fly away, and be at rest.—55:6

Oh That I Had Wings

THE POET WANTED TO GET AWAY FROM IT ALL, to "wander far off, and remain in the wilderness," get out of the city, get back to the quietude of nature.

He was very explicit of the agony that made him want wings: "I mourn." "The oppression of the wicked." "They cast iniquity upon me." "They hate me." "My heart is sore pained." "The terrors of death are fallen upon me." "Horror hath overwhelmed me." "I have seen violence and strife in the city." Poor man.

No wonder he wanted to "fly away, and be at rest."

At times we, too, have the same urge. The pressures of a complex society are disquieting, and our soul cries out for the quiet wilderness life. We want wings to fly away, but this is unreal. Opposition must be faced. Responsibilities must be met. Furthermore—

You cannot fly away like an eagle
with the wings of a wren.
—WILLIAM HENRY HUDSON

So maybe we had better stay put, fight it out and grow some stronger wings; by then we might want only temporary leaves to regain strength for a renewal of the struggles.

For it was not an enemy that reproached me;
then I could have borne it: neither was it he that hated me
that did magnify himself against me;
then I would have hid myself from him.—55:12

This Treachery Was Too Much

DAVID FELT THE RUMBLINGS OF REVOLUTION about him. His own son Absalom whom he dearly loved had risen in revolt. Multitudes forsook David in support of the rebellion. He discusses in the Psalm one of the rebels in particular—a traitor. His defection was one of the deepest disappointments and saddest sorrows the unhappy king was called upon to bear. While David trusted, "bloody treason flourished" over him. Anything else—he said he "could have borne," but this was too much for him. The turncoat was a man he had befriended; had trusted as a guide (friend); and had walked with him in fellowship to worship. It was a sore wound for David's heart. It outraged his sensibilities.

To place confidence—how bitter a thing it is when it crouches in treachery!

One of the necessary traits of a strong and wise character is loyalty—no selling a friend, not for money, not for glory, not for ambition. It's made of sterner stuff.

For the same reason David had his griefs we have had a few. We can hardly live (especially in public life) and not be Judas-treated. But be not dismayed. God can still bring us out on top.

The words of his mouth were smoother than butter, but war was in his heart: his words were softer than oil, yet they were drawn swords.—55:21

Smooth Butter and Sharp Swords

IN A CONTINUATION OF THE THEME on the treachery of David's chief adviser, the Psalm states, "He hath broken his covenant." This was a covenant of friendship with David in which they "took sweet counsel together."

Treachery lurks in honeyed words.

—DANISH PROVERB

The trust-breaker's words were masterpieces of deceit, excelling in smoothness like butter, surpassing in softness like oil, and exceeding in sharpness like swords. Lots of ability went to waste because he didn't have the character to be loyal.

While God sustains the righteous, He brings down the wicked. In this case, their days were cut short more than half. There was the suicide of the master deceiver, and the slaughter of David's rebel son, and many others.

Treachery, in the end, betrays itself.

David's faith in a confidant was shattered; but, with faith in God still intact, he closes the Psalm on a happy note of confidence: "I will trust in thee."

When friends stay and when friends betray, may our confidence in God—"I will trust in thee"—ever fill our hearts and keep us going.

Mine enemies would daily swallow me up:
for they be many that fight against me,
O thou Most High.—56:2

O Thou Most High

MOST HIGH. The original means high, exalted, and the translators understood the poet used it in reference to God in contrast to his foes. Other names and appellations bear out His Highness:

- ***God of Heaven.*** Universal God.
- ***Holy God.*** Pure. Guileless.
- ***God of Israel.*** Israel's God.
- ***Living God.*** Alive. Deathless.
- ***Merciful God.*** Kind. Good.
- ***God of All Comfort.*** Consoler.
- ***Eternal God.*** Timeless.
- ***Just God.*** Fair. Upright.
- ***Jehovah.*** I AM, the eternal living One.
- ***Father.*** Everything a father is.
- ***Creator.*** Originator.
- ***Almighty.*** Omnipotent.
- ***King.*** Supreme lawgiver.
- ***Savior.*** Redeemer of the sinful.
- ***Rock.*** Solid support. Firm defense.
- ***Shepherd.*** Provider. Protector.
- ***Judge.*** Factual. Merciful.
- ***I am.*** I AM WHAT I AM.

Hallowed be His name. Speak it with awe. Indeed, we need a personal relationship with Him but not a common and flippant one. For He is the Most High.

In God I will praise his word,
in God I have put my trust.—56:4

Praise His Word

GOD'S WORD IS INEXHAUSTIBLE. It has a bottomless profundity; we can spend a lifetime digging and never reach the bottom.

It is instructive: declares man's duties to God and man's obligations to man.

The power to protect is within it. Hide it in your heart and you will be shielded from every vice.

It sustains a spiritually hungry world. Sweet bread—that's what it is.

The Word reveals the nature of God Almighty to us. It makes known the Divine plan to snap the shackles of sin from human feet that we be free. Reveals the merciful hand that reaches down from heaven to wipe away humanity's tears and comforts us. Discloses the power over death by Him who said, "I am the resurrection and the life."

Would we be moved by sublimity, read it, imbibe it. Be true to it, and when music has lost its charm and poetry no longer stirs our souls, the Word of God—having been our way in life—will be our stay in death.

On the other hand, if we let our confidence in the Word be destroyed, we fill our future with darkness; we pull the sun out of our lives and the brightness of human hope is gone forever.

This I know; for God is for me.—56:9

God Is on My Side

THE AUTHOR BELIEVED GOD WAS FOR HIM, that He was taking his part. In the struggle between right and wrong, surely God is not neutral. His very nature dictates that He be on the side of right. Accordingly, if we are on the side of righteousness, then God is for us—this is how simple the matter of Divine partisanship is. God is no respecter of persons, but He is a respecter of faith, trust, obedience, uprightness and worship.

These are the reasons the God of Goodness was for this confident man, as stated in Psalms:

- "I believed" (116:10).
- "In thee do I put my trust" (7:1).
- "For I have kept the ways of the Lord" (18:21).
- "I was also upright before him" (18:23).
- "I will worship toward thy holy temple" (138:2).

It simply comes down to this: God is on the side of him who is on His side. So a timely, soul-searching question is, "Who is on the Lord's side?"

Once to every man and nation comes
the moment to decide,
In the strife of Truth with Falsehood
for the good or evil side.

—JAMES RUSSELL LOWELL

In the shadow of thy wings will I make my refuge, until these calamities be overpast.—57:1

Calamities

THERE IS ONE THING ABOUT CALAMITY—it passes. The psalmist mentioned this in the text. Elsewhere he stated, "the day of my calamity" (18:18)—day, something that ends. No night is so black but its lingering darkness gives way to the dawn of a new day. It did for David. It passed for Abraham. It spent itself for Joseph. And it can for you and me.

Sometimes we bring the calamities and problems on ourselves. At times, we are only the innocent victims of the actions of others. Still at other times, we may receive the "chastening" of our Father's hand because He loves us too much to leave us alone.

Usually, we never know for sure why we suffer calamity. But the *why* is not nearly so important as the *where.* Where will we go? Where will we turn for protection?

David turned to God and hid himself in the "shadow of thy wings." There he was secure.

God's wings, like a mother hen's, are still large enough and strong enough to protect. What about us? Where will we go for help?

My soul is among lions:
and I lie even among them that are set on fire,
even the sons of men, whose teeth are spears and arrows,
and their tongue a sharp sword.—57:4

Among Lions

THE LIONS WEREN'T BEASTS but "sons of men" who resembled lions: fierce, ferocious, savage men. When the author lay down for the night's rest, they were around him: beastly men, "set on fire," inflamed with hate, burning with anger. They had teeth like spears and arrows, and a tongue as sharp as a sword.

A cruel man is a two-legged, second-rate lion.

Yet, with these characters surrounding him, the psalmist was able to lie down and find repose. How did he do it? Trust. He slept under the shadow of the wings of the Lord. And with a fixed heart he declared, "In God have I put my trust: I will not be afraid of what man can do unto me."

In a very short time our society has degenerated into a series of horrors. Walking the streets in our cities at night is unsafe. The parks, once harmless places of relaxation, have been turned into forbidden jungles of violence. And moving away is no solution, for the threat is spreading.

What is the answer? David's behavior is the solution. Take precautions to preserve yourself and trust God for the rest. Don't live in fear with every breath a dread and every night a nightmare. There is a braver way.

Do ye indeed speak righteousness, O congregation?
do ye judge uprightly, O ye sons of men?
Yea, in heart ye work wickedness;
ye weigh the violence of your hands in the earth.—58:1,2

Unjust Judges

SOME QUESTIONS WERE PUT to the congregation of the sons of men, mighty ones, the judges. They were asked in mocking irony: Do you speak righteousness? Do you judge uprightly?

No! In their heart they devised wickedness and carried out the violence with their unclean hands.

Furthermore, these men were like a deaf cobra that could not be controlled or "charmed" by an enchanter's music. These self-serving judges were misusing their power and position, and nothing deterred their decadent decisions—no logic, no facts, no sympathy, no justice. They were pulling down the society they should have been upholding.

Thieves for their robbery have authority
When judges steal themselves.
—WILLIAM SHAKESPEARE

God give us just laws; and for their execution, give us honorable judges, men honorable in heart, men to whom it is fitting that we say, "Your Honor."

For, lo, they lie in wait for my soul:
the mighty are gathered against me;
not for my transgression, nor for my sin, O Lord.
They run and prepare themselves without my fault:
awake to help me, and behold.—59:3,4

Not His Fault

THIS WAS A TRYING TIME for the young hero. He was guilty of no treason, high crime or misdemeanor. But circumstances had placed him in the position where he was the object of the cruel envy of a proud king turned madman. Hence it became an obsession with King Saul to kill him.

The strife, the envy and hard feelings, were not the fault of David. It takes two to have peace, and he was only one. So in the Psalm he sang that the cruelty directed against him was not for any transgression or sin on his part. Not "my fault," he stated. In this matter he was absolutely innocent. He said in another Psalm:

> *For without cause have they hid for me their net in a pit, which without cause they have digged for my soul.*—35:7

However, a common error is to assume that where there is estrangement and strife both are at fault; and a grosser assumption is that perhaps both are equally at fault. The former is not always true, and the latter seldom is.

Let us do everything we can to stay on friendly terms with everyone—"if it be possible" (Romans 12:18). But with some, it will never be possible.

O God, thou hast cast us off, thou hast scattered us, thou has been displeased; O turn thyself to us again.—60:1

Despondency in Defeat

APPARENTLY THIS PSALM WAS WRITTEN following a defeat of the forces of Israel. It was composed before the fortunes of war turned in their favor, which they finally did, enabling them to occupy the country. But in their defeated state, despondency flowed from the poet's pen:

- "Thou hast cast us off."
- "Thou hast scattered us."
- "Thou hast been displeased."
- "Thou hast made the earth to tremble."
- "Thou hast showed thy people hard things."
- "O God, which didst not go out with our armies."

To be unpopular, loathsome, even cast off from society, is one of our worst fears. To be cast off from God is the worst calamity that can strike us. We can avoid God's displeasure when we share His heart—when what displeases Him displeases us. When this is true, our despair will blossom into hopefulness as it did for David. He said, "Through God we shall do valiantly: for he it is that shall tread down our enemies." God shall do the same for us. And as fortune rides the tides, in and out, we can handle it because of our faith in Him.

Give us help from trouble: for vain is the help of man.
—60:11

Vain Is the Help of Man

A PERSON MAY TURN AGAINST YOU and rend you. Your outstretched hand of goodness does not assure his gratitude. After entrusting him with your good name, he may prove to be a traitor; he may sacrifice your reputation for fear or favor; to the highest bidder he may let you go. The very people who were eager to do you honor when the crown of success looked so kingly on your brow may be the very first to nail you to the cross when failure comes.

Even if a person is true and loyal to the very end, he is limited in the assistance he can render. His advice may prove disastrous. His efforts to help may be too weak to sustain you. Sometimes he can do no more than sympathize. He is as powerless as you are.

The only absolutely unfailing source of adequate help is God, the One strong enough to help, the One *who never deserts you.* He is as constant as the rising and setting of the sun. He stands by when others forsake. And if fate drives you out into a cold, friendless world, He walks by your side and encourages you in every faltering step you take—to take another and another. And when the death scene comes, and helpless loved ones stand by weeping, He will take you by the hand and lead you into the better world. His help is the only help that fully suffices.

Have God and have all.

Hear my cry, O God; attend unto my prayer.—61:1

A Cry to God

IN CENTURIES GONE BY, the sixty-first Psalm was often sung in worship services. It is short, beautiful and a comforting sentiment when trouble comes.

David had enough troubles to break a man of lesser faith. We all have our ups and downs.

This life is not a pilgrimage on gentle, downhill roads marked with signs saying, "No Troubles," "No Sorrows," "No Efforts." The God who created us knew we would need some struggles that we may grow stronger. The great men whose illustrious names brighten the fading pages of history faced challenging difficulties, which brought out the heroic qualities within them. In their examples they give inspiration to the generations that follow.

Another thing we can be sure of—God has an open ear to the cries of believing children. "Hear my cry, O God," petitioned David. We may doubt others. We may doubt ourselves. But never doubt God. He will attend our prayers. Disaster may push us to "the end of the earth." But God is near and we may still cry out:

Lead me to the rock that is higher than I.

No matter how distressing our hardships are, God is near. He is the Rock of Shelter. Cling to Him.

From the end of the earth will I cry unto thee, when my heart is overwhelmed: lead me to the rock that is higher than I.—61:2

The Rock Higher Than I

THIS PASSAGE INSPIRED E. JOHNSON to compose one of the great hymns sung today by worshipers throughout the world.

O sometimes the shadows are deep,
And rough seems the path to the goal;
And sorrows, how often they sweep
Like tempest down over the soul.

O sometimes how long seems the day,
And sometimes how weary my feet;
But toiling in life's dusty way,
The Rock's blessed shadow, how sweet!

O near to the rock let me keep,
Or blessings or sorrows prevail,
Or climbing the mountain way steep,
Or walking the shadowy vale.

O then to the Rock let me fly,
To the Rock that is higher than I;
O then to the Rock let me fly,
To the Rock that is higher than I.

We fly to the Rock for a refuge, to reach a stronghold where safety may be found.

In our low vale we are exposed to every threat. If we would have security, we must get higher. A Savior no higher than ourselves would never elevate us any. But the Lord is "the rock that is higher than I."

Thou wilt prolong the king's life: and his years as many generations.—61:6

Prolong My Life

MAY THOU PROLONG THE KING'S LIFE. Here David prayed for his own days to be lengthened.

Life is one of our most precious possessions. In testing Job, Satan said, "Skin for skin, yea, all that a man hath will he give for his life" (Job 2:4). But he was wrong! Life is not as priceless as the soul. Not as valuable as honor. Not as great as God's cause. But it is more precious than gold. Hence, we spend money to protect it, change climates to keep it, and pray God to lengthen it. For when it is gone, it is "as water spilt on the ground, which cannot be gathered up again."

Life on earth means so much that one of the rewards God has offered is longer days: "Thou shalt keep therefore his statutes, and his commandments...that thou mayest prolong thy days upon the earth" (Deuteronomy 4:40). And, coming to the New Testament, Paul repeated the promise of longer days to those who honor their parents (Ephesians 6:2,3).

Now for a longer life, let us live the approved way and pray to Him who watches over it. For, excepting the soul and honor, its value is as Goethe stated:

Nothing is worth more than this day.

How long will ye imagine mischief against a man? ye shall be slain all of you: as a bowing [leaning] *wall shall ye be, and as a tottering fence.*—62:3

Leaning Walls and Tottering Fences

DAVID WAS SECURE ON THE ROCK: "He only is my rock" (verse 2). But his oppressors, having no foundation, were like a leaning wall and a tottering fence. For a little while such construction appears solid, but time soon disproves the hasty assumption. Time tries the foundation; if it is weak, the wall starts bending or the fence starts tilting, which aptly describes a life with no foundation.

These leaning-wall, tottering-fence people had no character on which to build. The Psalm says they imagined mischief, consulted to do harm, delighted in lies and spoke hypocritically (verses 3,4). Intellectualism without heart, cleverness without goodness, is a power only for mischief.

But when a strong character is the nature of a person, he is like an acorn that grows into an oak. Conditions may destroy the acorn, but they cannot divert it as long as it survives. While it lives, it defies man and beast, earth and sky, to produce an oak. Circumstances do not change its nature. So it is with a human being: a truthful, loyal character defies the circumstances to make the man. For what we become tomorrow we already are in character today.

Surely men of low degree are vanity,
and men of high degree are a lie:
to be laid in the balance, they are altogether
lighter than vanity.—62:9

Different Ranks

THE TEXT SPEAKS OF *MEN OF LOW DEGREE,* mere sons of Adam, commonly called common men, creatures of a vain and empty state. But worse than this, he points out, are *men of high degree* who are a lie, a false illusion, *lighter than vanity,* lighter than the *men of low degree,* for they are lacking in substance.

The matter of true worth or rank has become much confused. The person who is ranked the lowest in the eyes of the world may actually stand the highest in the sight of God. Worldly rank is only an empty bubble. God can change the rank of men rather quickly: "He hath put down the mighty from their seats, and exalted them of low degree" (Luke 1:52).

In God's sight, barring faith and accomplishment, no person is last or first—all rank the same. Real nobility is one of merit, something you make for yourself—with God's help.

Let none presume
To wear an undeserved dignity.
O! that estates, degrees, and offices
Were not deriv'd corruptly, and that clear honor
Were purchas'd by the merit of the wearer.

—WILLIAM SHAKESPEARE

If riches increase, set not your heart upon them.—62:10

Increased Riches

IF RICHES INCREASE—they may. If we enjoy health, work hard, practice thrift and exercise good judgment, our riches will increase.

Then there is the needed warning: *set not your heart on them.* Wealth is not a thing to be trusted, for it has wings and easily takes to flight. It is not something to love, for the love of it is the root of all evil (I Timothy 6:9,10).

But of course, many have been pierced because they didn't have it. The have-nots have also been covetous, wanting what is not theirs, which is a form of idolatry. They have been envious of successful people—another sin. They have borne false witness against industrious, saving people, accusing them of dishonesty and greed. Furthermore, they have slapped the hand that provided their blessings.

For instance, to buy a house, a family had to borrow thirty thousand dollars from a savings and loan company, which it got from a depositor. Every time someone borrows money, someone else had to save some.

Therefore, let us recognize there are possible pitfalls concerning wealth: those who have it may sin by trusting in it, and those who don't have it may sin by having the wrong attitude toward it and its possessor.

Thus will I bless thee while I live:
I will lift up my hands in thy name.—63:4

While I Live

DAVID PROBABLY WROTE THIS PSALM in the desert while being pursued by his son Absalom. A king in exile being hounded by a rebellious son—what a pitiful plight! But David was no ordinary man, and he did not respond to this crisis in an ordinary way. His heart overflowed, and his pen broke into praise:

• "O God, thou art my God." David knew who he was and whose he was. How often we forget who we are and consequently forget our Father, our spiritual family, our future.

• "My soul thirsteth for thee, my flesh longeth for thee in a dry and thirsty land, where no water is." David's desire for God was unending and unquenchable. How much time with God does it take to satisfy our thirst for Him? Depends on how thirsty we are.

• "Thy loving kindness is better than life." Better than life? How can this be? We tend to put life itself ahead of all other blessings. But David knew there was something better than life—it is love, love for God. Our Heavenly Father loves all of us; but without our loving Him, life is not worth living. It is only a long, inescapable ladder to nowhere.

• "Thus will I bless [praise] thee while I live." This was not praise confined to the easy times of life when everything was going well. David was no "fair weather praiser." His praise was a lifestyle, not a temporary emotion based on physical circumstances. "I will praise Thee as long as I live" was David's solemn promise. A lifetime commitment. May we make it ours.

While I remember thee upon my bed,
and meditate on thee in the night watches.—63:6

All Through the Night

ALL THROUGH THE NIGHT WATCHES David meditated on God. However, this was not unusual because he had spent the day doing the same thing. Only a person whose life has been touched by God could live as did David. He was consumed with a passion for God that most of us will never know.

It has been said that too often we ignore God all day and then ask Him to bless us all night. Is this a fair appraisal? Do we have our proportions out of balance? Do we live all day in a rush of activities and appointments in which God is not asked to participate? And if we think of Him at all, is it only briefly as we ask for a safe night of sleep? If so, then we have missed the message and meaning of Christianity.

David might be considered by some to be a genuine religious fanatic. He thought of God all day, he thought of God all night. He would probably be spurned by many people today because of his daily devotion to God. How many of us would like David if he were here today? Would he be just too "devoted" for today's standards?

David's heart was a passionate, fanatic heart totally consumed by God—all through the day and all through the night.

They encourage themselves in an evil matter:
they commune of laying snares privily;
they say, Who shall see them?—64:5

Encouraged to Do Evil

MISCHIEVOUS PEOPLE! They encouraged one another in a sinister scheme to destroy David's popularity and to promote open revolt: *They commune of laying snares privily.* In a spectacle of depravity and vice, they agitated horrendous living by suggesting that which is degraded and immoral. In an unwholesome relationship, marked with conceited claptraps, they pushed their ill-spent lives down a corrupt path.

How vicious for people to encourage each other to do wrong in any degree! But those bent on evil can always find something wrong to suggest. It begins even in youth. One boy dares another to fight the third boy, or tells him he is afraid to throw a rock through a window. On and on it goes—encouragement to do wrong.

We see it in mature life. Here is some common rhetoric, not very eloquent, but very common: "I wouldn't take that." "Why don't you get even?" "Have a drink. Prove to everybody you're a man." "Don't work if you can get out of it." "Sure, it's all right if you don't get caught." "You ought to get her told." "Now don't get too conscientious."

Leaving the unwholesome, we close with a thought upon the higher influence over each other:

And let us consider one another to provoke unto love and to good works.—HEBREWS 10:24

That they may shoot in secret at the perfect: suddenly do they shoot at him, and fear not.—64:4

Shooting the Innocent

LIVING AS PURE AND HOLY A LIFE as is possible will not keep us from being attacked. It did not protect David from slander and it will not us.

David was a man totally devoted to God. But his devotion did not protect him from his enemies' accusations.

Our Lord Himself was repeatedly attacked by Satan and Satan's henchmen. The Devil used every means and every trick to tempt Jesus into submission. He used the cunning, religious leaders of the day, and he used the unwitting disciples of our Lord.

So we must not let our devotion and desire for purity lead us into believing we will escape accusations, lies and slander.

While we are not totally innocent, "For all have sinned and fallen short of the glory of God," we are often innocent of the false charges thrown against us. "Innocent" victims are still being attacked today. But isn't it much better to be an innocent victim than to be guilty of shooting the innocent?

They search out iniquities;
they accomplish a diligent search:
both the inward thought of every one of them,
and the heart, is deep.—64:6

Searching to Harm

IN A FURTHER DESCRIPTION OF THE PEOPLE in the previous essay, they searched for iniquities—ways to harm a righteous man. And they found. In their blackguard endeavors they accomplished well-framed devices. With "much of Madness, and more of Sin," they plotted and plotted to harm and harm, to have their way. And maybe they did for a while. But the story is not finished. Their rotten words became a stench in the mouth, which caused others to ostracize them. They became known as harmers—not helpers—and harmers are not in demand. They swapped *manhood* for *doghood* to cringe and bite, but good people don't want that kind of a creature around.

There is a second part of the story: God interposed. God shot back—"But God shall shoot at them with an arrow" (verse 7). In their plan to wound another, they got wounded. Their words boomeranged. Their slander, their curses, came back to ruin and destroy them. Their throats were cut by their own tongues.

This tragedy is repeated daily. All of us have seen it. When we attempt to harm others, we are always harmed—even more so. Not always immediately, not always visibly, but count on it: sooner or later we suffer from our own mischief.

Blessed is the man whom thou choosest,
and causest to approach unto thee,
that he may dwell in thy courts:
we shall be satisfied with the goodness of thy house,
even of thy holy temple.—65:4

Satisfied Only in God

THE SOUL FINDS IN GOD what meets its needs. Nothing else will. Everything else leaves a void.

Unanswered questions leave us frustrated. Where did we come from? How did the world originate? The answer is God.

Though we are a little lower than the angels, we still are insufficient to guide ourselves. Only God completely fills our need for guidance. Life has its perils. When the storms beat, we need a rock for a refuge; and when our enemies' arrows are drawn, we need a protector.

Being spirit, we have an urge to worship. This requirement for human satisfaction is seen in the text. The psalmist said that he would be satisfied in the holy temple.

Life without hope would take the sun from our sky and the rainbow from our cloud. The longing question, "If a man die, shall he live again?" will not take *No* for an answer.

One question, more than all others,
From thoughtful minds implores reply,
It is, as breathed from star and pall,
What fate awaits us when we die?

Thanks be to the Most High, we can live fulfilling lives that satisfy—if we will seek Him.

Thou crownest the year with thy goodness;
and thy paths drop fatness.
They drop upon the pastures of the wilderness:
and the little hills rejoice on every side.
The pastures are clothed with flocks;
the valleys also are covered with corn;
they shout for joy, they also sing.—65:11-13

Crowned With Blessings

THERE IS ONE CROWN everyone has been given—the crown of God's goodness. He sends the rain on the just and the unjust.

His paths drop fatness—productivity and plenty. The wilderness blossoms with God's blessings. The rolling hills, touched by His artistic hand, rejoice in nature's charm. The green pastures are clothed with thriving flocks, created and sustained by the Great Provider—for us. The fertile valleys, crowded with corn ever so nourishing, respond to the gentle breezes and sing their own tune to the provisionary purpose of God.

He visits the earth and waters it. "The river of God" flows upon it. His "showers of blessing" fall upon us. Every good gift is from Him.

Truly, God has blessed saint and sinner alike with the goodness of nature. But God has even greater blessings—His very best—for a special group:

God knows, He loves, He cares,
Nothing His truth can dim;
He gives His very best to those
Who leave the choice to Him.

Come and see the works of God: he is terrible [awesome] *in his doing toward the children of men.*—66:5

Come and See

THE WORKS OF GOD HAVE EVER INSPIRED the poet's pen and the orator's tongue. They have filled eyes with astonishment and hearts with gratitude. The works of God! How magnificent! How breathless! How enduring! As stable as the hills, as moving as the earth! Warm like the sun, cool like the night!

His works are good and terrible, rewarding to His people, retributive to their enemies. To save His people, He has to subdue their enemies.

As an example, the author cited the deliverance of Israel through the Red Sea (verse 6). It's a thrilling story. When they came to the sea, pursued by the Egyptians, God sent a strong wind that divided the waters and dried the land, enabling the Israelites to go across with a wall of water on each side. But upon "the Egyptians the waters returned, and covered the chariots, and the horsemen, and all the host of Pharaoh that came into the sea after them; there remained not so much as one of them" (Exodus 14:28).

This story was a favorite among the Israelites and is a great source of comfort for us. The message of this miracle for today is that nothing shall stand in our way. With God, the seas become dry land, the waves stand in submission and we march on victoriously. Onward we go to the distant shore; and as we go we call to others, "Come and see."

*If I regard iniquity in my heart,
the Lord will not hear me.*—66:18

Sin Nullifies Prayer

PRAYER HAS ALWAYS MEANT MUCH to the children of God. It is a powerful avenue open to them, not open to those who regard iniquity in their heart. "Now we know that God heareth not sinners: but if any man be a worshipper of God, and doeth his will, him he heareth" (John 9:31).

When we cherish sin in our hearts, refuse to give it up, then our prayers rise no higher than our lips.

But in a finer vein, one of the most impressive statements on the changed life is "…ye were the servants of sin…" (Romans 6:20). They were sinners, but now they're not. This is the design and purpose of religion—to raise one above sin, which qualifies him to pray, unburdens him to live and prepares him to die.

It did for the composer. God heard him. "God hath heard me," he declared, "he hath attended to the voice of my prayer" (verse 19). The reason—he did not harbor sin in his heart.

Therefore, we need to ask ourselves:

Is thy heart right with God,
Washed in the crimson flood,
Cleansed and made holy, humble and lowly,
Right in the sight of God?

—E. A. HOFFMAN

*God be merciful unto us, and bless us;
and cause his face to shine upon us.*—67:1

His Shining Face of Mercy

It is proper to ask God to be merciful; for He is "the Father of mercies, and the God of all comfort" (II Corinthians 1:3).

How beautiful are the mercies of the Most High! "Like the drops of a lustre, which reflect a rainbow of colors when the sun glitters upon them, when turned in different ways...so the mercy of God is one and yet many; the same, yet ever changing; a combination of all the beauties of love blended harmoniously together."
—Charles Spurgeon

Man needs much mercy. Just a little will not suffice.

*It must be great mercy, or no mercy;
for little mercy will never serve my turn.*
—John Bunyan

While God is filled with pity and is anxious to extend mercy, its reception is dependent on us. "And his mercy is on them that fear him from generation to generation" (Luke 1:50).

After righteousness has been followed and God has been praised, man still needs mercy. If it were not for mercy, there would be no Divine way for man to pursue. A dying man was told, "You are going to receive the rewards of your labors." He replied, "I am going to receive mercy."

Then shall the earth yield her increase; and God, even our own God, shall bless us.—67:6

The More Productive Way

THE PSALM EXPRESSES A DESIRE that the way of God might be known to all nations. It voices a wish that all peoples might recognize the hand of God in the affairs of men and nations, and that they rejoice in this acknowledgment.

The prevalence of true religion—praise for God and regard for man—would greatly bless the temporal interests of the peoples: "Then shall the earth yield her increase" (verse 6). Indeed, true religion encourages the proper use of human lives and natural resources. It frees us from an unproductive course to follow a productive one. It gives us inspiration and direction to accomplish a purpose for which we were placed here, stated to Adam and Eve: "Be fruitful and multiply, and replenish the earth, and subdue it" (Genesis 1:28); to conquer the earth—not each other; to harness nature—not one another.

Today much wealth and many lives are being consumed by those who would force their will and way on others, and, in a reactive way, by those who feel the need to protect themselves.

How different it would be if all the peoples rejoiced in God's way. His way produces better harvests because we labor with honest hearts, right attitudes, true priorities, and God on our side. This makes us fruitful winners.

God setteth the solitary in families:
he bringeth out those which are bound with chains:
but the rebellious dwell in a dry land.—68:6

Emancipated

AS SEEN IN THE PSALM, God settles the solitary in families or houses. He gives a home to the outcasts and wanderers. Perhaps it refers to God's settling the nomadic Israelites in Canaan.

"He bringeth out those which are bound with chains." He loosed their chains and set them free. But the rebellious were not included; they were forced to "dwell in a dry land" of their own making, parched with their own rebelliousness.

God's principles favor the rights of man—oppose tyranny and oppression. The mistreated and trampled have cause to take heart. The God of mercy is a helper of the helpless, a Father to the fatherless and a defender of the widows (verse 5). His defense and protection especially cover those who need it most.

God's hand has moved with power to reshape the order of things for the good of His people. This is the encouragement the psalmist gave in the text.

Chains—the cruelest and most enslaving ones are not those made of iron but those forged by sin. Have we allowed God to set us fully free? For—

Not all are free who scorn chains.

—GOTTHOLD EPHRAIM LESSING

The Lord gave the word: great was the company of those that published it.—68:11

Women and the Word

WHAT WORD? Answers vary: "the word of command"; "the word of victory"; "the assurance of victory"; "the word to march." Whatever the word in the text is, it came from the Lord; that gave it unusual distinctions.

The host that proclaimed it was the choir of women. In that day there were choirs of women who sang the ancient war songs. Men did battle, and the women "that tarried at home divided the spoil" (verse 12). Whether in peace or in war, women have always had a significant role.

Where would the world be without the worthy women who have proclaimed God's word in song and deed? While man has been given the Divine injunction to be the spiritual leader in the home, where would most homes be were it not for the woman's constant profession of faith? And the church? Indeed, most churches would die were it not for a dozen good women who proclaim God's word through every deed and every action of their holy lives.

Therefore, it is fitting that we praise the faithful women who proclaim God's word!

Thou hast ascended on high, thou hast led captivity captive: thou hast received gifts for men; yea, for the rebellious also, that the Lord God might dwell among them.—68:18

Captured Captives

THERE ARE VARIOUS COMMENTARIES of men on this text. And while I sometimes find the comments of men appalling, I always find Paul appealing; so I quote him:

> *Wherefore he saith, When he ascended up on high, he led captivity captive, and gave gifts unto men. (Now that he ascended, what is it but that he also descended first into the lower parts of the earth? He that descended is the same also that ascended up far above all heavens, that he might fill all things.)*
>
> —EPHESIANS 4:8-10

Thus it is evident that Paul used the language in Psalms to describe the work, the glory and the triumph of the Messiah. In Christian relevance, it refers to Christ's converting Satan's captivity to His own captives. The Lord came down from His dwelling place on high, and after leading "captivity captive" returned to His seat; that is, He came to earth, died on the cross and ascended to heaven in triumph over all foes. It was a glorious victory. Now the bond captives of sin become the free captives of righteousness.

Freed of the chain of sin's slavery, let us thank God for our new-found freedom, made possible by Him who loved us and died for us to make us free.

Scatter thou the people that delight in war.—68:30

Scatter Those Who Delight in War

THIS IS A PRAYER concerning war and peace. Drive asunder the warmongers. Rid us of them. Peaceable people have ever prayed for peace (I Timothy 2:2).

In the silent city of the dead, as a folded flag is handed to a brokenhearted father and mother with the words, "From a grateful nation," they sob and silently pray, "Scatter thou the people that delight in war."

A little boy who misses a father who will never come home looks at his picture and prays, "Scatter thou the people that delight in war."

Grandmother, old and almost gone, requests to be driven to the military cemetery, and there amid a thousand ghastly crosses, cold and silent, is led to the grave of a grandson she loved more than life; and there, as she wipes the tears from dim and sunken eyes, she prays with thin and shrunken lips, "Scatter thou the people that delight in war."

Size up war any way you will, but don't say there is glory in it. You can say it is science—a science of destruction.

A battle is a terrible conjugation of the verb to kill—I kill, thou killest, he kills, we kill, they kill, all kill.

—THOMAS CARLYLE

Because for thy sake I have borne reproach; shame hath covered my face.—69:7

Reproach for Thy Sake

THE THING THAT PROVOKED ENMITY on the part of several people toward David was his consecration to God and his blessings from Him.

Here was a man whose conduct was such a contrast to theirs that it shamed them. He stood so much taller than they that it pained them to look up to him. His superior ability made their mediocrity look weak. His high ideal of returning good for evil showed up their wickedness and humiliated them. The high position of king, given to him by the Lord, contrasted their lower station too much for them to like him. His success turned their vicious tongues loose.

If we have not faced a plight similar to David's—of being scorned for our faith in God—why not?

Are our friends and associates so righteous that they would not dare ridicule our religion? Or is our faith so feeble and frail that no one knows we have any? Dead faith does not speak up for God and thus is never shamed for its activities nor ridiculed for its excellence.

If we have faced scorn for our faith, praise God that our faith was alive and visible enough to be noticed.

For the zeal of thine house hath eaten me up; and the reproaches of them that reproached thee are fallen upon me.—69:9

A Flaming Zeal

THE AUTHOR'S ZEAL FOR GOD'S HOUSE was a passionate ardor within him. He showed this in many ways. It burned within him and drove him forward.

Now let us observe how the passage was later used:

First, when Jesus drove the money changers out of the temple, "his disciples remembered that it was written, the zeal of thine house hath eaten me up" (John 2:13-17).

Second, relative to enduring persecution, Paul quoted the passage from Psalms and applied it to Jesus: "For even Christ," he said, "pleased not himself; but, as it is written, The reproaches of them that reproached thee fell on me" (Romans 15:3). In this particular passage he taught that just as Christ endured the calumnies of those who calumniated God, we, too, should be willing to bear abuse for His sake.

Zeal! What an energizer! It burns within and then loosens the tongue to speak, unshackles the feet to walk, and gives muscle to arms that otherwise would drop. All along the highway of life we see the stopped souls that ran out of zeal. And what about church buildings? When they become empty of zeal, they become empty of people. So let us keep the flame of zeal glowing.

They gave me also gall for my meat;
and in my thirst they gave me vinegar to drink.—69:21

They Gave Him Vinegar and Gall

WHAT DAVID CALLED A GALLING and bitter experience was literally fulfilled in the Messiah, as recorded by New Testament writers:

> *After this, Jesus knowing that all things were now accomplished, that the Scripture might be fulfilled, saith, I thirst. Now there was set a vessel full of vinegar; and they filled a sponge with vinegar, and put it upon hyssop, and put it to his mouth. When Jesus therefore had received the vinegar, he said, It is finished: and he bowed his head, and gave up the ghost.*
>
> —JOHN 19:28-30

The persecutors continued their course of maliciousness, but Jesus finished His earthly course of righteousness. He could say, "It is finished": a sinless life, His ordeal for human redemption. But what could they say?

Today mockers can contemptibly hand a cup of bitters to the Lord's disciples. They can taunt them with vinegary derision and galling scorn. They can nail the Divine cause to a cross of disbelief and depravity, but what do they later say? And where do they turn?

It is encouraging to note that while we cannot control what others do, we can—with God's help—control what we do.

I will praise the name of God with a song,
and will magnify him with thanksgiving.
This also shall please the Lord better than an ox
or bullock that hath horns or hoofs.—69:30,31

Better Than Sacrifice

He did not say material sacrifice is unimportant or unacceptable. He merely made a comparison. He compared formal giving to heartfelt thanksgiving and chose the latter. He prefers the inward feeling of the heart in preference to the precise offerings of the hand; it is better than an ox or bullock that hath horns and hoofs—a full grown one. And today praise and thanksgiving are better than greenback and gold.

The Almighty has His own priorities! In this age when money is so urgently needed in the church, let us not forget there are things better than temporal sacrifice:

- ***Thanksgiving.*** Stated in the text.
- ***Penitence.*** Mentioned in 51:16,17.
- ***Mercy.*** "For I desired mercy, and not sacrifice" (Hosea 6:6).
- ***Knowledge.*** "For I desired…the knowledge of God more than burnt offerings" (Hosea 6:6).
- ***Obedience.*** "Behold, to obey is better than sacrifice, and to hearken than the fat of rams" (I Samuel 15:22).

No one questions the propriety of sacrifice, but it is not the whole of godliness.

Let them be turned back for a reward of their shame that say, Aha, aha.—70:3

When the Laughter Is Over

THE WORLDLY RABBLE HAVE ALWAYS LAUGHED at the godly people. With ridicule and scorn, they laughed at David. They even laughed at our Lord Jesus.

Having no argument, the fool resorts to ridicule. It gratifies the little mind and eases the anger, but it proves nothing.

The important thing is for us to live as we should and leave the reaction to others, whether it be applause or mockery. It is ours to act, theirs to react. Job, feeling this way, said, "Suffer me that I may speak; and after that I have spoken, mock on" (Job 21:3).

The grasshopper mocks the ant, but it changes nothing. When the winter comes, the little ant that stuck with his duty can say:

Where be your gibes now?

—WILLIAM SHAKESPEARE

What difference does it make to the little canary if the old cat despises her singing? She can *meow* and *meow* all she likes, but the little singer still has her role to fulfill.

Likewise, it is imperative that the children of God keep on working and singing to the glory of our Maker, paying no mind to the sneers of men.

Be thou my strong habitation,
whereunto I may continually resort:
thou hast given commandment to save me;
for thou art my rock and my fortress.—71:3

The Design of the Commandments

THOU HAST GIVEN COMMANDMENT to save me. In the commandments of the all-wise God the author of the Psalm found help and salvation. Of course, faith in the commandments lay at the bottom of his rescue.

In the struggles today with our greatest enemy—sin—we need to recognize that God has given commandments to save us, and he who sins against them hurts himself (Proverbs 8:36). For every command of the Most High has been given to bless man: the one of restraint to Adam and Eve; the mandate to Noah to build an ark; the charge to Israel to cast off their slave chains; the Ten Commandments; and coming to the New Testament, the commands to obey the gospel, assemble for worship, respect civil law and be faithful—all are for the good of man.

In ages past, Moses recorded the classic statement on the purpose of the commandments:

> *And the Lord commanded us to do all these statutes, to fear the Lord our God, for our good always, that he might preserve us alive, as it is at this day.*—DEUTERONOMY 6:24

Now that expresses it exactly: *for our good,* but more than that—for our good *always.* Keep them and good will be our fortune.

For thou art my hope, O Lord God:
thou art my trust from my youth.—71:5

From My Youth

GOD HAD BEEN HIS TRUST AND HIS HOPE from his youth—a remarkable distinction. His defense was God. His hope was God. In God he placed his trust.

This is what youth is seeking today: something that gives meaning to life, something to trust, a confident relationship with a protector, hope for an otherwise dull life. Youth has to feel his way through a maze of problems; and in finding himself, he needs a trust that does not waver.

Youth is a time filled with potentials. Every hour of it trembles with destiny. It would be tragic to twist and warp a life so soon begun. For its formation it should be given to God, like clay is given to the potter, for His own shaping and molding. The Scriptures bear out this suggestion:

> *O God, thou hast taught me from my youth: and hitherto have I declared thy wondrous works.*—VERSE 17

> *Remember now thy Creator in the days of thy youth.*
> —ECCLESIASTES 12:1

Unless real quality is ingrained in youth's fiber, the years will expose them as ordinary stuff. Like cheap cloth assumes a different appearance when washed, they too will shrink and fade when later tested and run through the wringer.

Cast me not off in the time of old age;
forsake me not when my strength faileth.—71:9

Golden Years

THIS SEEMS TO BE A NATURAL and common feeling when old age starts creeping up on people; and apparently it had started overtaking the writer, for he alluded to it again in verse seventeen, "When I am old and gray-headed." In each instance he requested, "Forsake me not."

But age has its compensations:

• ***Wisdom:*** "Days should speak, and multitude of years should teach wisdom" (Job 32:7).

• ***Judgment:*** "At twenty years of age the will reigns; at thirty the wit; at forty the judgment," declared the wise old Benjamin Franklin.

• ***Experience that enhances faith and hope:*** "I have been young, and now am old; yet have I not seen the righteous forsaken, nor his seed begging bread" (37:25).

• ***Tolerance:*** On this behalf Goethe said, "One has to grow older to become more tolerant."

• ***Less pride and consequently less concern for what people think:*** it had this effect on Montaigne, as he stated, "I dare a little the more, as I grow older."

• ***The best of life:***

Grow old along with me, the best is yet to be,
the last of life for which the first was made.

—ROBERT BROWNING

For mine enemies speak against me;
and they that lay wait for my soul take counsel together,
saying, God hath forsaken him: persecute and take him;
for there is none to deliver him.—71:10,11

Weakness Invites Attack

AS SEEN IN VERSE TWENTY, the writer had experienced "great and sore troubles." His enemies took this to mean that God was no longer with him and, therefore, he would be an easy captive. They thought it was the opportune time to strike. Hit him when he can't hit back. Pull him down when there is no one to lift him up. Come upon him while he is weak and weary.

Their eagerness to overrun the weak supports the contention that weakness invites war, that aggressive nations feel freer to attack the unprepared. In recognition of this overbearing spirit, George Washington said:

> *To be prepared for war is one of the most effectual means of preserving peace.*

But the irreverent guessed wrong—God had not forsaken the psalmist. In a vein of confidence and protection he sang, "For they are confounded, for they are brought unto shame, that seek my hurt" (verse 24). Thus hardship does not prove Divine rejection. It can be the chastening of the Lord, the means of helping us.

Give the king thy judgments, O God,
and thy righteousness unto the king's son.—72:1

A Father's Prayer for His Son

THE PSALM REQUESTS THAT THE KING'S SON administer justice and righteousness to all (verses 1,2). This is the first responsibility of government.

It implores God for peace (verse 3). A reign of quietness and security would allow the people to chase their dreams with safety and joy.

It mentions the rights of the poor against oppressors (verse 4). Regardless of one's station in life, he has the right of governmental protection.

The prayer alludes to the fear of the Lord (verse 5). The most basic thing in law and order is the attitude in the heart; and the greatest influence for uprightness is the fear of God, which starts man on his whole duty (Ecclesiastes 12:13).

The reign is to be refreshing like gentle showers on freshly mown grass (verse 6). Liberty, freedom, opportunity, protection—all permit this.

It is a prayer that the righteous flourish in the abundance of peace (verse 7)—under an excellent ruler.

Whether one be a king or a peasant, he should pray for his sons and daughters to be righteous and to honorably discharge their duties in all the walks of life. How blessed is the child who has parents who pray for him.

And blessed be his glorious name for ever: and let the whole earth be filled with his glory. Amen, and Amen.—72:19

Blessed Be the Name

All praise to Him who reigns above,
In majesty supreme;
Who gave His Son for man to die,
That He might man redeem.
Blessed be the name,
Blessed be the name,
Blessed be the name of the Lord.

—W. H. CLARK

THERE ARE MANY GREAT NAMES THAT ADORN the pages of history. Just to read of their noble and heroic exploits sends a tingle down the spine. But how weak and imperfect they are in comparison to Him who is all-powerful, all-loving and all-enduring. Those historic characters lived for a time and then fell beneath the heaviness of their own blunders or the weight of their own years. They went the way of all the earth. But Jehovah is perfect and timeless; and when heaven and earth shall have passed away, He shall still be alive in perfection. And what about His love? We could sooner dip the ocean dry with a spoon than to exhaust it. Blessed be His name!

"Now unto the King eternal, immortal, invisible, the only wise God, be honor and glory for ever and ever. Amen" (I Timothy 1:17). May this sentiment of blessing and extolling His name frequent our lips forever.

But as for me, my feet were almost gone;
my steps had well nigh slipped.
For I was envious at the foolish,
when I saw the prosperity of the wicked.—73:2,3

A Narrow Escape

HERE IS A MAN who has had a narrow escape. He acknowledged that his feet were almost gone, that his steps had well nigh slipped. The thing that undermined his security was doubt.

Doubt gripped him because he took his eyes off God and looked to sinners. Envy swelled in his heart, crowding out faith. When he beheld the prosperity of the wicked, it seemed too unjust to reconcile with the acts of a just God. It was a painful experience that caused him to almost abandon his faith in the Almighty.

Later in the Psalm he confessed his mistake: "So foolish was I, and ignorant," like "a beast" devoid of reason, as stupid as a brute (verse 22).

But in his deeper thought, while in the sanctuary, he found the answer. He had placed too much emphasis on the physical, not enough on the spiritual. It had put him in slippery places. Indeed, the material-centered life is not what it seems—rather one of frustration and terror.

It's the counterfeit of prosperity that costs the most.

Measure not the work
Until the day's out and the labor done;
Then bring your gauges.

—ELIZABETH BARRETT BROWNING

And they say, How doth God know?
and is there knowledge in the Most High?—73:11

Does God Know?

THIS QUESTION HAS BEEN ASKED through the centuries by many in various circumstances. By those who wondered why God did not intervene to alter the state of affairs. And by those who lived in open defiance of His restrictions.

To the sinner one of the most horrifying things is that God knows, but to the obedient this is one of the most consoling facts.

It is *what* God knows that makes the difference. When one is aware that the God of heaven knows evil about him, he may seek relief by turning toward skepticism or by convincing himself God is weak and unknowledgeable. Thus his wish becomes his faith; so he begins to question God's existence or God's ability to know. The fault is not in a lack of Divine evidence but in the human heart. You can't blame the seed when the soil is bad.

Man can wish and wish, but God can't be disposed of by wishing He does not exist; neither will wishing hide anything from His sight. God always knows.

Blind unbelief is sure to err,
And scan God's work in vain;
God is His own interpreter,
And he will make it plain.
—WILLIAM COWPER

If I say, I will speak thus; behold, I should offend against the generation of thy children.—73:15

Say Nothing to Avoid Offense

THE WRITER HAD COME TO GRIPS with a perilous problem. His faith was shaken and almost abandoned after reflecting on the prosperity of the wicked in contrast with his own plagues (verses 3,14).

But to his credit, as seen in the text, he kept quiet about it rather than offend others. Whatever his own doubts were, he kept them to himself. He would not say anything that might lessen the believer's confidence in the Almighty.

However, most disbelievers are not content to hold their infidelity as a personal pain but rather want to make all others miserable by robbing them of their faith.

Nobody talks so constantly about God as those who insist there is no God.

—HEYWOOD BROUN

If God exists, there are many reasons to promote faith in Him. If He doesn't, why rob others of their hope?

Though the writer was temporarily reeling from doubts, he was approaching closer to greatness than he thought; for he had enough regard for the people to say nothing that might hurt them. This is a worthy example in every matter.

But it is good for me to draw near to God:
I have put my trust in the Lord God, that I may declare all thy works.—73:28

Nearer My God

IT IS GOOD FOR US TO DRAW NEAR TO GOD. Oh, how it fills our hearts with acclamation!

Nearer, my God to Thee,
Nearer to Thee!
E'en though it be a cross
That raiseth me;
Still all my song shall be,
Nearer, my God, to Thee,
Nearer to Thee.

Though like a wanderer,
The sun gone down,
Darkness be over me,
My rest a stone;
Yet in my dreams I'd be
Nearer, my God, to Thee,
Nearer to Thee.

Or, if on joyful wing
Cleaving the sky,
Sun, moon, and stars forgot,
Upward, I fly;
Still all my song shall be,
Nearer, my God, to Thee,
Nearer to Thee.

—SARAH F. ADAMS

This is the happiest association. The sweetest fellowship. For now. Forever.

A man was famous according as he had lifted up axes upon the thick trees.—74:5

Infamous Fame

WE HAVE IN THIS PSALM an outstanding example of infamous fame. They had built up a recognition for destruction. This is what they had done: Put Jerusalem in perpetual desolations. Plundered the temple. Raised tumults. With axes and hammers broke down the carved work—maybe for the overlaid gold. Set fire to the temple. Burned up the sacred meeting places. Their object was to destroy Israel altogether. In their brutality they violated things dear to God and His people. They demolished the holy with no more consideration than a woodsman with his axe in the forest.

Their celebrity was founded on how bad they were. Their distinction was their devastation. This is the only attention they got—their degeneracy. Their fame created itself out of something worse than nothing. For it is a thousand times better to live unacclaimed in righteousness and finally rest in an unknown grave than to be a headliner in criminality. When upright people are hurt and holy things are desecrated, how barbarous is the perpetrator.

Where none admire, 'tis useless to excel.

—LORD GEORGE LYTTELTON

I anger to think it was fame!

For God is my King of old, working salvation in the midst of the earth.—74:12

For God...

WITH JERUSALEM IN RUINS, the poet turned to his only recourse—God. For He who had done so much in times past would surely help them now:

• "Thou didst divide the sea by thy strength" (verse 13). He had divided the waters of the sea for Israel's crossing. For generations this had buoyed them when their spirits sank.

• "Thou breakest the heads of the dragons in the waters" (verse 13). The dragon was a symbol of Egyptian power but no match for the true God. Egypt's might was feeble compared to God's.

• "Thou driedst up mighty rivers" (verse 15), enabling them to pass over Jordan. Today He is our bridge over difficult places.

• "The day is thine, the night is also thine" (verse 16). He can see to protect us in the night as well as in the day.

All of this adds up to one irrefutable conclusion: God is mightier than men. And we can have Him in our corner. This puts *A Psalm in My Heart.*

O God, our help in ages past,
Our hope for years to come.
—ISAAC WATTS

O deliver not the soul of thy turtle-dove
unto the multitude of the wicked:
forget not the congregation of thy poor for ever.—74:19

God's Dove

IN THIS TEXT, ISRAEL IS REFERRED TO as God's dove, the mildest and softest of birds. A dove is gentle and harmless. And because of this extreme gentleness, a dove is easily captured, harmed or taken prey. Wild beasts easily make short work of the defenseless dove.

It is noteworthy, therefore, that God has often used the dove to tell us worthy things:

• It was a dove that God used to tell Noah when the waters of the flood had finally receded. The dove returned first with nothing, then with an olive branch—a symbol that the earth was alive and hospitable again (Genesis 8:8-12).

• It was a dove that God used to represent His Spirit when God spoke from the heavens, "This is my beloved son in whom I am well pleased" (Matthew 3:17).

• It was a dove that Jesus used to represent the innocence and purity that His disciples should possess. In sending out the twelve, He said, "Be ye therefore wise as serpents, and harmless as doves" (Matthew 10:16).

Today, God's doves, His people, must always maintain their purity and gentleness and make themselves available to be used by God in the communication of great truths. And since "birds of a feather flock together," they have no business flying with the hawks. Their contrasting dispositions do not make for affinity.

Arise, O God, plead thine own cause:
remember how the foolish man reproacheth thee daily.
Forget not the voice of thine enemies: the tumult of those that rise up against thee increaseth continually.—74:22,23

God, Plead Your Cause

LITERALLY, THE WRITER WAS BEGGING GOD to stand up for Himself, to fight back, to defend His honor.

Foolish people had mocked and reviled God. They made fun of Him. Thus the writer thought it was time for God to strike back, for God to take his hand out of His cloak and to destroy the revilers (verses 10,11).

It pains us to see our name and reputation being threatened and under attack. We leap to defend ourselves. We won't take it any longer. We counter-attack.

But when God's name is being dishonored, His holiness being derided, how do we respond then? Do we feel as keenly about His interests as we do our own?

While God is big enough to defend Himself and powerful enough to defeat the foolish, surely it rejoices His heart to see that we care about His reputation as much or more than we care about our own. God's cause should be our first cause. This gives the most gripping fascination. And the most lasting fame!

Unto thee, O God, do we give thanks, unto thee do we give thanks: for that thy name is near thy wondrous works declare.—75:1

Twice Thankful

GIVE THANKS, GIVE THANKS—the repetition emphasizes the intense feeling in the heart. There is nothing wrong with repetition. Nature does it all the time: the day and the night, the seasons, the rains, the foliage and the flowers. Repetition is a way of life for us: breathing, eating, sleeping, working; and another of our repetitious activities should be the giving of thanks.

It will increase our gratitude to meditate on our blessings and express our feelings in song, as Israel did. One of the world's favorites is:

O Thou fount of every blessing,
Tune my heart to sing Thy grace;
Streams of mercy, never ceasing,
call for songs of loudest praise.
—ROBERT ROBINSON

Everything grows by expression. Tell God you are thankful. And when man blesses you, thank him. It enhances lovability.

When Paul was in a storm-tossed ship, tossed to and fro by a mighty hurricane, he "gave thanks to God" (Acts 27:35). He certainly was not blessed at the moment with all he wanted (for the storm was raging), but he had the faith to see his blessings. And he was thankful. When we can see our blessings in the storm, we have made progress.

But God is the judge: he putteth down one, and setteth up another.—75:7

In His Hand Is Success or Failure

ONE OF THE STRONG SUPPORTS OF ISRAEL was their faith in the presiding power of God. This Psalm expresses that conviction.

"For promotion cometh neither from the east, nor from the west, nor from the south" (verse 6). It comes from above. Natural advantages can be thwarted and human alliances can be shaken by an overriding power. Exaltation can come from God alone. Prosperity depends more on Him above than on anything here below. Thus sometimes—

The race is not to the swift, nor the battle to the strong.

—ECCLESIASTES 9:11

The most elaborate plans can fail while success can spring out of almost nothing. God can lift up one and humble another. He is the sovereign.

Believing this, then we know that neither success nor failure has to be final. Armed with this conviction, life takes on new dimensions. Therefore let us follow His counsel, do our best and trust Him for the results. This will give us the mental attitude for success; and with it will come high aiming, energetic pushing, powerful pursuing and undiminished hoping.

For in the hand of the Lord there is a cup,
and the wine is red; it is full of mixture;
and he poureth out the same: but the dregs thereof,
all the wicked of the earth shall wring them out,
and drink them.—75:8

Drinking From His Cup

THIS PASSAGE IS IN KEEPING with the previous one which states God "putteth down one, and setteth up another." He holds the cup from which man must drink.

The contents vary. There is the sparkling, red wine mixed with spices to increase the quality—the better part. But there are the sediments the wicked must drink, wringing out the last murky drop. The containers were bags made of skins which lent themselves to wringing. The dregs were the strongest part of the mixture, representing the severest wrath of God. This portion was handed to the wicked.

Indeed, life has its dregs for the rebellious: hardships, disappointments, smiting conscience, frustration, paralytic disbelief and hopelessness. And in those dregs the disobedient drown themselves in misery.

All of us at times, however, have had to drink the distasteful. But one thing sure: we can renew our relationship with Him and ask for another cup.

The lesson from the dregs is a bitter one but helpful if it teaches us to ask for another cup that we may appropriate it to our sweetest taste.

Forget the past, live the present hour,
Drink from God's cup, your blessed dower.

At thy rebuke, O God of Jacob, both the chariot and the horse are cast into a dead sleep.—76:6

Rebuke

GOD'S "REBUKE" WAS A DEMONSTRATION of God's power. The psalmist was praising God's power over the great tools of war—the horse and the chariot. At God's rebuke, these once powerful weapons fell into the sleep of death.

Sometimes God rebuked with *interposing actions,* as seen in the text. And there are other instances: The plagues that were sent upon the Egyptians. And a storm was sent to stop the fleeing Jonah.

Other times, God rebuked with *reproaching words,* as revealed in the Bible: David felt the reproof of pointed rhetoric (II Samuel 12:1-7). Moses was rebuked in uncompromising terms because he did not sanctify God in the eyes of the people (Numbers 20:11). The Pharisees were reprimanded in sharp language for their hypocrisy (Matthew 23). Peter was censured in kind words for his little faith (Matthew 14:31).

If we need rebuke, let's not "kick against the pricks." It would be foolish to break the mirror because it reveals the wrinkles. The pain of rebuke is in its need, and its helpfulness is in the correction it works.

*Surely the wrath of man shall praise thee:
the remainder of wrath shalt thou restrain.*—76:10

Man's Wrath, God's Glory

MAN'S WRATH OCCASIONS THE PRAISE OF GOD and affords an opportunity for the Divine character to display itself.

The principle is seen in everyday life: A rebellious child breaks the heart of his parents, but his obstinacy does allow their wisdom to manifest itself. A murderer or robber grieves society, but he does occasion an opportunity for the commonwealth to show its strength in the administration of protective laws.

Also in another sense, the wrath of man is used to God's glory. His universal purpose requires Him to overrule all evil to His eventual good. The Just One transmutes the rage of man into His praise. The intended malice is utilized to the unintended glory of God.

As examples: 1) The treachery of Judas was turned to human redemption. 2) Heathen nations were used to discipline God's people. 3) The persecutors in the first century were employed to scatter the believers and thus spread the gospel far and wide.

Let this suffice us still,
Resting in childlike trust upon his will,
Who moves to his great ends unthwarted by the ill.

—JOHN GREENLEAF WHITTIER

But let's not confuse right and wrong. Man's fury is still wrong though God uses it to accomplish His holy purpose. The deed must be judged for what it is.

Vow, and pay unto the Lord your God:
let all that be round about him bring presents unto him
that ought to be feared.—76:11

Keep Your Vows

GOD'S PEOPLE ARE ADDRESSED in the passage. In time of great trouble they evidently made some vows to Him. Vows, under the spell of aroused feelings, are easy to make; and when some of the feelings wear off, they are easy to neglect. But a vow made in the storm should not be forgotten in the calm.

Vows to God are not to be taken lightly:

Better is it that thou shouldest not vow, than that thou shouldest vow and not pay.—ECCLESIASTES 5:5

The God of all honor exhorts men not to defer in keeping their vows but rather to "pay that which thou hast vowed" (Ecclesiastes 5:4).

Are you keeping your vows, the ones you made when your life was spared, when baby was born, when husband or wife lay at death's door, when you went back to work?

Vows should hold us to the stronger moments when we made them. Your vows are you; keep yourself by keeping them.

If a man vow a vow unto the Lord, or swear an oath to bind his soul with a bond; he shall not break his word, he shall do according to all that proceedeth out of his mouth.—NUMBERS 30:2

I call to remembrance my song in the night.
—77:6

Song in the Night

HERE IS A MAN IN THE GRIP OF TROUBLE who was trying to find some strength. Hence, he remembered when he sang in the night—when he had a psalm that darkness could not silence. Life had its problems and the night its shadows, but he could still sing. There were favors to cheer him and brighten his view in spite of the darkness that engulfed him. Though the night was black, he saw blessings that opened his mouth with praise. And he recalled those nights with the fond hope that what was might become what is. It is this kind of remembrance in the midnight hour that puts *A Psalm in My Heart.*

When the night is dark, look. Can't you see something to liven your heart? Sing on.

Sing on, ye joyful pilgrims:
The time will not be long,
Till in our Father's kingdom
We swell a nobler song.

Where those we love are waiting
To greet us on the shore;
We'll meet beyond the river,
Where surges roll no more.

Sing on, O blissful music!
With ev'ry note you raise,
My heart is filled with rapture,
My soul is lost in praise.

—CARRIE M. WILSON

I commune with mine own heart:
and my spirit made diligent search.—77:6

A Diligent Search

CONCERNING THE PAST and the present matter that lay before him, the author made inquiry which prompted him to ask the questions that follow (verses 7-9):

- "Will the Lord cast off for ever?"
- "Will he be favorable no more?"
- "Is his mercy gone for ever?"
- "Doth his promise fail for evermore?"
- "Hath God forgotten to be gracious?"
- "Hath he in anger shut up his tender mercies?"

After making the search and communing with his own spirit, the author absolved God. He never indicted the Most High. He rather freely admitted: "This is my infirmity." Whether the infirmity in this particular usage was something to bear or something he caused, it still remains that God never brought it on. If God is not to be blamed, then it follows that our ills are ordinarily the fruit of our own folly. It's all right to search for the source of our troubles, but be prepared for a little self-incrimination; for we may find them within ourselves. And then to God let us fly for pardon, strength and direction.

Thou leddest thy people like a flock by the hand of Moses and Aaron.—77:20

Like a Shepherd Lead Us

IN SPITE OF some depressing circumstances connected with the Psalm, it closes with a happy note on the pastoral work of the Almighty. It brings sweet satisfaction to meditate on the heartening truth that God is really the Shepherd of His people.

The sheep have their perils and need a shepherd devoted to their care. They require direction and protection, food and water, assistance in sickness, and a security that allows them to graze freely in the pastures by day and to sleep soundly in the fold by night.

The benedictions are many though the conditions are demanding. The tiresome journey to greener pastures is an ordeal but a necessary one to obtain the blessing. The restrictions of the fold are cramping but essential to the night's protection.

Flocks must be kept moving because of diminishing food and changing seasons. Sometimes they are led to the mountaintop, but before winter begins they must be led back to the valleys. So we sing:

Savior, like a shepherd lead us:
Much we need Thy tend'rest care;
In thy pleasant pastures feed us,
For our use Thy folds prepare.
—DOROTHY A. THRUPP

For he established a testimony in Jacob, and appointed a law in Israel, which he commanded our fathers, that they should make them known to their children: That the generation to come might know them, even the children which should be born; who should arise and declare them to their children.—78:5,6

From Generation to Generation

THE WRITER STATES IN THE THIRD VERSE that from the past generation they had learned of God: "Our fathers have told us." Furthermore, he declared that the fathers should teach the children, and the children, in turn, should arise and declare the Word to their children.

The Psalm gives these reasons for early teaching: 1) That they might know. 2) "That they might set their hope in God." 3) That they forget not "the works of God, but keep his commandments." 4) That they be not "stubborn and rebellious." 5) That they have a spirit "steadfast with God."

A person bends more freely in youth. And what is learned well in early life becomes ingrained and a part of one's lasting being. Today's adults are yesterday's children who were taught—or not taught—and it shows in either case.

'Tis education forms the common mind:
Just as the twig is bent, the tree's inclined.

—ALEXANDER POPE

And it is the responsibility of parents to bend the twigs.

The children of Ephraim, being armed, and carrying bows, turned back in the day of battle.—78:9

Deserters

THE TRIBE OF EPHRAIM WAS ONE of the large and leading tribes of Israel. They were well equipped and fully armed, but in the day of battle they turned back. They refused to stand with their brethren in the defense of the cause and the country. Favorably born, adequately armed, pledged to serve, yet when the day came to do battle they ran. What bravery in peace, what cowardice in war. What strength when it wasn't needed, what weakness when it was.

We never know our fiber until the crisis arises. The storm tests the structure and the zero hour the person.

To turn back when the going is rough, however, does not assign one to the role of a deserter forever. Peter is an example. Sometimes we rise above ourselves, other times we drop below our normal stance. This is largely what history is all about—those who fell below or climbed above, not those who stayed within the norm.

Our world is a battlefield. The war is one of ideas, morals and spiritual principles; and, like it or not, we are soldiers. Now this personal question: what kind are we? Like the children of Ephraim who "turned back in the day of battle"? Or like David, who went out to meet the giant? We know the kind we should be. To run, when truth is attacked, is treason to humanity.

And they sinned yet more against him by provoking the Most High in the wilderness.—78:17

Compounded Sin

THE CAUSE OF ISRAEL'S MULTIPLIED SINS was a lack of faith in God, as stated in verse twenty-two. Though God "had commanded the clouds from above, and opened the doors of heaven, and had rained down manna upon them to eat, and had given them of the corn of heaven," they still asked such faith-lacking questions: "Can God furnish a table in the wilderness? ...can he give bread also? can he provide flesh for his people?" (verses 18-24). The Most High had wrought streams out of the rock and dropped manna out of heaven; He had led them with a cloud by day and a fire by night; still they doubted and "limited the Holy One."

Their sin was all the greater because they had seen and received all the more. There was a growing disbelief. Doubt is sure to "add sin to sin."

"They tempted God in their heart." In a complaining and murmuring way they asked for food more tasty though they had manna, food fit for angels.

Doubt compounds sin, increasing the payments that must be met—

The sin ye do by two and two
Ye must pay for one by one.

—RUDYARD KIPLING

For he remembered that they were but flesh; a wind that passeth away, and cometh not again.—78:39

Only Human

THE PEOPLE OF GOD WERE FAR from perfect. "How oft did they provoke him in the wilderness, and grieve him in the desert! Yea, they turned back, and tempted God, and limited the Holy One of Israel. They remembered not his hand..." (verses 40-42).

"But he, being full of compassion, forgave their iniquity, and destroyed them not." This is compassion's nature—full of pity, mercy and forgiveness. Without His forgiveness all would be doomed.

God's compassion looked beyond the deeds and beheld the fleshly nature and weakness of sinners. *He remembered that they were but flesh,* that they were only human, that they were as weak as clay, that they were subject to temptation and error. He saw man as he is: no god, no angel, a fleshly creature whose spirit is willing but whose flesh is weak (Matthew 26:41).

The God of compassion took all this into consideration—their flesh, their trials, their temptations—and accordingly forgave them. This gives us the true view of man and God. Man can sin, but God can forgive. Let us, therefore, not lose sight of the need of this realistic approach to living.

Teach me to live and find my life in Thee,
Looking from my mistakes to the right way.
Let me not falter, but untiringly
Press on, and gain new strength and power each day.

He chose David also his servant, and took him from the sheepfolds.—78:70

From Pasture to Throne

GOD SENT SAMUEL THE PROPHET to the house of Jessie to anoint a king. They felt sure they had the very one—Eliab. After looking him over, the prophet agreed. "Surely the Lord's anointed is before him," he declared. A specimen to behold. But the God with the better eyes refused to go along. He rather explained: "Look not on his countenance, or on the height of his stature; because I have refused him: for the Lord seeth not as man seeth; for man looketh on the outward appearance, but the Lord looketh on the heart" (I Samuel 16:6-8).

Seven of the sons, one after another, passed before Samuel and the Most High rejected them all. Could there be an error? Are these "all thy children?" All that have a chance, thought their father. But there was another—the youngest, who was keeping the sheep. Well, they sent for him and, to their amazement, God said, "This is he." Though he was ruddy and handsome, he was chosen for his heart.

Now for some moralizing: when we measure a man, put the gauge to his heart. So let us keep ourselves strong within—there's the real standard.

Pour out thy wrath upon the heathen
that have not known thee, and upon the kingdoms
that have not called upon thy name.
For they have devoured Jacob,
and laid waste his dwelling place.—79:6,7

Praying Against Enemies

AN ATTITUDE THAT HAS BOTHERED SOME in their study of Psalms is the prayers against enemies. They have felt that they were vengeful and thus opposed to godliness. We do not wish to hide them, nor to stumble on them, but to learn the truth about them.

First, the spirit of resentment is natural in human beings when suffering is experienced, when honor is attacked and when religious issues dearer than life hang in the balance.

Second, bear in mind this was not a prayer of personal antagonism and revenge but rather a plea against kingdoms or nations that had not called upon God. It was not necessarily vindictive. It was rather an expression of intense care for the honor of God's name. Simply, it was a prayer that justice might be done which necessarily required reprimands to be meted out.

Third, it is a matter of easy logic to assume that whatever was proper for God to do was proper for man to pray. God's righteous judgment had been poured down on Israel's enemies many times. To commit the procedure to Him placed in His hand the *time* and the *how.*

O remember not against us former iniquities:
let thy tender mercies speedily prevent us;
for we are brought very low.—79:8

Former Sins

THE *AMERICAN STANDARD VERSION* renders the passage, "Remember not against us the iniquities of our forefathers."

One thing about sin: its effects remain around for a long time—to worry even the posterity of the sinner. That was true in this instance. The failures of their forefathers haunted them though there was assurance the often-sinning Israel was just as often forgiven. *Forgiving* includes *forgetting,* which has always been hard for people to fully grasp. The Lord's covenant promises His forgetfulness of the sins He forgives: "I will forgive their iniquity, and I will remember their sin no more" (Jeremiah 31:34). Blessed assurance! What a comfort!

Their fear of punishment for the sins of their parents may have surfaced because of a feeling of their own guilt. However, if one is forgiven, he should have no guilt complex. It is to God's honor that we feel clean after being laundered in His mercy.

Our fathers lived their lives and must answer for themselves. Now, as we live ours, let us think of our own responsibility, remembering, "The son shall not bear the iniquity of the father" (Ezekiel 18:20).

So we thy people and sheep of thy pasture
will give thee thanks for ever:
we will show forth thy praise to all generations.—79:13

A Thousand Tongues

IN A CONVERSATION PETER BOHLER HAD with Charles Wesley, he remarked, "If I had a thousand tongues I would praise Him with them all." Wesley loved the phrase and used it in writing the famous song *O for a Thousand Tongues to Sing*:

Oh, for a thousand tongues to sing,
My dear Redeemer's praise,
The glories of my God and King,
The triumphs of His grace!

My gracious Master and my God,
Assist me to proclaim,
To spread through all the earth abroad
The honors of Thy Name.

Yes, if we had a thousand tongues, each should be dedicated to praising the name of God. This was the spirit of the psalmist.

As long as we can praise and magnify the name of God, we can pass through a maze of trying, baffling difficulties. I have never known the daily praiser of God to lose his courage to pursue. A few setbacks? Yes. But in the end he triumphs. So may we, the sheep of His pasture, use the one tongue we have to praise Him forevermore.

Give ear, O Shepherd of Israel, thou that leadest Joseph like a flock.... —80:1

Three Prayers

THIS SIMPLE BUT ELOQUENT PSALM contains three distinct prayers, each concluding with the same thought: "Turn us again, O God, and cause thy face to shine; and we shall be saved" (verses 3,7,19).

The *first* prayer tenderly compares God's leadership to a shepherd that leads his flock. It beseeches Him to stir up His strength, to allow His countenance to shine upon them, and to save them. They needed to pray.

The *second* prayer is also based on their troubles. They were a people so sorrowful they were forced to live on a diet of tears. They had strife with their neighbors and were a laughing stock in their sight. They needed to pray.

The *third* prayer concerns God's former dealings with His people, represented by a vine that was planted, nurtured and made fruitful, but presently broken down and trampled. In this desolation they implore God to interpose, to behold and visit the needy vine, vowing to Him that if He alleviates their distress they will not turn back from Him. They needed to pray.

We have our problems, too, and the need of prayer is ever with us. Thus Vana R. Raye wrote:

Pray in the morning,
Pray at the noontime,
Pray in the evening,
Pray all the time.

*Thou hast brought a vine out of Egypt:
thou hast cast out the heathen, and planted it.*—80:8

Like a Vine

THE AUTHOR USED SOME POETIC IMAGERY in describing God's care of Israel. The vine which refers to God's people had been brought out of Egypt and planted in a new land. He had cast out the heathen to make room for the vine. The vine prospered, sending out its branches toward the Mediterranean Sea and the Euphrates River.

But the hedges which are usually around a vineyard were broken down, leaving no enclosure, exposing the grapes to be picked by all that passed by. Wild men, compared to swine and beasts, came in and devoured it (verses 12,13).

In asking for Divine help, they acknowledged they were at fault: "So will not we go back from thee: quicken us, and we will call upon thy name" (verse 18). *Will not go back from thee*—implies they had. *Will call upon Thy name*—suggests they had neglected this.

A practical lesson for us is: a vine should bear fruit; if it doesn't, it loses its right for special care and protection from the tiller. In a comparison of the disciples to branches, the Lord taught that they must bear fruit—or be severed:

> *Every branch in me that beareth not fruit he taketh away: and every branch that beareth fruit, he purgeth it, that it may bring forth more fruit.*—JOHN 15:2

I am the Lord thy God, which brought thee out of the land of Egypt: open thy mouth wide, and I will fill it. —81:10

Great Expectations

THE TEXT IS ONE OF GREAT EXPECTATIONS. Perhaps it is based on a true scene of nature. The poet probably had observed the little bird open wide its mouth to receive food from the parent bird. And in the sight of Him whose image we bear, are we not better than the fowl of the air?

The Psalm assured the people that they would not be disappointed in their hope. "And I will fill it" is the promise God made.

'Tis expectation makes a blessing dear.
—SIR JOHN SUCKLING

As we see from the text, faith in God makes us optimists. We who live in hope get ready to receive—just like a little bird.

One of the great rules of success can be stated in one word—expectation. We don't ordinarily get what we don't expect. So, for a fuller life, let us keep up our song of anticipation:

Through the night of doubt and sorrow
Onward goes the pilgrim band,
Singing songs of expectation,
Marching to the promised land.
—SABINE BARING-GOULD

So I gave them up unto their own hearts' lust.

—81:12

God Gave Them Up

THIS IS ONE OF THE MOST TRAGIC ACCOUNTS in all the Bible. Some well-favored people had to be given up. God withdrew from them, leaving them to follow their own stubborn will in their own lust. This is frightful. A similar fate is recorded in Hosea 4:17: "Ephraim is joined to idols: let him alone." No need to offer leadership to apostates who will not follow.

In this case they had to be given up. Of course, God is God and man is man, which is to say that God could have forced them to obey; but this would have denied man his lofty nature and made him no more than a puppet on a string. This would not have been in humanity's interest; for if man obeys at all, he must do it through his own volition.

And it was a continual refusal to hearken that finally caused God, as mentioned in verse eleven, to let them go their own way: "But my people would not hearken to my voice; and Israel would none of me." They would have none of God, which forced Him to have none of them. He doesn't think it proper to walk with those who will not honor His company.

Even today in the church, as unpleasant as it is, we have to follow the same course of withdrawal (II Thessalonians 3:6). This is God's way.

And they walked in their own counsels.
—81:12

Poor Counsel

THE FIRST PART OF THE VERSE, as seen in the previous essay, tells of a people so rebellious they had to be given up. They were allowed to do as they pleased. For in the end, their own decisions rebuked them. This, however, is God's way of dealing with hardened people. Examples are numerous: Israel clamored for a king and God gave them Saul (I Samuel 12). The prodigal was not hindered from going into a far country (Luke 15). By walking in our own counsels, we enter the lands of despair.

Now we see from the text that Israel, having rejected the Divine counsel, was left with no counsel but their own. Poor counsel indeed! If their counsel had been smart, they would not have given up God's instruction. Human advice—that's what they chose. We can get plenty of it free; but it will not be cheap if we follow most of it, for with every word a future will die.

They could have said a thousand times, "It's our life. We'll do as we please." Of course! But later when they had to suffer, it would have given no comfort to say, "This is our life." Yes, each has his life. And his misery. And his joy. So let's make it a life of joy and success by following God:

Because the foolishness of God is wiser than men.
—I CORINTHIANS 1:25

Oh that my people had hearkened unto me,
and Israel had walked in my ways!
I should soon have subdued their enemies,
and turned my hand against their adversaries.
...He should have fed them also with the finest of the wheat:
and with honey out of the rock should I have satisfied thee.
—81:13-16

It Might Have Been

THIS IS THE STORY of what might have been—neglected duties, lost opportunities. Israel's enemies would have been subdued. God's people would have been fed. But they missed what they could have had because they would not hearken. Much was at stake, and they lost it because they wouldn't listen. Deaf ears have denied legions the call to opportunity, and later all they could hear was, "It might have been."

Of all the sad words
Of tongue and pen,
The saddest are these:
It might have been.
—JOHN GREENLEAF WHITTIER

Oh, the haunting echoes of what might have been! Countless numbers who once were so close to a better way are now following courses of failure and sorrow. Oh! had they only hearkened to a better voice! But every new day presents another chance. Thank God for it! Let us learn from our *might have beens* and go out and meet the challenge of *what might be.*

They know not, neither will they understand.
—82:5

Ruling in Ignorance

THE MEN IN THE TEXT WERE MAGISTRATES. They had three distinctions, and all three were wrong: didn't know; topped by the second, didn't know they didn't know; and still worse, didn't care to understand. Their glory was in their superficiality, where they unashamedly rested their honor in unwitting decisions.

Blind and naked ignorance
Delivers brawling judgments, unashamed,
On all things all day long.
—ALFRED TENNYSON

Ignorance is a foe of justice. It's impossible to administer justice unless we have the complete facts. Judging with only a few facts is "like trying to tell what happens inside a house by watching what goes in by the door and what comes out by the chimney," declared Claude Bernard.

Though it's an official ignorance dressed in the ill-fitting clothes of an iller intelligence, it still hurts. The people want liberty, freedom and justice for all. They will swim the oceans to reach the land that offers it. And as they do, what a welcome sight is the Statue of Liberty, New York Harbor. But even a more encouraging and fortifying sight is the Book in the courtroom on which the witness places his hand. Let us go there basically to form our laws and from it get the morality and courage to render unbought decisions and unbiased judgments.

All the foundations of the earth are out of course [are shaken, *ASV*].—82:5

Destroying the Foundations

CIVIL INJUSTICE BREAKS THE FOUNDATIONS of society: spreads bitterness; inflames disrespect for law and order; and festers anarchy in the land. History is replete with what occurs when rulers rule too fiercely.

It seems paradoxical, but injustice can occur in a democracy—especially among people not organized to be heard; for politicians are not so sensitive to the voices of unorganized voters. Self-serving politicians can pave their pathway to victory with special considerations for those who can turn out the votes. This can saddle some citizens with galling inequalities while it gives the favored a flash-in-the-pan glee. Yes, flash-in-the-pan jubilation. For nothing can endure that is not based on honesty, fairness and justice for all.

A government red with blood will someday turn ghastly pale in death. Blood—that's life. And the sacrifice of wealth—that's also life. For it takes so much life to produce a dollar. Life can be taken on the field of labor as well as on the field of battle. One is a once-for-all sacrifice, the other a day-by-day bleeding. When government demands too much, it destroys the incentive to produce, undermines its foundations and topples its own prosperity.

Let us, therefore, hold dear the sacred view that government should exist for the benefit of the governed—not the governors.

I have said, Ye are gods: and all of you are children of the Most High. But ye shall die like men, and fall like one of the princes.—82:6,7

Death Knows No Pedigree

RULERS ARE CALLED "GODS" because of their role in humanity's affairs. But beneath those royal robes is a mortality as fragile as the obscure peasant. The king is subject to heart failure, stroke, ruptured appendix, malignancy and all other ills, plus creeping old age, like the mass of mankind. Renown will not ease the pain of disease nor stop it from taking its toll. The pale horse with its rider called Death is galloping not far behind him as well as us.

Seeing that death a necessary end,
Will come when it will come.
—WILLIAM SHAKESPEARE

Death knows no pedigree or position. I was more deeply impressed with this fact and with man's frailty and superficial values when I visited the old home of Andrew Jackson. After going through the dwelling place of the heroic president, popularized for his stonewall courage, I went out to the family burial ground. There I stood and meditated at the grave of a man who held the highest office in the land. Then I walked over to the grave of his trusted slave. There I searched my soul as I pondered the state of man. And I thought—it doesn't make much difference when the end comes whether you are president or slave, rich or poor, acclaimed or unnoticed, for all must die and sleep in the same dust.

They have taken crafty counsel against thy people, and consulted against thy hidden ones.—83:3

Hidden Under Thy Wings

THE HIDDEN ONES WERE THE PEOPLE OF GOD whom He was protecting and keeping safe from their enemies.

God has always hidden and protected His people, even when they did not know it. Yet, there are times when we want to fly away: get away from the grind, the greed, the superficiality of a society that aches because of its self-caused pains. This craving of the soul for a place of concealment was expressed by the psalmist in beautiful language: "Oh that I had wings like a dove! for then I would fly away, and be at rest" (55:6). What we really want to get away from is not the here but the strain of what's here. We are beset by problems. We feel so alone, so vulnerable, so unprotected. Friends forget us and fail us. Our time and energies are overtaxed. The road is rocky, and the way is hazy.

But we must not lose heart! God continues to shelter and shield His children, if we would only accept His refuge and His goodness. So, in the poetic wording of David, let us pray: "Keep me as the apple of the eye; hide me under the shadow of thy wings" (17:8). And let us sing:

Hide me, O my Savior, hide me
In Thy holy place;
Resting there beneath Thy glory,
O let me see Thy face.

—FANNY J. CROSBY

That men may know that thou, whose name alone is JEHOVAH, art the Most High over all the earth. —83:18

Jehovah

THERE IS SO MUCH TO LEARN from the names of God:

Jehovah: This was the holiest name of God, so much so that the early Hebrews did not even pronounce it. The name originally came from a Hebrew verb meaning "to be." Jehovah is the One, the One who always was and always will be. But more than that, He is also the "Becoming One," the One who becomes the answer to our every need.

Jehovah-jireh: After Abraham demonstrated his faith in raising his hand to offer Isaac, God provided a ram as a substitute sacrifice for the boy. In grateful recognition, Abraham called the place "Jehovah-jireh," which means "God will provide" (Genesis 22:14). God has provided a Lamb for us and daily provides for our needs.

Jehovah-nissi: After the victory over the Amalekites, Moses built an altar and called the place "Jehovah-nissi," which means "God is our banner" (Exodus 17:15). The Lord is still our Conqueror. It is under His banner that we find the victorious life we all seek but few find.

Jehovah-shalom: When Gideon was finally convinced that God wanted to use him to lead the Israelites and guaranteed him peace in the midst of war, he built an altar and sacrificed to the Lord. He called the place "Jehovah-shalom," which means "God is our peace." Peace, if we are to find any of it, still comes from God and God alone.

Praise Jehovah—our I Am, our Provider, our Conqueror, our Peace!

They go from strength to strength,
every one of them in Zion appeareth before God.—84:7

Inner Strength

WHILE GOD OFTEN GAVE HIS PEOPLE physical strength to defeat physical enemies, inner spiritual strength was always necessary and much preferred.

Accordingly, Moses spent a lot of time getting the Israelites ready for the Promised Land. In his last farewell address to them before they left for Canaan and he left for Mount Nebo, Moses told the people, "As thy days, so shall thy strength be" (Deuteronomy 33:25). In other words, they would have strength for all their days if they continued to trust in God. And so will we.

To find strength for our days there is probably no greater passage to turn to than Isaiah 40:29-31:

> *He that giveth power to the faint; and to them that have no might he increaseth strength. Even the youths shall faint and be weary, and the young men shall utterly fall; But they that wait upon the Lord shall renew their strength; they shall mount up with wings as eagles; they shall run, and not be weary; and they shall walk, and not faint.*

God gives strength to the weary and the weak and the powerless. We expect young athletes to be able to run forever, but they eventually will stumble and fall. God's people, though, will be renewed from an inner strength unseen by human eyes. Like a tree that flourishes because of unseen roots, so we will be fortified from unseen forces.

God's people will walk faithfully without fainting, run the race without tiring and soar like eagles without wings!

For a day in thy courts is better than a thousand.
I had rather be a doorkeeper in the house of my God,
than to dwell in the tents of wickedness.—84:10

One Day With God

A DAY SPENT IN THE COURTS OF GOD will do more to bring peace and satisfaction to the soul than a thousand days spent in worldly indulgence, social-mixing, honor-looking, self-seeking and money-chasing combined.

When we start reviewing the past, we find that those days spent seeking pleasures were rather empty and disappointing. The satisfactions we sought were always beyond us, and when we got there they were still beyond us. They were the fleeing mirages that kept ahead of us.

We find internal peace in a relationship—not in seeking it, for it is a by-product. The communion of our spirit with the Great Spirit, believing in Him, hoping in Him, brings a special delight not experienced in common pastimes.

Out of the hardness of heart and of will,
Out of the longings which nothing could fill,
Out of the bitterness, madness, and strife,
Out of myself and all I called life,
Into the having of all things with Him!
Into an ecstasy full to the brim!

Wilt thou not revive us again:
that thy people may rejoice in thee?—85:6

Revive Us Again

THE PETITION, "REVIVE US AGAIN," implies that there was life, but it also suggests that their spiritual life had declined and was in need of revival. The causes of this cooling state were many; and as they were removed, the fervor of the soul would be restored.

Those people were like a countryside swept by the wintry blasts: cold, barren, in need of spring's revival. Their zeal had lost its glow. The once-burning fire within them was not just some dying embers. They had left their first love; it was no longer first.

In the plea for renewal, the poet gave this reason: "that thy people may rejoice in thee." Clearly, the joyous life is incompatible with a weak, inactive religion.

A soul-stirring awakening is needed throughout the land. Oh, the warmth, the zeal, the invigoration, if we would live in a constant revival with no changing seasons, no winter—perpetual, spiritual summer. Then there would be the voice of a vibrant life, the jubilee of salvation, the song of holiness and the hallelujah of praise. Great results would follow. Needing a revival, Israel sang of it. So should we:

Revive us again: Fill each heart with Thy love;
May each soul be rekindled with fire from above.
Hallelujah! Thine the glory; Hallelujah! Amen;
Hallelujah! Thine the glory; revive us again.
—WILLIAM P. MACKAY

Mercy and truth are met together; righteousness and peace have kissed each other.—85:10

The Kiss of Reconciliation

THE STORY OF AN UNUSUAL TRIAL has been told. It occurred in a land that demanded unyielding penalties for the disobedience of laws. A young man who had destroyed both eyes of another was brought to trial. The law required an eye for an eye—two in this case. The trial judge was his own father, who was torn between the conflicting cries of mercy and truth. Mercy pleaded for acquittal. But truth had to be honored—his son was guilty. Finally the father-judge said, "As your judge I must uphold the law. The verdict is: two eyes must be given for the two destroyed. But, as your father, I offer one of mine to help meet the demands of justice."

Mercy and truth met together and found a way of reconciliation. They do not necessarily conflict with each other. Human governments, however, have ever had the issue of assessing the proper proportions of each.

God has no such problem; for mercy permits an escape from justice—because change occurs in the heart of the offender, and this is what God wants. So in what seems to be an estrangement and alienation between mercy and truth, God unites them and, like alienated friends kiss when reconciled, they, too, kiss for they have been brought together in the loveliness of a cherished and effectual unity.

Bow down thine ear, O Lord, hear me:
for I am poor and needy.... —86:1

Utterances of a Distressed Soul

HERE ARE THE EARNEST UTTERANCES of the trustful but distressed poet, as expressed in the Psalm:

• "O Lord, hear me." And he believed God would. "Thou wilt answer me," he confidently stated.

• "I am poor and needy." But the poorer the state of man, the richer can be the mercy of God.

• "Preserve my soul." The Creator is also the Preserver. "O thou preserver of men" (Job 7:20).

• "Save thy servant that trusteth in thee." Trust is one of the most necessary attributes in religion.

• "Be merciful unto me." He asked that his unworthiness be disregarded. This was a common request of the psalmist; and rightly, for this is what we all need. Our human frailties require it.

• "I cry unto thee daily." The cry of the mouth was merely the echo of the heart's need.

• "Rejoice the soul of thy servant." He pleaded that sorrow and anxiety be replaced with joy and peace.

So trust, faint heart, thy Master!
He doeth all things well,
He loveth more than heart can guess
And more than tongue can tell.

Among the gods there is none like unto thee, O Lord; neither are there any works like unto thy works.—86:8

The Incomparable God

A COMPARISON of the one God to false gods was only an accommodation to the superstitions of men—not that they exist, except in the misconceptions of men. In a land where many people were devoted to heathen gods, the poet paid tribute to the true God by stating, "there is none like unto thee" and ascribed to Him these distinctive traits:

- "For thou, Lord, art good."
- "Ready to forgive."
- "Thou wilt answer me."
- "A God full of compassion."
- "Plenteous in mercy and truth."
- "Thou art great."
- "Doest wondrous things."
- "Thou art God alone."

For there is "one God and Father of all, who is above all," uncaused, invisible, spiritual, described in one word—love. He is not limited to the do-nothing role of the so-called gods. What men call gods are not gods. They are not self-existent, all-knowing, all-powerful beings. They are only man-made, and to serve them is idolatry.

Teach me thy way, O Lord; I will walk in thy truth: unite my heart to fear thy name.—86:11

Unite My Heart

A FEW YEARS AGO A MAN CAME TO MY OFFICE for consultation. He bore all the signs of a distraught, desperate creature. His skin was tormented with a nervous rash. His eyes showed loss of sleep. His voice was unsteady. His hands were shaky. After conversing for a while, I said, "Your trouble is a divided heart. You are trying to follow two ways of life that completely contradict each other. You have too much conscience to do wrong, but not enough consecration to do right. You can't serve two masters in the same heart. *No man can serve two masters* is an incontrovertible principle of happiness and success. By making God the master-passion of your heart, you can pull your shattered life together. In fact, this is the only satisfactory remedy for the contradictions and rivalries that now rage within you.

"Your problem is as old as man—and as human. Many great men have suffered the pain that is yours, including David. You can learn from him. You should pray his prayer (we turned and read from Psalms): *unite my heart to fear thy name.* And you should live as you pray. You will never have peace and security until you unify your heart."

The Lord shall count, when he writeth up the people, that this man was born there.—87:6

The Divine Count

GOD WOULD HONOR THOSE BORN IN ZION. When a census of the people was taken or an enrollment was made, those whose birthplace was Zion would be given special distinction.

Some practical truths from the text are:

First, there is great distinction for those born into his church, the spiritual Jerusalem. It is God's house or family—"the house of God, which is the church of the living God" (I Timothy 3:15)—and we are born into it, born again, which is an absolute requirement of this preferential recognition (John 3:3). In this we enjoy a nobility of birth—which neither degenerates nor improves by ancestors—that is strictly personal. Truly, to live nobly and die nobly befits such a noble birth.

Second, God is interested in counts. Luke recorded that three thousand were added to the church in one day (Acts 2:41). We should never depreciate numbers when they apply to people, for every person is an invaluable number.

Third, God does have a personal and complete knowledge of His people. God's "book of life" is the spiritual biography of us all. So when the saints go marching in, may we be among that number.

O Lord God of my salvation, I have cried day and night before thee...for my soul is full of troubles: and my life draweth nigh unto the grave. I am counted with them that go down into the pit: I am as a man that hath no strength. Thou hast laid me in the lowest pit, in darkness, in the deeps. Thy wrath lieth hard upon me, and thou hast afflicted me...Thou hast put away mine acquaintance far from me; thou hast made me an abomination unto them...Mine eye mourneth by reason of affliction...They came round about me daily...they compassed me.—88

The Most Mournful Psalm

THIS PSALM HAS BEEN CALLED the most mournful of the Psalms, the saddest of all. It is unlike the most of the sad Psalms which relate to sickness and sorrow, defeat and disappointment, in that they generally end with a ray of hope, a cheerful note and a triumphant rhetoric. But not this one.

The poet expected to die, but didn't anticipate it. His heart was filled with gloom, showing no consolation.

The writer felt an intense, personal distress, a heart full of trouble. Have we not all at times felt like we were the living dead?

When the psalmist needed his friends most, they were not there. Actually, he was an "abomination unto them." They fled at his presence. Sound familiar?

Yet this distressed man held on. He prayed daily. In all his troubles he recognized the hand of God. His faith carried him onward as he kept his pace to the grave. And with faith in God we also can handle depression, we can triumph over every trouble and mount every obstacle.

I am afflicted and ready to die from my youth up: while I suffer thy terrors I am distracted.—88:15

Afflicted

SOME SEVERE AILMENT HAD RACKED the poet's body for years. His trouble and affliction had been of long continuance—"ready to die from my youth up." His strength was nearly gone. He didn't think he could endure much longer. Moving toward death, he was tormented with terrors. He was afraid.

Beset with fears, he said, "I am distracted." Exhausted. Bewildered. It was hard to pursue a normal, settled course of straight thinking because he was possessed with fears. He was the victim of contending feelings. Composure was gone, and so was clear thinking.

The deathbed is not the best place to weigh the claims of religion, or to write wills, or to reconcile any of the differences of life. The better time is in the vigor of heath when the mind is sharp and the thinking is clear. Then when sickness comes and our thinking is impaired, we will have nothing to do but to enjoy the comfort of long and faithful lives spent in God's service and the anticipation of a better tomorrow—immortality. And as the end draws nearer, each of us can confidently answer, "Must I go?" with the hope, "Let me go."

O Captain! my Captain!
My fearful trip is done!
The ship has weather'd every rock,
The prize we sought is won.
—WALT WHITMAN

With my mouth will I make known thy faithfulness to all generations.—89:1

God Is Faithful

GOD PROVES HIS FAITHFULNESS DAILY. Every morning the sun climbs up over the eastern hills and, in the quiet splendor of a new dawn, proclaims, "God is faithful."

Gentle clouds form and water the earth. And soon the rainbow beautifully stretches across the sky, and that reminds us of a covenant made long ago—that God would never send another flood to destroy the earth. The unfailing message of the graphic rainbow is clear: "God is faithful."

Little birds fly, and we remember the hopeful words of Jesus, "Your heavenly Father feedeth them. Are ye not much better than they?" And then we acclaim, "God is faithful."

The mere act of writing a letter and dating it (A.D.—in the year of our Lord) marks the fulfillment of God's promise to send the world a Redeemer. With grateful hearts we praise, "God is faithful."

Night falls, and the beauty of a billion stars bursts forth. They radiate God's glory and silently testify to the word of God that keeps them in orbit (II Peter 3:7). Again we laud His name, "God is faithful."

Now, amid the shadows before we slumber, each should pray: "Dear God, help me to emulate Thy faithfulness, to be true to my word. Assist me to keep my promises to my religious commitment, my family, my friends, my business connections, and to myself."

God is greatly to be feared in the assembly of the saints, and to be had in reverence of all them that are about him.
—89:7

Fearing God the Right Way

THE FEAR THAT GOD ENJOINS UPON US is not the ordinary fear—terror, horror, fright and dread. "God hath not given us the spirit of fear; but of power, and of love, and of a sound mind" (II Timothy 1:7). The fear we should have of God is a constructive fear—reverence, awe and respect. The Bible states that we should "serve God acceptably with reverence and godly fear" (Hebrews 12:28); however, the words "godly fear" are rendered "awe" in the *American Standard Version.* Hence, the fear we should have is:

- The awe of God's greatness.
- The reverence of His name.
- The veneration of His authority.
- The attitude that prefers to please Him.
- The submission to His will.
- The adoration that bows in worship.

In the command to fear God, it was not intended that we be terrorized at the thought of Him; for we are also commanded to love God, which is not compatible with fright. For "perfect love casteth out fear." The fear of God and the love of God complement each other, and as they enlarge in the heart they give power to religion by providing the motives for the closest walk with God.

Remember how short my time is:
wherefore hast thou made all men in vain?—89:47

How Short Is My Time

LIFE IS BRIEF. "Man that is born of a woman is of few days" (Job 14:1). And those few pass so quickly. Time moves on crutches only for youth; a little later it flies on jets. So there's not but one reasonable conclusion:

Make Haste to Live

Make haste, O man! to live,
For thou so soon must die;
Time hurries past thee like the breeze;
How swift its moments fly.
Make haste, O man! to live.

Make haste, O Man! to do
Whatever must be done;
Thou hast no time to lose in sloth,
Thy day will soon be gone.
Make haste, O Man! to live.

The useful, not the great,
The thing that never dies;
The silent toil that is not lost,
Set these before thine eyes.
Make haste, O Man! to live.

Lord, thou....
—90:1-4

Blessed Thoughts of God

WE HAVE IN THIS PSALM some of the loftiest theological concepts—blessed thoughts of God:

• ***His personal relation to man:*** "Thou hast been our dwelling place in all generations." "For in him we live, and move, and have our being" (Acts 17:28). It would make no sense to have an impersonal God; the thesis that He exists requires a second—that we live in Him.

• ***God's almighty power:*** "Thou formed the earth and the world." There had to be a super power behind creation, for it could not have created itself.

• ***His eternal existence:*** "Even from everlasting to everlasting, thou art God." He is a self-existent Being, uncaused, unchangeable. He "was set up from everlasting, from the beginning, or ever the earth was" (Proverbs 8:23).

• ***His rulership:*** "Thou turnest man..." (verse 3). It is a natural role for God to rule man.

• ***God's timelessness:*** "A thousand years in thy sight are but as yesterday when it is past" (verse 4). To Him who always existed and always will, how could it be otherwise? Time for Him will not run out.

One thought I have—my ample creed,
So deep it is and broad,
And equal to my every need—
It is the thought of God.

—FREDERICK LUCIAN HOSMER

*The days of our years are threescore years and ten;
and if by reason of strength they be fourscore years,
yet is their strength labor and sorrow; for it is soon cut off,
and we fly away.*—90:10

Fleeting Years

THIS IS A MELANCHOLIC MEDITATION on the fewness of man's years. Threescore. By reason of strength, fourscore. But whether the strength is little or much, "it is soon cut off, and we fly away." Our years are like a passing shadow, a fleeting breath, the folding of a shepherd's tent—time to move on.

God stands winding His lonely horn,
And time and the world are ever in flight.
—WILLIAM B. YEATS

Consequently, it was incumbent upon the psalmist to exhort: "So teach us to number our days, that we may apply our hearts unto wisdom" (verse 12). Fill our days with the best and worthiest living. Therefore it is fitting that we ask ourselves:

Out of eternity
This new day is born;
Into eternity
At night will return.

Here hath been dawning
Another blue day;
Think; wilt thou let it
Slip useless away?
—THOMAS CARLYLE

Establish thou the work of our hands upon us; yea, the work of our hands establish thou it.—90:17

Pray for Your Work

THIS PORTION OF THE PSALM INVOKED the favor of God upon their plans and purposes. It was a prayer of the heart that accompanied the work of the hands. The repetition of the request indicates how intense the feeling was.

In rebuilding the walls of Jerusalem, the builders prayed as well as worked. "The people had a mind to work" and a mind to pray: "we made our prayer unto our God" (Nehemiah 4:6,9). The two powers that raise walls, tame wildernesses, erect cities, ascend heights and enlarge the kingdom of God are work and prayer.

When we work and pray, there is the combination of man's labor and God's help. This is enough.

"But is my work worthy of praying the blessings of God upon it?" you ask. Does it sustain your family? Does it help others? Does it aid the cause of God? If the answer is "Yes" to any of the questions, then you should work hard and pray much.

Sing, pray, and swerve not from your work;
But do thine own part faithfully;
Trust his rich promises of grace,
So shall they be fulfilled in thee.
—GEORGE NEUMARCK

He shall cover thee with his feathers, and under his wings shalt thou trust: his truth shall be thy shield and buckler.

—91:4

Under His Wings

ONE OF THE MOST BEAUTIFUL and comforting images of God's protection is found in this verse.

Under His wings. God takes cares of us like a mother hen takes care of her chicks. She nurtures them, nestling them gently under her large wings. She protects them from harm, from outsiders, from the cold—from all that would threaten her tiny offspring. It is no dreary duty but a joy. She gives her newly hatched a sense of identity and teaches them how to live.

On His wings. But God does even more. In Deuteronomy 32:11 we read that God is like a mother eagle, which "stirreth up her nest, fluttereth over her young, spreadeth abroad her wings, taketh them, beareth them on her wings." When God sees that we are old enough to fly, He stirs up the nest, breaks up everything we have thought dear and privileged. He expands our world and shows us how to fly. He shoves us out of the nest for us to try our own wings. All for our good. And ever watching as we fall, He glides under and scoops us up on His wings and carries us to safety. Over and over until we have learned to fly.

If mother hens and mother eagles work this hard and show this much love, don't you think our Father, the God of the universe, can do as much and more for us?

For he shall give his angels charge over thee, to keep thee in all thy ways. They shall bear thee up in their hands, lest thou dash thy foot against a stone.—91:11,12

Protected by Angels

SATAN QUOTED THIS PASSAGE when he tempted Christ, urging Him to fling Himself down from the pinnacle of the temple (Matthew 4:5,6). Satan applied the Psalms text to that occasion, but Jesus didn't for He didn't jump. While the Bible teaches aid by the angels, it does not teach that man should allow Satan to interpret the occasion and the extent. Satan is hardly a correct interpreter of Scripture; rather, his skill is in perverting Scripture to his own purpose.

The devil can cite Scripture for his purpose.
—WILLIAM SHAKESPEARE

Since man is "a little lower than the angels," then the angels are in a higher position than man. In their exalted position, they are the "ministering spirits" of God.

As the servants of God, they feel a deep interest in man. Thus the Savior says, "There is joy in the presence of the angels of God over one sinner that repenteth" (Luke 15:10).

Because he hath set his love upon me....

—91:14-16

God Blesses Those Who Love Him

JEHOVAH IS THE SPEAKER. He states the blessings He will grant to the person who loves Him, namely:

- "Deliver him" from evil (verse 10). Individually, each needs some kind of deliverance.
- "I will set him on high." Exalt him. Honor him. God smiles on those who love Him.
- "He shall call upon me, and I will answer him." Prayer is a privilege not everyone enjoys for spiritual reasons. Only the person who loves God has the Divine promise that God will answer—not always as he asks, but always in the way that is best.
- "I will be with him in trouble." There will be trouble, but God will be with him when it comes.
- "With long life will I satisfy him." This is very understandable. The life prescribed by true religion—calmness, moderation, temperance, faithful industry and freedom from excesses—contributes to health and longer days.
- "Show him my salvation." The previously mentioned blessings are temporal, but this one is spiritual, reaching beyond the grave, for now and for ever.

Oh! the triumph of loving God!

O Lord, how great are thy works! and thy thoughts are very deep. A brutish man knoweth not; neither doth a fool understand this.—92:5,6

How Great Are Thy Works

SOMETHING GREAT IS GOING ON. Are we observant enough to see it? Do we have the faith to recognize the power behind the greatness? And the gratitude to praise God for it?

The grandeur and enormity of His works overwhelm us; and though we meditate on them the longest and the fullest, we're still just primary students forced to say, "Thy thoughts are very deep." Too deep for complete comprehension! They have a vastness and eternity that swallow up our littleness and temporality. Job's question is still only rhetorical: "Canst thou find out the Almighty unto perfection?" (Job 11:7). But we don't have to fully understand God to appreciate Him, no more than a child has to know all about cake to like it.

His works are beyond our perfect comprehension, but we do understand their source and appreciate them. This is something "a brutish man knoweth not." "Neither doth a fool understand this." The stupid person, like the brute, does not have the rationality to relate creation to Divinity. Stupefied by sin, his concept of the marvelousness of God's counsels and works is very minimum. But whether a person sees it or not—

There lives and works a soul in all things,
And that soul is God.

—WILLIAM COWPER

They shall bring forth fruit in old age.
—92:14

Fruit in Old Age

THIS IS ENCOURAGING. Beautiful. Years of industry, sobriety, temperance and sound thinking form a fruitful way of life that is not apt to be broken by just some birthdays. There is, of course, a lessening of physical strength, but it is offset by the enhancement of other powers.

As a rule, the generals are older men; so are bank presidents and executives of other large businesses. Furthermore, age is a qualification of bishops or elders in the church. Age must have something going for it. God thinks so, and so does man. The people demand maturity, seasoning, experience and wisdom of the person who fills the most responsible job; they don't care if he is no longer able to triumph in football or to win the mile run in a track meet. They want something from his mind and heart, and they feel that the years enrich both. And they are right!

With aged men is wisdom, and in length of days understanding.
—JOB 12:12

Those who get wiser with time qualify themselves to bring forth a special fruit in old age.

For age is opportunity no less
Than youth itself, though in another dress,
And as the evening twilight fades away
The sky is filled with stars invisible by day.

Thy testimonies are very sure.

—93:5

God's Testimonies Are Sure

ALL OF GOD'S TESTIMONIES ARE TRUE: every word He spoke, every command He gave, every promise He made and every prophecy He uttered. And in their surety they:

• Make the simple wise: "The testimony of the Lord is sure, making wise the simple" (19:7).

The Bible is an invaluable and inexhaustible mine of knowledge and virtue.

—JOHN QUINCY ADAMS

• Rejoice the heart: "The statutes of the Lord are right, rejoicing the heart" (19:8). But in contrast, all joys based on unrighteousness are superficial and short-lived.

• Enlighten the eyes: "The commandment of the Lord is pure, enlightening the eyes" (19:8).

• Warn man: "Moreover by them is thy servant warned" (19:11).

• Bless those who keep them: "Blessed are they that keep his testimonies" (119:2). This is the verdict of history.

In a society of imperfect and changeable people, it is heartening to have something sure and certain—the testimonies of God, our heritage forever (119:111). And when we near the journey's end may we be able to repeat this blessed expression: "I have stuck unto thy testimonies" (119:31).

Holiness becometh thine house, O Lord, for ever.
—93:5

Holiness in God's House

HOLINESS IS CLEANNESS ON THE INSIDE, without which no dimming of lights, or bowing in prayer, or retiring in solitude or keeping quiet will make a person that way.

Holiness should prevail in the house of God. There truth should be the cardinal distinction and righteousness the dominant influence. God's house should be free of corruption, worldliness, politics, pride, ostentation, respect of persons, hate and hypocrisy. Sincerity and purity should characterize those within it.

Let us bear in mind, we get the crowd we appeal to. Appeal to those who prefer vaudeville and that's what we get—but not for long, for we are not good enough actors to hold them. But contrariwise, appeal to the spiritual and we get them—and their continued support, for the appeal is to the heart.

Since people become like what they worship and how they worship, this is God's plan for man:

Worship the Lord in the beauty of holiness.
—I CHRONICLES 16:29

So this is our prayer:

Take my life and let it be
Consecrated, Lord, to Thee.
Take my moments and my days;
Let them flow in ceaseless praise.
—FRANCES RIDLEY HAVERGAL

Understand...when will ye be wise?

—94:8-10

When Will We Be Wise?

THE PSALMIST FINALLY HAD ENOUGH from the senseless, foolish blowhards. They were arrogant; they had murdered widows and orphans. They needed to be confronted.

Therefore, the psalmist posed four questions designed to stop the evildoers in their tracks:

1) ***He that planted the ear, shall He not hear?*** God can hear all the shouts and whispers of all peoples. After all, He is the One who created the ear.

2) ***He that formed the eye, shall He not see?*** Do you think you can hide from God's eyesight? Our eyes, marvelous though they be, are as blindness compared to the eyes of God.

3) ***He that chastiseth the heathen, shall He not correct?*** If God can punish and bring down the heathen empires of the world, is it not possible for Him to discipline a few rebellious servants?

4) ***He that teacheth man knowledge, shall He not know?*** We get pretty smart and sometimes assume we are even smarter than we are. But God is the source and author of all wisdom. Our tiny storehouses of learning are insignificant compared to His.

As asked in the text, when will we be wise? When we realize that the all-hearing, all-seeing, all-correcting, all-knowing God is smarter and stronger than we are. It's really very simple.

Blessed is the man whom thou chastenest, O Lord, and teachest him out of thy law; that thou mayest give him rest from the days of adversity.—94:12,13

Rest From Adversity

BLESSED OR HAPPY IS THE PERSON who understands God's plan of ups and downs, who knows that our earthly stay requires some "bread of adversity and water of affliction," who understands that—

Prosperity is not without many fears and distastes; and adversity is not without comforts and hopes.

—FRANCIS BACON

When we are strengthened with the positive view, engendered by God's teachings on reverses, then when trouble abounds we will have the hope to be calm and the confidence to continue. Reverses are easier to take when we realize they can be the means to a higher end.

Sweet are the uses of adversity,
Which, like the toad, ugly and venomous,
Wears yet a precious jewel in his head.

—WILLIAM SHAKESPEARE

Thus every setback must be judged in the light of how it affects us.

Whatever our troubles are, they will pass. And oh! the rest from adversity, how sweet it will be! And just as the winter beautifies the spring, so adversity will sweeten our prosperity.

Unless the Lord had been my help,
my soul had almost dwelt in silence. When I said,
My foot slippeth; thy mercy, O Lord, held me up.—94:17,18

When I Was Slipping

IF IT HAD NOT BEEN FOR GOD—for God's guidance to direct, for God's promise to sustain, for God's comfort to cheer, and for God's mercy to rescue, the poet would have fallen. He had been in a slippery place and had almost lost his balance. A little longer and he would not have been able to stand. If relief had not come, he would have gone down to the grave of silence. But, in that threatening hour, the mercy of God held him up.

In a similar statement the author said, "I had fainted, unless I had believed to see the goodness of the Lord in the land of the living" (27:13). His belief saved him from despair—they never fill the same heart.

How frail is man without the help of God. How invincible he is with it. So in traversing the slippery ground let us fully believe in God, watch for the threatening places, draw near to Him, pray for His help, and balance ourselves with His Word in our hearts.

And that gives security.

Shall the throne of iniquity have fellowship with thee, which frameth mischief by a law?—94:20

No Fellowship

THE QUESTION IS AN EMPHATIC NEGATIVE—No! God does not sit on thrones with the rulers of iniquity. The oppressors of mankind do not have His fellowship. They frame laws to further mischief. They condemn the innocent blood (verse 21). Consequently, God shall make them to fall into the snare of "their own iniquity, and shall cast them off in their own wickedness" (verse 23).

Here are some other pertinent questions asked in II Corinthians 6:14-17:

What fellowship hath righteousness with unrighteousness?
What communion hath light with darkness?
What concord hath Christ with Belial?
What part hath he that believeth with an infidel?
What agreement hath the temple of God with idols?

None! So "come ye out from among them, and be ye separate, saith the Lord."

As seen, fellowship requires more than association, more than contact; it requires unity, unity of beliefs, unity of aims. "Can two walk together, except they be agreed?" (Amos 3:3). This is the prerequisite of fellowship—agreement, like views, like goals. And this unity of spirits with God and with others is one of earth's sweetest joys.

O Come, let us worship and bow down: let us kneel before the Lord our maker. For he is our God; and we are the people of his pasture, and the sheep of his hand.—95:6,7

Pasture People

GOD LIKES THE IMAGERY OF SHEEP and shepherds and has used it often in Scripture.

In the analogy, we are always the sheep and always in need of guidance. Sheep are not brilliant thinkers. They will stand in their drinking water and pollute it with their own wastes. They will eat the grass to the roots and then dig up the roots and eat them, leaving barren land. They have little sense of direction. Furthermore, they are totally incapable of defending themselves against danger. Yet there is hope, not in their merit but in the ability and goodness of their shepherd.

This is a rather accurate analogy of us. We also have a shepherd—the Good Shepherd. He knows the sheep, He knows them intimately by name. He leads them and they, knowing His voice, follow. He keeps them together for their protection. He directs them in safe and pleasant places. But if danger comes, the Good Shepherd stands and defends the sheep. The hired hand, however, works only for wages and will run at the first sign of trouble. But not the Good Shepherd. He lays down His life for the sheep, if necessary. And for us it was necessary: Jesus the Good Shepherd died for us. He is always there, always protecting, always leading.

Now it is our job to be the good sheep.

Today if ye will hear his voice, harden not your heart, as in the provocation, and as in the day of temptation in the wilderness.—95:7,8

Harden Not Your Heart

PAUL NOT ONLY QUOTED THIS PASSAGE, he attributed its source to the Holy Spirit: "Wherefore as the Holy Ghost saith, To-day if ye will hear his voice, harden not your hearts, as in the provocation…" (Hebrews 3:7,8). "The Holy Ghost saith"—not man! Thus the New Testament writer placed the stamp of inspiration on Psalms. It is an inspired message—not human folklore.

Today! The commands of God relate to the present. They are too important to be postponed.

Harden not your heart. It is an act of will. It is voluntary. And there are many ways we can do it: 1) Refusing the call of God hastens the petrifying process. 2) Our every effort to have our own way firms the mind in false reasoning. 3) Every doubt sets up the hardening action. 4) Resisting right dulls the sensitivity and makes it easier the next time. 5) Trying to justify wrong sears the conscience a little deeper. 6) A heart that beats only for self hardens a little with every throb. And 7) a heart that is filled with hate, how like iron it becomes.

But if we can harden our hearts, we can also soften them; let us do the latter.

Sing unto the Lord, bless his name;
show forth his salvation from day to day.—96:2

From Day to Day

From day to day is God's plan for us. It is simple. All that is required of us is to do our duty daily. It's a plan for the *now.* One of constancy. One of practicality. One of appropriation.

Every day presents its opportunities; seize them.

Each day brings its responsibilities; shoulder them.

Every day showers its blessings; thank God for them.

Every day brings us closer to the end; rejoice in it.

Life is wrapped up in today. Now is the time to be good and happy. As did the psalmist, so should we sing today, praise God's name today, and show salvation today to a world in need of the Savior.

So this is our prayer:

Only today is mine,
And that I owe to Thee;
Help me to make it Thine;
As pure as it may be;
Let it see something done,
Let it see something won,
Then at the setting sun
I'll give it back to Thee.

—Henry Burton

He shall judge the people righteously.
—96:10

Righteous Judgment

JUSTICE GRAY OF THE SUPREME COURT once said in a lower court to a man who would have been sentenced, except for a technicality: "I know that you are guilty and you know it, and I wish you to remember that one day you will stand before a better and wiser Judge, and there you will be dealt with according to justice and not according to law."

How assuring to the people of God! How frightening to those who are not!

God the Creator, God the Provider, is also God the Righteous Judge, better and wiser than man. He is the all-pure, never-corruptible, all-knowing, all-merciful Judge of souls. "He shall judge the world with righteousness, and the people with his truth" (verse 13).

Judgment Day will be a day of great rejoicing for the people of God, rewarding time, the crowning day.

> *Henceforth there is laid up for me a crown of righteousness, which the Lord the righteous judge, shall give me at that day: and not to me only, but unto all them also that love his appearing.*—II TIMOTHY 4:8

It will be the day for which we have lived to hear Him say, "Well done, good and faithful servant…enter thou into the joy of thy lord" (Matthew 25:23).

Confounded be all they that serve graven images, that boast themselves of idols: worship him, all ye gods.
—97:7

Graven Images

CONFOUNDED BE THE IDOLATERS. Let them be ashamed. Let them be disappointed. Let them learn that their idols are not real gods. May their boasting be in vain.

The heathen had their idols, but the people of God at times have also drifted into idolatry. The Israelites once made a golden calf and said, "These are thy gods, O Israel, which brought thee up out of the land of Egypt" (Exodus 32:8). Of course, they knew the golden calf which could not walk did not bring them out of Egypt. So the calf was only a symbol of deity, which constituted idolatry.

Then why did the people resort to image-making? Because they wanted a concrete manifestation of an invisible being. Man thinks it is difficult to remain close to a being he cannot see with the naked eye, so he creates some symbol to represent the being. But this is not needed, for our relationship to God is one of faith, not of sight (II Corinthians 5:7).

The Ten Commandments forbid the making and worshiping of images:

> *Thou shalt not make unto thee any graven image, or any likeness of any thing that is in heaven above, or that is in the earth beneath, or that is in the water under the earth: Thou shalt not bow down thyself to them, nor serve them.*—EXODUS 20:4,5

Light is sown for the righteous,
and gladness for the upright in heart.—97:11

Gladness for the Upright

I HAVE NEVER HEARD of a School of Happiness; yet we evidently can be taught some principles that help us to develop gladness, for the Bible gives them—and surely to some avail.

The righteous person sows for himself a harvest of joy. It springs up and thrives around him. The happy people are reaping what they have sown.

By sowing the seed of thinking, we gather happiness. Solomon made it plain that as one "thinketh in his heart, so is he."

> *No man can be happy who does not think himself so; for it signifies not how exalted soever your station may be, if it appear to you bad.*
> —LUCIUS ANNAEUS SENECA (8 B.C.-A.D. 65)

Sow the seed of righteousness, and it gives an approving conscience, which is an absolute requirement of happiness. For if the conscience bites, joy writhes and dies in pain.

By sowing the seed of trust, we reap optimism and become the "glad in the Lord." Our trust brings us peace.

Sow the seed of helpfulness. It brings satisfaction. We find happiness by taking an interest in people. "It is more blessed to give than to receive" (Acts 20:35).

*O sing unto the Lord a new song;
for he hath done marvelous things.*—98:1

Our Marvelous God

THE STORY GOES THAT A KING IN THE ORIENT once set before his three sons three sealed urns, one of gold, the second of amber and the third of clay. He asked them to pick the one that appeared to contain the greatest treasure. The eldest chose the golden vase whereon was written "Empire." When he opened it he beheld it full of blood. The second chose the vessel of amber on which was written "Glory." He opened it and found it full of the ashes of men who had only made names for themselves. The third son selected the vessel of clay which had the word "God" engraved on the bottom. Within it was a single Scripture verse: "Which doeth great things and unsearchable; marvelous things without number" (Job 5:9). The wise men in the king's court voted the third was the most valuable, basing their decision on the belief that it contained the whole of everything that is precious and priceless.

How right they were!

Everything about God is marvelous: His self-existence. His omnificence. His omnivision. His omnipotence. His love. His mercy. His forgiveness.

To think upon His marvelous works inspires within us a new song: a song of praise and thanksgiving.

In all eternity no tone can be so sweet
As where man's heart with God in unison doth beat.

—JOHANNES SCHEFFLER

Make a joyful noise unto the Lord, all the earth:
make a loud noise, and rejoice, and sing praise....
Let the sea roar, and the fulness thereof; the world,
and they that dwell therein, let the floods clap their hands:
let the hills be joyful together before the Lord.—98:4-9

Let Creation Praise Him

LET THERE BE one grand and continuous chorus of praise to our glorious God. May the saints declare His glory from pole to pole and from shore to shore. May everything in nature—the heavens, the snow-capped mountains, the green valleys, the roaring seas, the sparkling dewdrops, the singing birds, the flashing lightning, the desert sands, the quiet dawn and the golden sunset—shout the praise of the Creator.

It was customary in a mountainous country, as the sun was going down, for a man on one of the peaks to shout loudly through his horn, "Praise ye the Lord." Higher up the mountains another and another would take up the sublime anthem until the mountains rang with the praises of God.

Hallelujah! Here. There. Everywhere. Today. Tomorrow. Forever. For it is one exercise that will continue in the next world.

As a little boy lay critically ill, his older brother tried to teach him to say, "Hallelujah." But death came before he learned it. When the older one was told of his passing, he silently stared into nothingness for a few moments and then said, "Johnny can say 'Hallelujah' now, Mother."

Exalt ye the Lord our God, and worship at his footstool; for he is holy.—99:5

For He Is Holy

IN THREE DIFFERENT VERSES the Psalm exalts the holiness of God as a leading characteristic of the Just One.

Isaiah, in moving and beautiful eloquence, also emphasizes this Divine trait: "Holy, holy, holy, is the Lord of hosts: the whole earth is full of his glory" (Isaiah 6:3).

A modern poet was inspired by Isaiah's passage to write this tribute—a popular hymn—for today's worshipers:

Holy, holy, holy! Lord God Almighty!
Early in the morning our song shall rise to Thee;
Holy, holy, holy! merciful and mighty!
God over all, and blest eternally.

Holy, holy, holy! tho' the darkness hide Thee,
Tho' the eye of sinful man Thy glory may not see;
Only Thou art holy! there is none beside Thee,
Perfect in pow'r, in love, and purity.

—REGINALD HEBER

It is natural for people to become like what they praise, worship, or imitate. Accordingly, we become holy by becoming "partakers of the divine nature" (II Peter 1:4). Not to the fullest degree but to the extent we "follow holiness" (Hebrews 12:14) and are counted holy or "sanctified through the offering of the body of Jesus Christ" (Hebrews 10:10). Now from the redeemed come, "Holy, holy, He is holy!"

They called upon the Lord, and he answered them… they kept his testimonies, and the ordinance that he gave them.—99:6,7

Pray and Obey

IN SPEAKING OF SOME outstanding men—Moses, Aaron and Samuel—the composer stated that they prayed to God and kept His testimonies. They prayed and obeyed.

This is a worthy pattern for us to follow—pray and obey—whereby we are given a ready hearing before the throne of God:

> *And whatsoever we ask, we receive of him, because we keep his commandments, and do those things that are pleasing in his sight.*—I JOHN 3:22

The believer cannot afford to dispense with the privilege of prayer. It is effectual, first, because God answers prayer. Of all the truths taught in the Scriptures, perhaps there is none more verified by human experience than this—that God answers prayer. Second, it is fruitful because of the therapeutic value afforded the praying person by expressing his deepest and most locked up feelings.

God answers prayer, but only if we have the disposition to obey; otherwise our lisped words are in vain. Hence this question is ever fitting: "And why call ye me, Lord, Lord, and do not the things which I say?" (Luke 6:46).

I may as well kneel down
And worship gods of stone,
As offer to the living God
A prayer of words alone.

—JOHN BURTON

*Thou wast a God that forgavest them,
though thou tookest vengeance of their inventions.*—99:8

The Forgiving God

YEARS AGO A DISTRESSED WOMAN CAME to our home on a Sunday afternoon. Caught up in sin, remorseful, ashamed, she felt her only escape was suicide.

"If you believe the way I do, you could get a new start in life," I suggested.

"What do you mean?" she inquired.

"I believe in the God of forgiveness."

It was this thought—the thought of forgiveness—that took the woman's mind from self-destruction and enabled her to find her better self in a new life.

It was heartening to the psalmist to recall that God forgave Moses, Aaron, Samuel and other greats (verse 6). They were not perfect; they were sinners; yet God showed them mercy and forgave them. He manifested displeasure at their follies; nevertheless He pardoned their shortcomings and answered their prayers.

God cannot overlook sins, but He can forgive them. This is our hope and our greatest attainment—forgiveness:

> *Forgiveness is man's deepest need and highest achievement.*
>
> —HORACE BUSHNELL

It is more than the remission of sins—it is the restoration of a broken fellowship. Cleansed of guilt and reunited with our Maker, we have a new slate and a new opportunity—all because God is forgiving.

Make a joyful noise unto the Lord, all ye lands. Serve the Lord with gladness: come before his presence with singing. Know ye that the Lord he is God: it is he that hath made us, and not we ourselves; we are his people, and the sheep of his pasture. Enter into his gates with thanksgiving, and into his courts with praise: be thankful unto him, and bless his name. For the Lord is good; his mercy is everlasting; and his truth endureth to all generations.—100

God and Man

THIS PSALM PERTAINS TO GOD'S GREATNESS and man's duty:

God's greatness:

- "The Lord he is God."
- "It is he that hath made us, and not we ourselves."
- "The Lord is good."
- "His mercy is everlasting."
- "His truth endureth to all generations."

Man's duty to God:

- "Make a joyful noise unto the Lord."
- "Serve the Lord with gladness."
- "Come before his presence with thanksgiving."
- "We are his people, and the sheep of his pasture."
- "Enter into his gates with thanksgiving."
- "Enter…into his courts with praise."
- "Be thankful unto him."
- "Bless his name."

So it's God and man, man and God, the story of civilization.

*Know ye that the Lord he is God:
it is he that hath made us, and not we ourselves.*—100:3

He Made Us

I LOOK AT MY WATCH, knowing that every tick is more than a tick of time, that it is a tick to the genius of its maker—for it never made itself.

As the light from the lamp drives out the darkness, I know the light bulb never made itself—it shines to the glory of its inventor.

I turn on the TV and I know it is the product of a manufacturer, that it never made itself.

Neither did my house evolve. It's the work of a builder. In recognition of this fundamental truth, the Bible says, "For every house is builded by some man; but he that built all things is God" (Hebrews 3:4).

In keeping with the same common sense, our text gives this explanation of the origin of man: God created him; he never made himself (Genesis 1:27; 2:7).

This is reasonable. And therefore as long as watches, light bulbs, televisions and houses are unable to make themselves—have to be made by a superior power—just that long I must hold to the idea that we are the creation of a Higher Power.

So this is my song:

Thou art the workman, I the frame;
Lord to the glory of Thy name
I raise my voice in lofty strain,
I praise, I sing this old refrain.

I will…
—101

Thirteen Resolutions

THE PSALM GIVES the fixed determinations of a king:

- "I will sing of mercy and judgment."
- "I will behave my self wisely in a perfect way."
- "I will set no wicked thing before mine eyes."
- "The work of them that turn aside, it shall not cleave to me."
- "A froward [perverse] heart shall depart from me."
- "I will not know a wicked person [evil things, ASV]."
- "Whoso slandereth his neighbor, him will I cut off."
- "Him that hath a high look…will not I suffer."
- "Mine eyes shall be upon the faithful of the land…."
- "He that worketh deceit shall not dwell within my house."
- "He that telleth lies shall not tarry in my sight."
- "I will early destroy all the wicked of the land; that I may cut off all wicked doers from the city of the Lord."

These were the resolutions of a great king. Don't you think they would be appropriate in our own lives?

For my days are....

—102:3

The Days of Man

THE BIBLE CONTAINS SOME VERY DESCRIPTIVE and meaningful statements on the days of man:

1) "My days are consumed like smoke" (verse 3).

2) "My days are like a shadow that declineth" (verse 11).

3) "I am withered like grass" (verse 11).

4) "Shall wax old like a garment" (verse 26).

5) "They were but flesh; a wind that passeth away, and cometh not again" (78:39).

6) "We spend our years as a tale that is told" (90:9).

7) "As the days of a tree are the days of my people" (Isaiah 65:22).

8) "For we...are as water spilt on the ground, which cannot be gathered up again" (II Samuel 14:14).

9) "For what is your life? It is even a vapor...appeareth for a little time...vanisheth away" (James 4:14).

10) "He...like a flower...is cut down" (Job 14:2).

As the life of a flower, as a breath or a sigh,
So the years that we live, as a dream, hasten by.

—LAURA E. NEWELL

11) "Are not his days also like the days of a hireling [looks for his reward]?" (Job 7:1). The award awaits us. This life is only the beginning.

I am like....

—102:6,7

Like Birds

AT TIMES LIFE CAN GET EXTREMELY ROUGH. The blues can sink us low. We can feel so lonely. The poet, no less human than the rest of us, was caught up in this very human experience of melancholy when he wrote the Psalm. He stated, "I am in trouble"; "my heart is smitten, and withered like grass, so that I forget to eat my bread." Then he compared himself to three sorrowful birds:

1) "I am like a pelican in the wilderness." This bird is a striking image of grimness and loneliness. Its solemnity and austerity are most visible. David referred to it to illustrate his own depression.

2) "I am like an owl of the desert." The owl is known as a bird that dwells in solitary places. Just to look at it is enough to give us the blues; and to hear its doleful cry in the night strikes a tune of desolation within us.

3) "I watch, and am as a sparrow alone upon the housetop." David watched through the sleepless nights. Grief would not let him sleep. He likened his state to the sparrow. When it loses a mate it will sit on the housetop alone and mourn in sad bereavement.

All of this called for a conquering faith and a persevering patience, which he expressed in the last verse. David survived and so can we.

I said, O my God, take me not away in the midst of my days.—102:24

Let Me Live

THIS PRAYER FOR MORE DAYS gets down to where we live...and die. Hezekiah stated, " O Lord, by these things men live" (Isaiah 38:16).

Even throughout life, 'tis death
that makes life live.
—ROBERT BROWNING

We don't like the idea of getting old, but we prefer it over the alternative. Life smiles at its problems and pulls back from the grave. Because for every ounce of gall there is a ton of honey, and for every thorn there is a garden of roses. The urge to live is especially compelling when so many of our plans have not yet come to fruition.

The psalmist's supplication grew out of his fear that he might not live to see the restoration of Zion (verse 13). He was concerned that his plight might cut him short of his unrealized dreams.

A prayer for longevity is proper, but the specific answer must wait on the will of God. Now as we pray for more days, let us properly use the ones we have and trust Him who is the giver and taker of life for whatever lies ahead.

Bless the Lord, O my soul, and forget not all his benefits.
—103:2

Forget Not His Benefits

DAVID WAS RESOLVED NOT TO FORGET the wonderful things God was doing for him. And in the Psalm, verses 3-5, he mentioned the following benefits from God: forgiveness, restoration of health, rescue from danger, kindness and mercy, things that satisfy the mouth, and renewal of youth.

One of David's outstanding virtues was his thankfulness. It is definitely one of the requisites of a lofty life and one the psalmist constantly mentioned; for instance:

> *Enter into his gates with thanksgiving, and into his courts with praise: be thankful unto him, and bless his name.*
> —100:4

Gratitude signifies a greatness of heart. Definitely so! It has a good memory—does not forget.

An appreciativeness on the part of the recipient is commended and lauded the world over; however, ingratitude is despised and rebuked as one of the most despicable sins. Ingratitude reveals that one is lacking in goodness and nobility. It is a glaring flaw in character.

So in the language of David, we say to ourselves: "forget not all his benefits"—nor the blessings from man. For gratitude is one of the sweetest flowers that blossoms in the garden of virtue.

Like a father pitieth his children, so the Lord pitieth them that fear him.—103:13

Like a Father

IF A SON SHOULD LEAD A REVOLUTION to unseat his father that he might occupy the throne; and if the son should lose his life in the struggle, that loving father would lament and mourn his passing in overwhelming grief. David is our example. When he learned the fate of his revolutionary son, he "was much moved, and went up to the chamber over the gate, and wept: and as he went, thus he said, O my son Absalom! my son, my son Absalom! would God I had died for thee, O Absalom, my son, my son!" (II Samuel 18:33). The heartbreak and depth of feeling have been described by Longfellow:

There is no far nor near,
There is neither there nor here,
There is neither soon nor late,
In that Chamber over the Gate.
Nor any long ago
To that cry of human woe,
"O Absalom, my son!"

That 'tis a common grief
Bringeth but slight relief;
Ours is the bitterest loss,
Ours is the heaviest cross;
And forever the cry will be,
"Would God I had died for thee,
"O Absalom, my son!"

Like a father, God weeps for His children.

*For he knoweth our frame;
he remembereth that we are dust.*—103:14

God Knows We Are Weak

HE KNOWS HOW WE ARE MADE. He fashioned us—of dust. He understands our feebleness and is sympathetic toward our weakness. He knows that we are frail and may break under pressure, that we are weak and may yield to temptation. This is special reason for his compassion toward us. Would that men were as considerate of one another's frailty.

When the issues call for rugged strength and we seem so breakable, it is assuring to recall that He pities our humanity.

When our work is imperfect and our life is stained with sin, though our intentions are pure and our efforts stir from faith and spring from love, it is then that we are in dire need of the pity that comes from Him who knows our frame. It is a boon to drooping spirits to remember that all men are made of the same dust and that to the apostles who evidently had some superior traits, Jesus said:

> *Watch and pray, that ye enter not into temptation: the spirit indeed is willing, but the flesh is weak.*
>
> —MATTHEW 26:41

He who knows the weakness of His children has in every age owned them, directed them, blessed them and forgiven them—as they believed and obeyed. Hence, imperfect people are able to maintain a blessed relationship with Him—provided they try.

O Lord my God, thou art very great.
—104:1

Our Wonderful World

THE PSALM LAUDS GOD for the wonders of this world He has given us.

Light is our benefaction, and the heavens stretch out like a canopy.

We have seas of water and stretches of dry land with permanent boundaries because the waters that once stood above the mountains fled at the rebuke of God.

The springs that run from the hills remind us of a hidden source of water ready for our tapping.

The growing grass for cattle and the thriving herbs for man are provisions of God. And the trees flourish in beauty and usefulness.

The moon adds to the beauty and efficacy of our world, and the sun rises and sets with dependability.

The seas are filled with innumerable things and perhaps contain benefits that we have not yet appropriated.

So inviting and productive is the earth that man goes forth unto his work and labors in hope.

"O Lord, how manifold are thy works! in wisdom hast thou made them all: the earth is full of thy riches" (verse 24).

Our world is too necessary to be ungrateful for it and too wonderful to misuse it. As tenants, may we be good stewards.

These wait all upon thee; that thou mayest give them their meat in due season. That thou givest them [what] *they gather: thou openest thine hand, they are filled with good.*—104:27,28

The Open Hand of God

WE WAIT UPON GOD THE GREAT PROVIDER for our blessings. Having no means of our own, we are wholly dependent on Him. We are needy creatures, but His hand is open to us. From it we are "filled with good."

In rapturous wonder we praise His name, saying, "Thou openest thine hand, and satisfiest the desire of every living thing" (145:16). And we pray:

> *My times are in thy hand; deliver me from the hand of mine enemies, and from them that persecute me.*—31:15

> *Let thine hand help me.*—119:173

And now with all our fears allayed we put our hand over in His big, open hand. For He has said, "I…will hold thine hand, and will keep thee" (Isaiah 42:6).

A little girl, walking home one dark night with her father, suggested, "Take my hand, Papa! I can take only a little piece of yours, but you can hold all of mine." In his strong grasp she seemed comforted, but suddenly asked, "Papa, are you afraid?" When he assured her he wasn't, she confidently stated: "All right! If you're not, I'm not."

My meditation of him shall be sweet:
I will be glad in the Lord.—104:34

Sweet Meditations

I SHALL FIND A SWEET JOY in meditating on the character and works of God. This is the purpose of these 365 devotionals on the Psalms. The ageless Psalms are such unique and rich sources for contemplation.

The very first Psalm says this of the blessed man: "His delight is in the law of the Lord; and in his law doth he meditate day and night." That there could be delight in such musing tells us of a heart that beats in tune with the heart of God.

In the world's great art galleries the lovers of art will spend hours before a single masterpiece. They go away and return the next day. In spellbound ecstasy with charmed eyes they survey the wondrous beauty. Through prolonged meditation it seems to them the world stops and they get off, and standing there in rapturous thought they discover new beauties and new joys.

This is what happens in meditation. We close our eyes to the beckoning scenes to see one sight. We deafen our ears to a thousand calls to hear one voice.

Close up his eyes and draw the curtains close;
And let us all to meditation.

—WILLIAM SHAKESPEARE

All his wondrous works.

—105:2

Responding to God's Providence

WHAT SHOULD OUR RESPONSE BE to the providential wonders of God? The answer is given in the Psalm:

- ***Gratitude:*** "O give thanks unto the Lord." Thank the tree that bears your fruit, and the bridge that carries you safely over, and the sun you take for granted, and the God man often forgets.
- ***Publication:*** "Make known his deeds among the people." As much as we have in us, tell it because we have something to say that compels us to say it.
- ***Praise:*** "Sing unto him, sing psalms unto him: talk ye of all his wondrous works." Men, worthy or unworthy, are praised because they die; but God never dies. Praise Him because He lives and for ten thousand other reasons.
- ***Joy:*** "Let the heart of them rejoice that seek the Lord." God's motto for us is:

Enjoy living.

- ***Endeavor:*** "Seek the Lord, and his strength: seek his face evermore." "Seek, and ye shall find." The non-seekers are the non-finders in every field.
- ***Remembrance:*** "Remember his marvelous works that he hath done; his wonders, and the judgments of his mouth." Remember! For exuberance of personality and renewal of soul, remember. Never forget!

And he...gave them the lands of the heathen:
and they inherited the labor of the people;
that they might observe his statutes, and keep his laws.
Praise ye the Lord.—105:44,45

The Purpose of Prosperity

THE DESIGN AND PURPOSE of all the guiding, protecting, feeding and sustaining of those so few and weak (leading them to the promised land) was "that they might observe his statutes and keep his laws." The end of God's providential care was to establish a God-fearing nation, a nation with character, moral, spiritual and holy. By keeping His laws, they could partake of His own holiness and thereby achieve the ideal that God had set for them.

Today the principle is the same. We are given life, breath and all things that we might glorify Him. Life has a greater end than counting birthdays.

Hence when prosperity smiles upon us, may it correct us—not corrupt us; and may we use it—not abuse it. For its purpose is lofty, and its effect is revealing. It won't take long for it to show what a person is.

As God's blessings continue to drop upon us, let us remember: *we are prospered to serve.* Every blessing is a mercy-drop from heaven. Receive it graciously. Use it advantageously.

They angered him also at the waters of strife,
so that it went ill with Moses for their sakes:
Because they provoked his spirit,
so that he spake unadvisedly with his lips—106:32,33

Extenuating Circumstances

MOSES WAS GUILTY. No question about it. This is why "it went ill" with him. But there were mitigative circumstances.

This is what occurred: the people complained and blamed Moses when things got rough with them. One of their trials was no water to drink. In supplying this need, God ordered Moses to gather the congregation together and to speak unto the rock, promising that water would gush forth. But under the strain of all their murmurs and reproaches, Moses went beyond the command of God and said, "Hear now, ye rebels; must we fetch water out of this rock?" (Numbers 20:10). Then he "smote the rock twice."

This was God's reaction: "Because ye believed me not, to sanctify me in the eyes of the children of Israel, therefore ye shall not bring this congregation into the land which I have given them" (Numbers 20:12). But Moses had been provoked, which justly needed to be considered; so God permitted him to glimpse the land though he could not enter.

Here are two morals from the story:

First, one man's sin may cause another to sin.

Second, when one's mistake is the result of another's incitement, we should soften our censure of it. Provocation begs consideration.

Nevertheless he regarded their affliction, when he heard their cry.—106:44

A Nevertheless God

THE "NEVERTHELESS" OF GOD'S MERCY is the theme of the whole Psalm. The Israelites were in dire and constant need of mercy because their sins were so grievous and numerous.

They "were brought low for their iniquity." Sin is very degrading. There is nothing elevating about it. When sin has triumphed over us, it has always pulled us from our lofty position and trampled us in the mire.

The worst thing God could have done to them was to do nothing—leave them alone—but He did not ignore them. They were on His heart, the object of His attention; and consequently He chastened them, giving "them into the hand of the heathen" (verse 41) for their good. In spite of all their sins He regarded their affliction when He heard their cry. They were His children. And he forgave them when they came back to Him. Oh! what mercy spared Israel! A mercy equaled only by the mercy that spares us. And it is welcome like the warm sunshine that follows a freeze.

Let the redeemed of the Lord say so,
whom he hath redeemed from the hand of the enemy.—107:2

Let the Redeemed Say So

THE REDEEMED—they are especially qualified to say so. Having been rescued by the loving mercy and the outstretched hand of God, they are prepared to say so.

The redeemed—in this particular usage it refers to a deliverance from danger, probably to the deliverance from Babylonian captivity (Isaiah 43:3,4). But more, there was a blotting out of their sins: "I have blotted out as a thick cloud, thy transgressions, and, as a cloud, thy sins: return unto me; for I have redeemed thee" (Isaiah 44:22).

The redeemed—we belong to this number if we have been washed in the blood of the Lamb. This is our assurance; so let us sing it:

Redeemed

Redeemed—how I love to proclaim it.
Redeemed by the blood of the Lamb;
Redeemed thro' His infinite mercy,
His child, and forever, I am.

I know I shall see in His beauty
The King in whose law I delight;
Who lovingly guardeth my footsteps,
And giveth me songs in the night.

Redeemed by the blood of the Lamb;
His child, and forever, I am.

—FANNY J. CROSBY

Oh that men would praise the Lord for his goodness, and for his wonderful works to the children of men!—107:8

Praise the Lord

THIS VERSE IS GIVEN VERBATIM three more times in the Psalm (verses 15, 21,31). Four times in one Psalm should impress the mind of the reader with the urgency of the message. Those who have been blessed by the wonderful works of God should praise Him for His goodness—not just in words, but in life.

Neither should the praise of God be just a little temporary expression of emotion, but rather a life-feeling. David viewed it as a lifetime attitude, avowing: "As long as I live: I will sing praise to my God" (104:33).

Nor should it be lip service. David's whole being was committed to the praise of God: "I will praise thee, O Lord, with my whole heart" (9:1). When man's whole being pulsates with thanksgiving and praise, he approaches an ideal that each should have. Aware of this, we pray for a fuller life of praise:

Fill Thou my life, O Lord, my God,
In every part with praise,
That my whole being may proclaim
Thy Being and Thy ways.

Not for the lip of praise alone,
Nor e'en the praising heart,
I ask, but for a life made up
Of praise in every part.

—HORATIUS BONAR

A mouth of praise is a good thing, but a life of praise is better.

And are at their wit's end.

—107:27

At Their Wit's End

THE CONTEXT PRESENTS A MARITIME SCENE. A ship is struck by a storm which stirs up high and hammering waves. The soul of the mariners is "melted because of trouble." Fearful, seasick, reeling "to and fro like a drunken man," they "are at their wit's end." All their wisdom is swallowed up. No human power avails. Helpless, feeling that God is their only rescue, they pray; and He speaks peace to the storm, and the waves are settled.

Sometimes we, too, are at our wit's end. Our little sea turns angry and we become fearful, sick and dismayed. Everything fails. Problems seem to have no solution. Helpless, we do what men should be doing all along—earnestly pray. For prayer is needed in smooth waters as well as in stormy seas. And the God who calmed the briny deep for the Israelites and stilled the waters for the disciples can quiet those raging waves that threaten us.

Master, the tempest is raging!
The billows are tossing high!
The sky is o'er shadowed with blackness;
No shelter or help is nigh,
"Carest Thou not that we perish?"

—MARY A. BAKER

Yes, He cares. Remember—when man is at his wit's end, it could be God's beginning of help.

O God, my heart is fixed; I will sing and give praise, even with my glory.—108:1

The Fixed Heart

HIS MIND IS MADE UP. No vacillation. His slogan is: *All steps ahead.* No turning back. When success smiles and when failure frowns, when friends stand by and when they betray, when praised and when condemned. Hence, the fixed heart does not depend on outward circumstances…but on an inward state.

The fixed heart brings the whole man into the effort, uniting and coordinating his labors; and this awakens the slumbering giant:

Every human mind is a great slumbering power until awakened by keen desire and by definite resolution to do.
—EDGAR ROBERTS

The fixed heart holds us to a purpose.

When my resolution is taken, all is forgotten except what will make it succeed.
—NAPOLEON I

The fixed heart makes for favorable winds. Otherwise—

When a man does not know what harbor he is making for, no wind is right.
—LATIN PROVERB

The fixed heart, summed up, is the way of success.

The secret of success is constancy of purpose.
—BENJAMIN DISRAELI

Give us help from trouble: for vain is the help of man.
—108:12

Worthless Help

DAVID KNEW THAT THE STRENGTH OF MAN was no match for God. He knew that all human help was really worthless in comparison to God's loving heart and helping hand. He knew the source of his strength—God.

David also knew that "vain is the help of man." We look to people for help, for friendship, for support, for comfort; and many times they do help us to the extent of their ability. But eventually all human forms of assistance and support fail us. Only God never disappoints us.

But to have God's help we must give up our exalted views of self-sufficiency and the mocking panaceas of others. How many times have we depended on ourselves or others in vain. And finally as a last resort, we turned to God for help. Our God should not be the God of last resorts but often is.

We must become more settled in our dependence on God and ask for His assistance. A young boy tried in vain to build a bird-house. But he couldn't cut the boards evenly. He couldn't drive the nails straight. Finally, he came into the house, frustrated and depressed, and blurted out, "I can't build it. I can't do it. I've tried everything." His father listened for awhile and then gently reminded him, "You haven't done *everything* yet. You haven't asked me to help you."

Surely that's the way God looks at us and our feeble attempts to build our lives without Him. We cry in frustration that we have done everything. But have we asked God?

Through God we shall do valiantly:
for he it is that shall tread down our enemies.—108:13

The Valiant

BRAVERY—HOW HUMANITY LOVES IT. The world salutes the brave man, regardless of his weaknesses. For bravery alone we're willing to pin a medal on him. But the coward, though he has a thousand virtues, is held in contempt. And justly so. For his faintheartedness nullifies his excellencies.

A great deal of talent is lost to the world for the want of a little courage.

—SYDNEY SMITH

O spirit of courage! what you can do for me! In every hour of danger you can favor me in the struggle.

Fortune favors the brave.

—VIRGIL (70-19 B.C.)

In a world crowded with fears and dreads, anybody with a plan to generate a little more courage is welcome.

The surest place to find it, as David declared, is in God. Through Him we gather strength to go forth with spirit and courage. With God at our side, we say, "I will fear no evil." Not that we always win according to our wishes, but we always try.

It is better to suffer a few defeats than to live in that dismal cowardice that knows neither victory nor defeat.

The courage to try and try, again and again, enrolls our names among the valiant.

They compassed me about also with words of hatred; and fought against me without a cause.—109:3

Enemies Without Cause

DAVID SPOKE OF ENEMIES HE HAD NOT CAUSED. They had hurt him severely. Because of the injury they had done to him, it caused some to look upon him and shake their heads.

But he had not caused the enmity. Instead, he had treated them kindly, but his love was recompensed with hate and his goodness was rewarded with evil.

This is not an uncommon reaction—enemies for no cause. Here are the despicable reasons for it:

- Having what another likes may drive him to fight you.
- Holding to truth may alienate those who don't want it.
- Knowing something bad about a person makes him despise you.
- Being harmed by another tends to make him hate you.
- The feeling that you are a threat to one's job, honor or success may prompt him to detest you.
- An inferior person's trying to feel bigger or cleaner can cause him to disparage you.
- Seeking an outlet for frustration may move the frustrated to pick on you.
- The feeling that one is dependent on you may cause him to loathe you.

The Lord said unto my Lord, Sit thou at my right hand, until I make thine enemies thy footstool…. —110:1-7

The New King

IF WE BELIEVE IN PROPHECY, here is a Psalm for us to proclaim, one in which we can exult. It is Davidic in authorship and prophetically Messianic in subject. We say this because Jesus attributed its authorship to David and its fulfillment to Himself:

> *While the Pharisees were gathered together, Jesus asked them, saying, What think ye of Christ? whose son is he? They say unto him, The son of David. He saith unto them, How then doth David in spirit call him Lord, saying, The Lord said unto my Lord, Sit thou on my right hand, till I make thine enemies thy footstool? If David then call him Lord, how is he his son? And no man was able to answer him.* —MATTHEW 22:41-46

The Psalm touches on the Messiah's kingdom, His priesthood and His final victory over the power of evil. It sets forth His glory and the conquest that someday shall be His. He shall exercise judgment over all the nations and shall rule until all enemies are made His footstool (put down).

We are told that His subjects *willingly* accept His rulership (verse 3). Our King, in recognition of human volition, says, "If any man will come after me…" (Matthew 16:24). A basic and fundamental requirement is "If there be first a willing mind." So let us rid ourselves of all rebellious urges and willingly turn to Him and make Him the King of our lives.

All his commandments are sure. They stand fast for ever and ever, and are done in truth and uprightness.
—111:7,8

Something Sure

IN A WORLD OF CRUMBLING STANDARDS, "the commandments of God are sure," and "stand fast for ever and ever." They are true, for He is truth. They are the criterion, for He is the standard. They shall endure, for He shall be around to see that they do.

His commandments (except in some rites and ceremonies) have not changed. His moral injunctions have withstood the testing of time. The frustrations and defects of humanity have not relegated them to a place of irrelevancy. The more defeats we suffer the more convinced we become that we need to get back to a *Thus saith the Lord.* Laid low by imperfect, human views, we see the need of society's adhering to a sure and workable standard, lest we turn mad and destroy ourselves.

His regulations have been the bread of life, the pilgrim's staff, the mariner's compass and the soldier's sword. They have fed us. They have steadied us. They have directed us. They have defended us.

Say what you will, it is easy to see the practicality of "Thou shalt not kill," "Thou shalt not steal," "Thou shalt not bear false witness," "Honor thy father and thy mother" and all other moral directives. They are as relevant today as yesterday and shall be as urgent tomorrow.

Holy and reverend is his name.

—111:9

Reverence His Name

THIS IS NO LIGHT MATTER. Man *can* and *must* hold the name of God in awe and exaltation. As we touch and taste the works of God, let us lisp the praise His holy name requires.

When we look at nature, stirred by its grandeur, we exclaim, "Holy and reverend is His name."

As we read the Scriptures, blessed by their practicality, we declare, "Holy and reverend is His name."

Having been laundered in the fountain of mercy and cleansed in the waters of forgiveness, we exuberantly say, "Holy and reverend is His name."

Convinced that victory belongs to those who walk with God, we proclaim, "Holy and reverend is His name."

So awake, my soul, in joyful exclamation and pay the tribute His name so richly deserves. I know that I can no more do His name justice than I can count the stars. But I *can* reverence it! I *can* venerate it! I *can* refrain from degrading it in vain and ugly speech!

It chills my blood to hear the blest Supreme
Rudely appealed to on each trifling theme;
Maintain your rank, vulgarity despise;
To swear is neither brave, polite, nor wise.
You would not swear upon the bed of death;
Reflect! Your Maker yet may stop your breath.

—WILLIAM COWPER

Blessed is the man that feareth the Lord,
that delighteth greatly in his commandments. . . . —112:1

Fear and Delight

AT FIRST, THIS MAY SEEM LIKE A STRANGE MIXTURE—fear and delight. But the psalmist knew what he was talking about.

Fear: When we properly understand what it means to fear God, then we have nothing in this world to be afraid of. To "fear" God is to respect Him, reverence Him, be in awe of Him as our Father. It is not the dread of being in His presence or the fright of His return. Healthy fear respects God and hopefully looks forward to His coming again. It is a blessed condition.

What do we fear? Is it poverty? A lack of popularity? A loss of power? These scares we can overcome by having a respectful fear of God.

Delight: Blessed are those also who delight in God's commandments. Most of us don't find much delight in obeying rules. We look for delight in freedom from rules and in the do-as-you-please philosophy which says, "World, don't hem me in." Some even delight in seeing how close they can get to the fires of sin without getting burned. And they learn nothing from their scorched eyebrows and parched lips.

The truly blessed life, however, comes from knowing when to pursue and when to stop, what to partake and what to refuse, what to fear and what to enjoy. Too bad we sometimes get confused.

Wealth and riches shall be in his house.

—112:3

Wealth and Riches

IN A CONTINUATION OF PSALM 112, the writer goes on to mention wealth as a tangible blessing of true religion. The Bible has much to say about wealth—how to make it and how to use it.

There are numerous principles throughout the Bible that inevitably promote prosperity:

1) ***Work:*** "If any would not work, neither should he eat" (II Thessalonians 3:10).

2) ***Vision:*** "Where there is no vision, the people perish" (Proverbs 29:18).

3) ***Enthusiasm:*** "Whatsoever thy hand findeth to do, do it with thy might" (Ecclesiastes 9:10).

4) ***Analysis:*** "For which of you, intending to build a tower, sitteth not down first and counteth the cost…" (Luke 14:28-30).

5) ***Time*** element: "Go to the ant…Consider her ways, and be wise…provideth her meat in the summer, and gathereth her food in the harvest" (Proverbs 6:6-8).

6) ***Thrift:*** "Gather up the fragments that remain, that nothing be lost" (John 6:12).

Prosperity has a price. But poverty costs more. And even more costly is wealth held to its owner's hurt (Ecclesiastes 5:13). Hence, let us keep the materials God has provided in perspective. May they be a blessing, not a curse.

Surely he shall not be moved forever: the righteous shall be in everlasting remembrance. He shall not be afraid of evil tidings: his heart is fixed, trusting in the Lord. His heart is established,he shall not be afraid, until he see his desire upon his enemies.—112:6-8

Bad News

THE BLESSED OF GOD ARE SECURE, unshakable people. They are not chaff moved by the wind. They are not driven by restlessness, frustration and defeat. They are stable, solid and firm because their roots are grounded in God and His Word.

As a result, one of the distinct characteristics of godly people is that they are not afraid of bad news. This is true for several reasons. They know that the words "good" and "bad" are often very inaccurate. What we call "bad" may actually be for our good. We need new eyes—the eyes of God—to see what is really helpful or harmful.

Also, with their roots deep in God, they know that nothing on this earth can really topple them. When facing serious illness, crippling disease or financial disaster, the believers know that those seeming hurts are small in comparison with their relationship with God. They still have the one really important asset of life—God.

Secure in God, the blessed believer has a new view of the world. It's like standing on top of a tall mountain peak and watching the tiny cars scurry about down below. The problems and pain of everyday living are still real, but they have lost their size. They have ceased to plague us. We are steadfast, secure.

Praise ye the Lord. Praise, O ye servants of the Lord, praise the name of the Lord. Blessed be the name of the Lord from this time forth and for evermore. From the rising of the sun unto the going down of the same the Lord's name is to be praised. The Lord is high above all nations, and his glory above the heavens. Who is like unto the Lord our God, who dwelleth on high, who humbleth himself to behold the things that are in heaven, and in the earth! He raiseth up the poor out of the dust, and lifteth the needy out of the dunghill; that he may set him with princes, even with the princes of his people. He maketh the barren woman to keep house, and to be a joyful mother of children. Praise ye the Lord.—113

He Is Able

WE HAVE GIVEN IN FULL THIS PSALM which has proven to be very popular in church services.

Praise to God is "from this time forth and for evermore." "From the rising of the sun unto the [its] going down"—from the farthest east to the farthest west.

Why such timeless and universal acclamation for God? Because God is able! Though He "dwelleth on high," God is never too far away or too busy or too preoccupied to "humble himself," as the text states, and come to our help. No distance can ever hide our needs from God's eyes.

In contrast to the problems of rulers and nations, the barrenness of one woman may have seemed insignificant. But the God who could lift up a ruler and bless a nation could also bless a barren woman. Sarah knew it, Hannah knew it, and so did Elizabeth.

God is able to handle our problems, big or small!

When Israel went out of Egypt....

—114:1-8

Over and Over Again

THIS IS ONE OF THE MOST POETIC of all the Psalms, more like the poetry of the modern poet. In it, nature's wonders are personified, pictured alive and responsive to the presence and power of the Omnipotent One, and in such eloquent and lofty rhetoric. The psalmist portrays the sea as having eyes that saw Israel approaching and then fled for their passage; and Jordan, accommodating as it were, pulled back for them to cross over into the promised land. Referring to the agitations of Sinai's peaks when God gave the Law, the poet pictures the mountains skipping "like rams, and the little hills like lambs" leaping for joy. The whole earth trembled because God was there. And in this graphic style it states that the rock Moses struck was turned into a standing water and the flint was made a fountain.

This impressive language was employed to celebrate the praises of God in delivering Israel from Egyptian bondage. How many times those people sang and quoted the same old stories again and again. In an uncomplimentary contrast, however, we are so easily bored and tire so quickly of hearing old truths. But they never tired because they were ever grateful for their deliverance. They never grew weary of talking about it. They never took it for granted. Consequently, they never relegated it to a passe time and buried it in a dusty history.

Maybe we should be more grateful for our deliverance.

Not unto us, O Lord, not unto us,
but unto thy name give glory, for thy mercy,
and for thy truth's sake.—115:1

Not for Our Glory

WHEN WE PROPERLY RELATE OURSELVES to God, we put ourselves in the background.

We wear the Lord's name to glorify Him—not ourselves.

We shine to His glory—not to be applauded.

We give of our means because we have given ourselves—not to be seen of men.

We pray to be heard of God—not to be acclaimed by others.

Now these personal questions:

Why attend church? To worship God or to hold up our reputation?

Why construct a new church building? To glorify God or to exalt ourselves?

Why give? To please God or man?

Why seek a church office or position? To serve God or to dignify ourselves?

If we follow a make-believe religion to impress people, our only reward will come from people—none from God (Matthew 6:5).

He that does good for good's sake seeks neither praise nor reward, though sure of both at last.

—WILLIAM PENN

Their idols are silver and gold, the work of men's hands....
—115:4-8

Idle Idols

THE DENUNCIATION OF IDOLS is a common characteristic of Psalms. This was necessary because these people lived in the midst of idolatry where the scorning of idol-deities was constantly needed.

In the Psalm there is a contrast in the powerful God and the powerless idols. It says of God, "he hath done whatsoever he pleased." But all that could be said of the idols is:

"They have mouths, but they speak not.

"They have ears, but they hear not.

"Noses have they, but they smell not.

"They have hands, but they handle not.

"Feet have they, but they walk not."

Idle idols—they have the organs, but not the sensibilities.

They are the deified representations of a people's own frailties and passions. And a study of a nation's gods will give you a nation's history.

Idols are only "the work of men's hands." Having been made by man, they are inferior to him; and if there should be any worshiping of either, the idols ought to worship man. So to make idolatry all the worse, it is practiced in reverse.

He will bless them that fear the Lord, both small and great.

—115:13

The Small and the Great

"NOBODY BIG. NOBODY LITTLE. Everybody same." These are the leveling words some young boys painted inside their little, unpretentious clubhouse.

Quite appropriate. At least they represent the feelings of God. To Him all look alike. Money doesn't impress Him—He has all there is. Neither does education—He knows everything. So the *small* and the *great* stand the same height in His sight. Accordingly, He blesses all who fear Him, both *small* and *great.* Surely God loves the *small,* for there are so many of them; and the mighty should, for if there were no little ones there would be no big ones. God also loves the *great,* for He made them, too.

Many *greats* in the Bible stand out in faith. But as a whole, the little people have been more inclined to honor God. Since human nature is the same, therefore there must be exterior causes which affect the hearts of one group more than another: money, power, popularity, intellectual pride and the cares of the world.

Great men are not always wise.

—JOB 32:9

So if we permit the things of the world to blind us, don't blame God if we can't see Him.

The heaven, even the heavens, are the Lord's: but the earth hath he given to the children of men.—115:16

But the Earth Belongs to Us

BECAUSE OF OUR FINITE THINKING, God has pictured Himself in the heavens though He reigns and rules everywhere. When the Roman general Pompey conquered Jerusalem, he was surprised to find the Most Holy Place in the temple to be an empty room. He didn't know that our God is not a physical object. He is not confined by the time and space dimensions as are we. God lives and rules throughout His universe.

But the earth He gave to man as a home. And in man's down-to-earth living he is to employ his skills, earn his bread and live out his days in hope of a home better than earth. However, man's poor job as keeper of the earth has defiled it. Unquestionably—"The earth also is defiled under the inhabitants thereof; because they have transgressed..." (Isaiah 24:5). Believing that the last best hope of earth is in man's conformity to the Landlord's wishes and to nature's restrictions, we say:

There is no sense, as I can see,
In mortals such as you and me
A-faulting nature's wise intents
And locking horns with Providence.

For if we would justify our brief moment here, we as tenants must respect our Landlord.

I believed, therefore have I spoken.

—116:10

Energetic Faith

PAUL USED THIS PASSAGE to emphasize the faith that proclaimed the gospel despite all opposition. He said, "We having the same spirit of faith, according as it is written, *I believed, and therefore have I spoken*; we also believe, and therefore speak" (II Corinthians 4:13). It is a powerful, energetic force.

The faith of the psalmist found a tongue. He could not be silent. His faith spoke.

Furthermore, his faith found legs. He declared in the previous verse, "I will walk before the Lord in the land of the living."

Talk and walk—the effects of faith.

Faith moves: "By faith Noah…moved…prepared an ark" (Hebrews 11:7). Faith is the great, vigorous force that will move our mountain—at least tunnel through it. For faith doesn't stop at the mountain; it grabs a shovel.

Faith is the force of life.

—TOLSTOY

Over the entrance to the Temple of Life are these words:

Ye must have faith.

I said in my haste, All men are liars.

—116:11

Hasty Words

HIS FAULT IS A COMMON ONE—hasty words, hasty charges. Many things precipitate fast speech:

Illness. Tormented by suffering, we may say things we would not normally say. Feeling neglected, we may be tempted to impugn the character of others.

Disappointment. Occasionally we shall be disappointed in others. We may reach the hasty conclusion that all persons are liars and cheats. But no one instance should indict the whole race.

Projection. A charge against another may be only the expression of one's own guilt.

Anger. Rash words come fast from hot tempers.

Ignorance. It's faster and easier to assassinate character than to investigate.

Hate. Give the hater the slightest chance and he will jam the air waves with calumny; and if the chance doesn't come, he will make it.

Protection. One may accuse another of lying to protect himself in his own lies.

In conclusion, "be slow to speak." And if it's something bad about somebody else, be a thousand times slower.

Be not rash with thy mouth, and let not thine heart be hasty to utter any thing before God.

—ECCLESIASTES 5:2

I will pay my vows unto the Lord now in the presence of all his people.—116:14

Open Religion

THERE ARE TWO KINDS OF HYPOCRISY: 1) The showing of religion to gain praise. 2) The hiding of religion to escape censure. The latter is more popular in this age. In either case, one is failing to be his true self; and this is hypocritical.

God went public with His religion. In its very nature it relates to others, which negates secrecy.

Serving God is visible. "Let your light so shine before men, that they may see your good works, and glorify your father" (Matthew 5:16). As a devotee of God you are light, and the purpose of a light is to shine. Don't conceal it. Don't hide your light.

Let us beware of two extremes: proud ostentation and false humility. We are opposed to pretentious parade and just as opposed to feigned modesty. But there is a true and sincere ground between the two in which one practices open religion to the glory of God. No affectation. Just the real thing.

Be yourself, and be the person you hope to be.
—ROBERT LOUIS STEVENSON

Precious in the sight of the Lord is the death of his saints.
—116:15

Precious Death

TO THE HEAVENLY FATHER the death of His children is precious. It is essential to the accomplishment of His merciful and eternal purpose.

After Adam and Eve sinned, the compassionate Got put them out of the Garden of Eden, separating them from the Tree of Life lest they should live forever in a state of sin and rebellion. Death became a little extra grace for man, giving him the way to reach a new and deathless life that he can live in perfection.

In death there is the separation of the two beings: fleshly and spiritual. "Then shall the dust return to the earth as it was: and the spirit shall return unto God who gave it" (Ecclesiastes 12:7). That is what death is—separation! not extinction! And over there the Lord shall clothe man's spirit with a new body like His own glorious body.

There is no real death; what looks like it is transition. So when a loved one is called away, we ought not to count our grief more than his relief. He has gone home. It is precious.

I cannot say, and I will not say
That he is dead! He is just away.
—JAMES WHITCOMB RILEY

O praise the Lord, all ye nations: praise him all ye people. For his merciful kindness is great toward us: and the truth of the Lord endureth forever. Praise ye the Lord.—117

The Shortest Psalm

THIS IS THE SHORTEST PSALM, but not too short to reveal some foundation truths.

It recognizes God in national life. However, in this age some think He doesn't belong there. They say, "God, there's no place for You in the halls of Congress or in the assemblies of the United Nations. Run along to the little chapel; that's your field. Stick to Your business, and we'll stick to ours." What blasphemy! What shame! We can't assign God to only a little role in a chapel. He is the God of the universe.

The Psalm gives special reasons for praising Jehovah. For His merciful kindness and His truth that endure forever. Our salvation requires both mercy and truth, praise His name; one without the other will not suffice. Nations rise, touch a little glory and fall. But God lives. So does His mercy. So does His truth.

Blessed Assurance!

Watching and waiting, looking above,
Filled with His goodness, lost in His love.
This is my story, this is my song,
Praising my Savior all the day long.

—FANNY J. CROSBY

The Lord is on my side; I will not fear:
what can man do unto me?—118:6

The Lord on My Side

THERE NEVER HAS BEEN a more assuring statement uttered by mortal man than this: *The Lord is on my side.* And He was. For God is no passive spectator of our struggles with Satan. He does not sit on the sidelines of neutrality, watching to see who wins before He does anything. He is involved with us in our fighting.

The psalmist declared, "The Lord taketh my part with them that help me" (verse 7). Indeed, he had friends who aided him; but God was working with them, making their gestures and labors productive in the poet's behalf.

With God on his side, he fearlessly asked, "What can man do unto me?" For if God is for us, who can be against us?

No care can come where God doth guard;
No ill befall whom He doth keep;
In safety hid, of trouble rid,
I lay me down in peace and sleep.

But before God will take our side, take up our struggle and scatter our enemies, we must be on His side. He will not fight for us if we are on the wrong side. To do so would be to fight Himself. Hence, we need to ask, "Who is on the Lord's side?" (Exodus 32:26).

The stone which the builders refused is become the head stone of the corner.—118:22

The Rejected Stone

THIS IS A POETIC FIGURE that alludes to the construction of a building. The masons cast aside the stones they consider unfit to go into the walls. It compares to any individual who is rejected by others.

It describes David who was despised among the sons of Jessie, but raised to be the ruler of Israel. But the analogy was fulfilled in the largest sense by the Messiah. Though "his own received him not," He was destined to become the King of Kings and the Prince of Peace. Jesus applied the Psalm to Himself:

> *And he beheld them, and said, What is this then that is written, The stone which the builders rejected, the same is become the head of the corner?*
>
> —LUKE 20:17

Oftentimes the very person in whom others see no attainment climbs the highest. The child who is considered dense may later turn the light on for millions; Thomas Edison did.

Though all men should turn us down, there is still the opportunity for the grandest honor and service. We can be living stones in the church of God (I Peter 2:5).

This is the day which the Lord hath made; we will rejoice and be glad in it.—118:24

Look Well to This Day

THERE IS NO DAY LIKE TODAY.
The Lord made it. For you and me.
It is the day to rejoice and be glad.
The day to work and pray.
And serve and grow; dream and hope.
Today I shall grow taller!
For I shall walk with God.

An Exhortation to Dawn

Listen to the Exhortation of the Dawn.
Look well to this Day! For it is Life,
The very Life of Life.
In its brief course lie all the Verities
And Realities of your Existence.
The Bliss of Growth;
The Glory of Action;
The Splendor of Beauty.
For Yesterday is only a Vision.
But Today well lived makes every Yesterday
A Dream of Happiness.
And every Tomorrow a Vision of Hope.
Look well, therefore, to this Day.
Such is the Salutation of the Dawn.

Blessed are they that keep his testimonies, and that seek him with the whole heart.—119:2

Power of the Word

IN THIS MASTERPIECE ON THE WORD OF GOD, Psalm 119, the poet said, "My tongue shall speak of thy word" (verse 172). Concerning its efficacy, here are eleven distinct functions:

Cleanses: "Wherewithal shall a young man cleanse his way? by taking heed…to thy word" (verse 9).

Guards against sin: "Thy word have I hid in mine heart, that I might not sin against thee" (verse 11).

Counsels: "Thy testimonies also are my delight, and my counselors" (verse 24).

Gives hope: "Remember the word…upon which thou hast caused me to hope" (verse 49).

Quickens: "Thy word hath quickened me" (verse 50).

Puts a song in the heart: "Thy statutes have been my songs in the house of my pilgrimage" (verse 54).

Makes wise: "Thou through thy commandments hast made me wiser than mine enemies…my teachers…the ancients" (verses 98-100).

Feeds the soul: "How sweet are thy words unto my taste! yea, sweeter than honey to my mouth" (verse 103).

Gives light: "Thy word is a lamp unto my feet, and a light unto my path" (verse 105).

Gives joy: "Thy testimonies…a heritage for ever…they are the rejoicing of my heart" (verse 111).

Provides the only infallible way: "I esteem all thy precepts concerning all things to be right" (verse 128).

I will keep thy statutes.

—119:8

Resolutions Related to the Word

KNOWING THAT THE BLESSINGS of the commandments are derived from keeping them, the poet's mind was made up to abide by them to the very end: "I have inclined mine heart to perform thy statutes always, even unto the end" (verse 112). Resolved, he said:

- "I will ***meditate*** on thy precepts" (verse 15). There is power in meditation. As we meditate, we become.
- "I will ***delight*** myself in thy statutes (verse 16). Our delights show our true self and the things to which we are attuned.
- "Thy law: yea, I shall ***observe*** it with my whole heart" (verse 34). Whole heart! A divided heart pulls us apart and puts our nerves on edge.
- "I will ***speak*** of thy testimonies" (verse 46). What the heart doesn't speak, the heart is not apt to have.
- "I will ***never forget*** thy precepts" (verse 93). To forget the Word is but to forget our map, our food, our protection and our hope.
- "I will have ***respect*** unto thy statutes continually" (verse 117). For "I esteem all thy precepts concerning all things to be right" (verse 128).

We have to resolve to improve. So for the better life, let us strengthen ourselves with higher intents.

Wherewithal shall a young man cleanse his way? by taking heed thereto according to thy word.—119:9

Security for Youth

YOUTH IS SO SUSCEPTIBLE TO TEMPTATION and exploitation. In the lad and lassie days, passions clamor for indulgence. The young mind, not satisfied with old truths, seeks something new, something different from what the fathers followed; and this makes him an easy victim of doubt and unbelief. Impatient with control, youth has a tendency to cast off all restraint. Untaught and inexperienced, it is easy for him to be ensnared.

Another problem is youth's vulnerability to reaction. He sees the world very idealistically, which makes it easy for him to march. He experiences the imperfect conditions around him, and he wants to make changes. Everything should be perfect, and he shall make it so—now! He has not lived long enough to understand that this is not a perfect world and very seldom, if ever, do we find perfect solutions. As solutions drag on, this tries his patience and sometimes drives him into a reactionary behavior.

How do young people find their way through a maze of dangers besetting them? The same way we all do. By taking heed to God's Word (verses 10-16).

How shall the young secure their hearts,
And guard their lives from sin?
Thy word the choicest rules imparts
To keep the conscience clean.

'Tis like the sun, a heav'nly light,
That guides us all the day;
And, thro' the dangers of the night,
A lamp to lead our way.

I will run the way of thy commandments, when thou shalt enlarge my heart.—119:32

The Enlarged Heart

THE COMPOSER BELIEVED GOD WOULD GRANT him the necessary grace to expand his heart. The heart must have something to stimulate its growth, and a powerful stimulant is the word of His grace. With God's Word working in the human heart—developing faith, hope, love, humility and unselfishness—that heart is sure to expand.

The Word produces faith, and faith enlarges the heart. A big faith can make a mighty big heart that opens a bigger world.

Hope is another heart expander. However, when hope is lacking, the heart starts shrinking. Indeed, every shrunken heart lost hope. So don't take great expectations from me.

Also, love is a vigorous influence in the heart that urges its growth. Where love is, there's no lack. Stand back, therefore, all you things that would deny me of love.

Humility is likewise a factor in heart development. We must guard against haughtiness, for it constricts the heart.

Additionally, unselfishness swells the heart.

In conclusion, what humanity needs is bigger hearts. For a good heart is better than all the heads in the world.

I thought on my ways, and turned my feet unto thy testimonies.—119:59

I Thought on My Ways

THE POET GIVES US THE FIRST STEP in turning to God—reflection. He thought on his ways and stopped his course of folly. He examined himself, and what he saw he didn't like.

He had gone too far without thinking, which describes a lot of traffic on the highway of life. He had lived with presence of mind but absence of thought. Not thinking denies one the fuller life. For there can be no harvest-time of character without a seed-time of thought.

Thinking on one's conduct has the power to stop the evil and right the wrong. When the thief thinks on his ways, the peasant gets his cow back.

> *There is always hope for an individual who stops to do some serious thinking about life.*
>
> —KATHERINE LOGAN

Thus, as we would expect, the first step in the Prodigal Son's long journey home was his coming to himself (Luke 15:17). Only after getting a person to think upon his condition—his guilt and its consequences—can we hope to change him.

Therefore, we need to stop to think and think to stop. If there are bad things in our lives, a little thinking will help us see it's so.

I am a companion of all them that fear thee, and of them that keep thy precepts.—119:63

Companions

LIKE VIEWS AND GOALS MAKE COMPANIONS. Where there are similar ideals there is an affinity. The psalmist brought this out in the text, stating that he was a companion of all who feared the Lord and kept His testimonies. They shared in a common interest and toiled in a common cause. This generated a magnetic power that pulled them together. For this reason they were always glad to see one another.

They that fear the Lord will be glad when they see me.
—119:74

A person tells on himself by the company he keeps. When all of a church member's best friends are outside the church, it indicates where his heart is. The seekers of God prefer one another. The association gives them strength in their calling.

Two are better than one.
—ECCLESIASTES 4:9

Indeed, it is revealing that the psalmist's commitment to God was so meaningful that it produced a special fondness or an attraction to all God's children, even the ones he did not know. Are we affected the same way? And does meeting one, at home or abroad, strike a note of joy?

Before I was afflicted I went astray:
but now have I kept thy word.—119:67

Sweet Afflictions

THE PSALMIST APPRAISED HIS SUFFERINGS as blessings in disguise. His affliction let him see life from a different vantage, and it reclaimed him from straying. He admitted that it had been good for him:

> *It is good for me that I have been afflicted; that I might learn thy statutes.*—119:71

In time of health and prosperity, he had held false values, forgotten his duty, neglected the right and embraced the wrong.

This is the experience of millions.

Hence, affliction is often necessary to call us back to our finer self. Adversity is a better keeper of the Word than prosperity.

There are lessons to learn in illness that we never learn in health. We become cognizant of blessings we had just taken for granted. Prayer becomes sweeter. The Bible more meaningful. Going to church is no longer a formality. Friends are dearer. Just a walk in the yard is a delight. And a ride in the car is a thrill. The whole world is more beautiful. And the desire to do right is multiplied many fold. When this occurs, then surely we, too, can say, "It is good for me that I have been afflicted."

Thou art good, and doest good: teach me thy statutes.
—119:68

The Good Do Good

GOD DOES GOOD BECAUSE HE IS GOOD. It is not mere policy! Not bare wish! Not simple sentiment! It is the natural outpouring from a natural, inexhaustible reserve of goodness. Just as the fountain gives what it is, so does God.

The same principle of bringing forth fruit in keeping with the tree is true of man.

> *A good man out of the good treasure of his heart bringeth forth good things.*—MATTHEW 12:35

So the secret of doing good is being good; then it comes naturally. One might better try to fly than try to be good when he is bad.

> *True goodness springs from a man's own heart.*
> —CHINESE PROVERB

Even though there is much around us that is evil, the world still prefers the good person; and because "a good man's pedigree is little hunted up," we don't care when or where or of whom a person was born. We simply want honorable associates, honest workers, upright teachers and just judges.

Thou through thy commandments
hast made me wiser than mine enemies....
I have more understanding than all my teachers:
for thy testimonies are my meditation.
I understand more than the ancients,
because I keep thy precepts.—119:98-100

What Makes Us Smart

THE WRITER WASN'T BOASTING, just stating a fact. He wasn't exalting himself. He was lauding the Word of God.

The commandments had made him wiser than his enemies. The Word gives a wisdom far above the cleverness of the worldly wise. It is as Moses stated:

> *Behold, I have taught you statutes and judgments.... Keep therefore and do them; for this is your wisdom and your understanding in the sight of the nations, which shall hear all these statutes, and say, Surely this nation is a wise and understanding people.*
>
> —DEUTERONOMY 4:5,6

He had more understanding than all his teachers; that is, the teachers of secular knowledge. They were wise in their fields of worldly training but unwise in unworldly matters. Instructors can be well versed in their specialty but very lacking in wisdom and spiritual knowledge.

He had a deeper understanding than the ancients or the aged. It was due to keeping the Divine precepts. "Years should teach wisdom," but sometimes the aged don't learn.

> *Antiquity is no help against stupidity.*
>
> —MARTIN LUTHER

Order my steps in thy word:
and let not any iniquity have dominion over me.—119:133

Who Rules My Life?

THE POET PRAYS THAT NO SIN RULE OVER HIM, that no passion enslave him. Even a little sin is so subtle it will not stay little long.

Sin multiplies. He that will serve one sin will have to serve many.

No person is prepared in heart to keep himself pure if he has granted himself the privilege to indulge in a few or even one sin. It is no restraint at all just to refrain from the sins that have no appeal to us. We are all against the sins that give us no pleasure. Obeying only what suits us is hardly obedience at all.

No man is master of himself who is slave to sin.

It is our task to master the sin—not allow the sin to master us. The great issue of life is which is to be master. That's all.

I am small and despised: yet do not I forget thy precepts.
—119:141

Little Big People

I AM SMALL. The word *small* could mean small in number, or small in years, or small in rank.

And *despised.* Treated with contempt, passed by, loathed. It may have come as the result of rank, age, poverty or religion. Regardless of the cause, the pain of being despised surely hurt. It is hard to take reproach and ridicule.

Little—but he remembered the precepts of God. This made him big. Little in the eyes of men. Big in the eyes of God. The perfect God and the imperfect man have completely different standards of littleness and bigness, which make it possible for the same person to be so little and so big.

Life is made up of *littles* that are valuable. The day is filled with little beams of the sun, and the night is magnificent with the little twinklings of the stars. When nature chose to give the world something rare and beautiful, she made it little: little diamonds, little pearls and little gold nuggets. Even the Sermon on the Mount is little, but the person who obeys it becomes a giant.

Let us not despise the little people. They may be the keepers of the precepts. And in that case, they are giants the world is too blind to recognize.

Deliver my soul, O Lord, from lying lips, and from a deceitful tongue.—120:2

Lying Lips

EVERY PERSON who has been misrepresented and maligned has cried out with anguish, "Deliver my soul, O Lord, from lying lips." There are few hurts more painful and widespread than slander.

And when it occurs, what do we do? The origin cannot always be traced; and if it could, the perpetrator often becomes all the more bitter and, behind your back, vilifies us for approaching him. This only makes a bigger tale that adds a tinge of credibility to that which is false. Even if the slanderer should repent and try to right the wrong, the calumny has gone on the wind like feathers on a windy day.

Poor person! Retaliation will not help. Even if we wished, how could we black that which is already jet black? The calumniator fights in ways we cannot engage. Like the skunk, he gives off an odor that righteous people find hard to encounter. Like the wolf, he has fangs not to be matched with soft hands.

Our friends won't believe the rumor. And our enemies won't have it any other way. So maybe, about all we can do is to pray. And here's our prayer: From fabricators, gossipers, talebearers, anonymous writers, senders of newspaper clippings and all liars, dear Lord, deliver us.

My soul hath long dwelt with him that hateth peace. I am for peace: but when I speak, they are for war.—120:6,7

Takes Two to Make Peace

THE POET HAD BEEN EXPOSED to the strife of people known for their warlike disposition. When he spoke to them of peace, they were for war. No proposal would satisfy them. They were averse to peace, set on hostility. There was nothing the psalmist could do to prevent it.

To be exposed constantly to a quarrel—in marriage, in the home, in business, or in world affairs—is extremely bitter. It is trying to live with maladjusted people always ready to pick a fuss.

Takes two to make peace. But what about the maxim "Takes two to make war"? Takes two to make attack and counterattack. However, one can attack and though the attacked refrains from hostility, it is still war—just one-sided strife. One person can cause trouble, but it takes two to make peace.

How sorry a thing is war.

But peace can never rule the day unless peace rules the hearts of both.

I will lift up mine eyes unto the hills, from whence cometh my help. My help cometh from the Lord, which made heaven and earth. He will not suffer thy foot to be moved: he that keepeth thee will not slumber. Behold, he that keepeth Israel shall neither slumber nor sleep. The Lord is my keeper: the Lord is thy shade upon thy right hand. The sun shall not smite thee by day, nor the moon by night. The Lord shall preserve thee from all evil: he shall preserve thy soul. The Lord shall preserve thy going out and thy coming in from this time forth, and even for evermore.—121

Unto the Hills

PSALMS 120-134 ARE CALLED the Songs of Ascents or the "Pilgrim Psalms" because they were sung by travelers on their way to worship in Jerusalem. Psalm 121 was often sung as they came into view of the hills surrounding Jerusalem. They were still far from Jerusalem but not far from Jehovah, and just to come in sight of those hills quickened their assurance.

They knew that the "Keeper of Israel" was watching over them. Like a rich man keeps his treasure and a general keeps a city, God watches over and protects us. We are secure. We can sleep in safety because our God never sleeps. He never drowses while we are talking to Him and never slumbers during our time of trial. We need to be spared the blistering sun and the chilly nights and kept from slipping as we travel through the treacherous places of life.

The future is too uncertain not to have the assurance of which the Psalm so beautifully speaks, for one thing we struggling creatures need is help.

I was glad when they said unto me,
Let us go into the house of the Lord.—122:1

Worship Makes Me Glad

WORSHIP SHOULD MAKE US GLAD—not bore us. For we were born to worship, and this innate desire is fully satisfied only in worship to Jehovah our God. Worship does several things:

• ***In worship, we remember.*** We remember that God is over our lives, our world and our future. We remember from where our strength comes and from whom our blessings flow. We remember how God has blessed us, provided for our needs and leads us gently, patiently, through the wilderness.

• ***In worship, we are refreshed.*** God is omnipresent and is with us always. We are never out of His mind. However, God is very often out of our thoughts and our minds; and it is very refreshing for us to put all other thoughts aside to focus more clearly and singularly upon our Father. Then in quiet meditation and communion with God, we find peace. We find the calmness and serenity that our hearts desperately seek and seldom find. Indeed, worship refreshes the soul for the future struggles.

• ***In worship, we realize.*** Having remembered the source of our strength, having been refreshed by solitude with our Maker, we realize more fully than ever before what is important in life. Without the cataracts of frantic living and the myopia of unconfessed sin, we see our priorities more clearly. We see what is important and who is important. Our eyes are opened to the neglected opportunities and missed blessings around us.

Truly, worship is a marvelous, invigorating experience!

Peace be within thy walls, and prosperity within thy palaces. For my brethren and companions' sakes, I will now say, Peace be within thee.—122:7,8

For the Sake of Others

IT WAS HIS PRAYER THAT THERE BE PEACE in Jerusalem, that tranquility prevail in the rulers' palaces.

The particular reason was *For my brethren and companions' sakes.* Because some dwell there, others go there to worship, and all derive hope from the city. Thus he earnestly prayed, "Peace be within thee." For there their dreams and hopes were entwined.

The religion of God requires that we be concerned with others: "Look not every man on his own things, but every man also on the things of others" (Philippians 2:4).

It is reputed that on the bells of a New England university are inscribed these words:

For him who in art beautifies life, I ring;
For him who in letters interprets life, I ring;
For the man of science who widens knowledge, I ring;
For the philosopher who ennobles life, I ring;
For the scholar who preserves learning, I ring;
For the preacher of the fear of the Lord, I ring.

But the one statement that strikes the major chord of humanity's heart is that on the first bell:

For him who in any station seeks not to
be ministered unto, but to minister, I ring.

Unto thee I lift up mine eyes,
O thou that dwellest in the heavens.—123:1

The Lifted Eyes

THIS IS ONE OF THE BLESSINGS OF MAN—the ability to lift up his eyes. The animals have no longing that prompts their eyes to look heavenward. But man is different. With eyes of faith, he penetrates the veil of space and lifts his vision in search of the unseen.

Lifted eyes indicate a heart that is very expressive:

• ***Signifies reflection.*** The individual ponders the issues of life; helpless, he looks up to Him who rules and blesses man.

• ***Testifies to faith.*** The infidel's vision is never above the earth.

• ***Bespeaks obedience.*** The lifted eyes manifest obedient service: "Speak, Lord, I will hear. Command, I will obey."

• ***Suggests humility.*** The proud have eyes that see only themselves and their own glory.

• ***Indicates need.*** Going around with our heads down is a good way to shrink our perspective. Bitter trials and vexing problems leave us in need of a longer and broader view, achieved only by lifting our eyes to God.

• ***Denotes hope.*** The person desires and expects something this earth cannot supply.

The visionary eyes will give us a view of God and man; and this is what religion is all about—seeing God and serving man.

Behold, as the eyes of servants look unto the hand of their masters, and as the eyes of a maiden unto the hand of her mistress; so our eyes wait upon the Lord our God, until that he have mercy upon us.—123:2

As the Eyes of a Servant

THE ILLUSTRATION IS AN APT PORTRAYAL of the believer's relationship to his God—that of a servant. The eyes of the servant and maiden are constantly set on the master and mistress to catch their every expression, ready to obey their wishes on the slightest signal.

We, too, need eyes focused on our Master and a disposition that prays, "Not my will, but Thine, be done."

There are, however, differences in the relationship and servitude, which should prompt our services to come more gladly and freely. Our Master, being perfect, never issues an unreasonable order; is more understanding, more protective; and offers superior rewards, even eternal life. Since good servants are made by good masters, this makes us the greatest and bestows upon us the grandest honors—a nobility that outranks kings who are not His servants. By all means, to serve our Master is not slavery; it is rather the highest form of liberty. And best of all, our service can continue in the next world. And when everything else has passed away, what a joy it will be to hear Him say:

Well done, thou good and faithful servant...enter thou into the joy of thy lord.—MATTHEW 25:21

If it had not been the Lord who was on our side,
when men rose up against us;
Then they had swallowed us up quick.... —124:2,3

God for Us

THERE WAS UNMISTAKABLE EVIDENCE that God had interposed and delivered them when they were assailed by their enemies.

The determining factor in their success was God. He was on their side. If it had not been for Jehovah, they would have been pulled down by opposing forces. God tilted the balance of strength in their favor.

The one all-important lesson to learn from Israel's successes and failures is that when God was on their side, they were strong and invincible; but when God was not with them, they were weak and vulnerable.

With God on our side, we have the Almighty to bear our burdens, stand by us in distress, dry our tears in time of sorrow, and give us strength in time of temptation. He will fight for us, and that means victory.

With God on our side, we cannot lose; without Him, we do not deserve to win.

Our soul is escaped as a bird out of the snare of the fowlers: the snare is broken, and we are escaped.—124:7

Escaped

LIKE A BIRD CAUGHT IN THE SNARE of the fowler, they escaped. The net was broken and they were free. This happens when the snare is not as strong as the struggling bird; and, in the application of the illustration, it occurs when the snare is too weak to hold a robust people made strong by the power of God. For their help is "in the name of the Lord" (verse 8).

It may be that we have been caught by a number of ensnarements that restrict our freedom, snares from which we desperately need to escape. ***Doubt*** confines us to only what we see, hear, touch, taste and smell; for we are devoid of faith. ***Superstition*** locks us within walls of unsupported fears. ***Hate*** binds us to a slavish and miserable life. ***Unforgiveness*** tightens the hold on the soul and squeezes the life out of it. ***Worry*** paces us in a narrow cage. ***No vision*** clips our wings and holds us to where we are.

All kinds of fowlers with every kind of a snare are out there, but with God's help we can break loose.

May our yearning to escape cause us to cry out in the language of Lot:

O let me escape thither, and my soul shall live.
—GENESIS 19:20

They that trust in the Lord shall be as mount Zion, which cannot be removed, but abideth for ever.—125:1

Unmovable Like a Mountain

THE DEVOUT JEW BEHELD MOUNT ZION with all its stability as a symbol of the dependability of God and as a promise of what he could become if he trusted Jehovah. This everyday scene, always there, always unchanged, conveyed a message to the Israelites—one that all humanity needs to hear.

Trust in God provides a firm foundation that saves us from slipping and tottering. It is only when trust is broken that the child of God becomes movable, as seen in the Scripture: "Take heed, brethren, lest there be in any of you an evil heart of unbelief [doubt, distrust] in departing from the living God" (Hebrews 3:12). Distrust is the earthquake that sends the rumblings through the soul and shifts it. However, when our trust in Him is full and undivided, we stand unmovable like a mountain.

I Shall Not Be Moved

Though the tempest rage round me,
Through the storm, my Lord, I see;
Standing like a mountain holy,
I shall not be moved from Thee.
I shall not be moved,
Anchored to the Rock of Ages,
I shall not be moved.

—ALFRED H. ACKLEY

Do good, O Lord, unto those that be good, and to them that are upright in their hearts.—125:4

Reward the Good

BECAUSE THEY ARE GOOD, REPAY THEM with good, give them the reaping of their sowing. This was the prayer of the psalmist. It is in keeping with the scriptural principle that like deserves like.

I cannot hold to the pessimism that good people do not profit from their goodness. Good for the evil and evil for the good is contrary to all the workings of nature.

Things are drawn together by a natural affinity. The good man draws good. And he should. For he is fit to receive. "Righteousness tendeth unto life" is a law of God (Proverbs 11:19).

Good, better, best;
Never let it rest
Till your good is better,
And your better best.
—OLD MAXIM

Good is sure to come back to us for being our best. There are many rewards. The most good that comes, however, is comfort in the hour of death. When Sir Walter Scott lay dying, he called for his son-in-law and biographer and said, "Lockhart, be a good man. Be virtuous, be religious, be a good man. Nothing else will give you any comfort when you come to lie here."

When the Lord turned again the captivity of Zion, we were like them that dream.... —126:1-3

A Dream Come True

THE ECSTASY WAS CAUSED by the Lord's returning the Israelites from captivity. The poet stated, "We were like them that dream." It seemed too good to be true. But it was. Their redemption from captivity was real; it was marvelous and full of joy.

This is how it affected their personality:

"Then was our mouth filled with laughter." They had something to cause them to laugh, and they did.

"And our tongue with singing." Their happiness was expressed in songs, which is a natural way to show a rapturous feeling. In an assembly of people whose dreams have come true, there is always joyful singing.

"The Lord had done great things for them." They knew it. They felt it. They expressed it.

Dream! Be sure to dream! Then turn it over to the Fulfiller of Dreams. Back of the dreamer there is the God who makes the dream come true, for—

If God be for us, who can be against us?
—ROMANS 8:31

With His help, we can see what men have only dreamed of seeing.

They that sow in tears shall reap in joy.
He that goeth forth and weepeth, bearing precious seed,
shall doubtless come again with rejoicing,
bringing his sheaves with him.—126:5,6

Bringing in the Sheaves

IT WAS A WORK OF TOIL AND TEARS, but there was joy in bringing in the sheaves.

The sower's work is sometimes so burdensome that he sows in tears yet reaps in joy. Many endeavors are beset with difficulties and require long, laborious hours; but the joy of success more than compensates for the care and toil. This is true of the farmer's perspiration, the businessman's caution, the worker's loyalty, the teacher's patience, the student's application, the parent's training, the minister's proclamation and the missionary's concern—sometimes sowing in tears, always reaping in joy, bringing in the sheaves. This is stated so beautifully in the song:

Bringing in the Sheaves

Sowing in the morning, sowing seeds of kindness,
Sowing in the noontide and the dewy eves;
Waiting for the harvest and the time of reaping,
We shall come rejoicing, bringing in the sheaves.

—KNOWLES SHAW

Except the Lord build the house, they labor in vain that build it. Except the Lord keep the city, the watchman waketh but in vain.—127:1

Except the Lord Build the House

GOD HAS A BLUEPRINT FOR CONSTRUCTION and security that cannot be ignored without failure finally coming, no matter what the skill, or strength or industry of the worker may be.

As people build a home, a business, a school, a nation or a local church, a dependence on God as the builder should be uppermost in their minds.

Except the Lord build the house, they labor in vain that build it should be our motto. Churchmen should not be tempted to ignore God, to substitute the human for the Divine. We are too prone to discard the old, scriptural plan for something less demanding. The material for the church is living stones, redeemed and sanctified; but the get-a-crowd-at-any-price builders throw caution to the wind and use crumbling stones of impenitence, irreverence and worldliness. They swell church rolls and shrink sanctuaries.

As William Cowper stated, too often men have:

Built God a church, and laugh'd His word to scorn.

The inconsistency of such a builder was voiced by James Russell Lowell:

For though he builds glorious temples, 'tis odd
He leaves never a doorway to get in a god.

Lo, children are a heritage of the Lord: and the fruit of the womb is his reward. As arrows are in the hand of a mighty man; so are the children of the youth. Happy is the man that hath his quiver full of them: they shall not be ashamed, but they shall speak with the enemies in the gate.—127:3-5

Children a Heritage

THE PROSPERITY OF A FAMILY AND A NATION depends on children. They are the reward of God. The lesson is enforced by an illustration: as arrows in the hand of a mighty man, children protect their aged parents; and when the father's cause is contested, they stand in the gate to take his part.

They protect the couple from selfishness. The parents are absorbed with the welfare of their offspring.

Children protect the home from boredom. With their hurts and ills, curiosity and learning, joys and smiles, sorrows and tears, each day bursts anew with challenges that bring a special interest.

Flesh of their flesh protects the home from separation. Surely there should be other reasons for togetherness, but children do tend to unify the parents. Drawn together by an object of mutual love and held by two tiny hands, one in the hand of the mother and the other in the hand of the father, they renew their commitment to each other.

Children protect the parents in old age. Nature has a way of balancing things. The little ones are cared for in their helpless state; and when years have passed and parents become helpless, they have their children to stand by and assist them.

Blessed is every one that feareth the Lord; that walketh in his ways. For thou shalt eat the labor of thine hands: happy shalt thou be, and it shalt be well with thee. Thy wife shall be as a fruitful vine by the sides of thy house: thy children like olive plants round about thy table.—128:1-3

A Lovely Home

A FAMILY ***possessed with the fear of the Lord.*** This is a basic for the ideal home. The temperance, prudence, industry and thrift that go with keeping the commandments of God definitely bless the family.

A family that enjoys the labors of their own hands. Work brings a unique happiness, a satisfying contentment. It gives a feeling of accomplishment and independence, a sense of worthwhileness, which holds up their heads and allows them to look the world in the face.

A family with a fruitful wife. She is willing to do more than her part. A pleasant, industrious, thrifty, cooperative, helpful wife who loves her husband and her children is a precious blessing. He who finds her finds a good thing (Proverbs 18:22).

A family blessed with the patter of little feet. The "children are like olive plants" round about, growing up to take the place of the older ones when time takes its toll. They are stimulating blessings. They scatter sunshine and give strength.

Be it ever so humble, there's no place like home.

—JOHN HOWARD PAYNE

Behold, that thus shall the man be blessed
that feareth the Lord.... Yea, thou shalt see
thy children's children, and peace upon Israel.—128:4-6

A Grandfather's Delight

THE PROMISE TO THE GOD-FEARING MAN to see "thy children's children" is literal and one of the happiest experiences of life—to hold and love flesh of his flesh. "Children's children are the crown of old men" (Proverbs 17:6).

The very word *grandfather* speaks volumes. He is old enough to realize that the newly arrived child from the hand of God is a link between two worlds. Grandfather can especially enjoy the childish sweetness, warm companionship and wide-eyed adoration of the grandchild. The years have seasoned him for it.

The godly man finds a distinct gladness in the thought he is leaving behind a pious lineage he hopes will continue. He rejoices in the expectation that his unfeigned faith will be handed down to succeeding generations. It is a sign of man's spiritual nature that it gives him joy to extend his life in the lives of his posterity.

Give us grandchildren!
Strong, healthy, talented ones:
Grandsons whom high hope inspires,
Granddaughters whom virtue fires,
Grandsons who honor their fathers,
Granddaughters who love mothers,
True, pure, faithful, useful ones;
Give us grandchildren, I say,
Give us grandchildren.

Many a time have they afflicted me from my youth, may Israel now say: Many a time have they afflicted me from my youth: yet they have not prevailed against me. The plowers plowed upon my back: they made long their furrows. The Lord is righteous: he hath cut asunder the cords of the wicked.—129:1-4

They Survived the Hardships

OPPRESSIONS! BITTER OPPRESSIONS! The enemy was unmercifully cruel. "They plowed upon my back," making long furrows, states the composer. The Israelites' oppressors had attempted to hold them in bondage with strong cords.

However, the violence directed against God's children failed. They withstood the afflictions in a commendable and heroic way. It is amazing how much punishment human beings can take when their will is forged by an unbreakable faith. They could say, "Yet they have not prevailed against me."

Other individuals and nations passed through similar trials and bore them courageously, and perhaps they were the bigger and purer because they suffered.

On this point, Job said:

> *But he knoweth the way that I take: when he hath tried me, I shall come forth as gold.*—JOB 23:10

Endurance was their crowning quality. It showed a Divine grandeur.

Let them all be confounded and turned back that hate Zion. Let them be as the grass upon the housetops, which withereth afore it groweth up: wherewith the mower filleth not his hand; nor he that bindeth sheaves his bosom. Neither do they which go by say, The blessing of the Lord be upon you: we bless you in the name of the Lord.—129:5-8

Grass on the Housetop

THIS IS A PRAYER THAT GOD INTERPOSE and confound the enemies of Israel, turn them back, "let them be as the grass upon the housetops." The housetops were covered with earth where seeds would germinate and begin to grow but later would wither because of the soil's shallowness—an apt illustration of feebleness.

It was customary when persons passed the harvest field to say to the reapers, "The blessing of the Lord be upon you." It was a token of goodwill, an expression of achievement and a hope of prosperity; but such a greeting to the owners of grass on housetops was inappropriate. Thus, the psalmist's prayer in regard to the haters of Zion was that they be like housetop grass, that they not be given a prosperity that would evoke the congratulations and appreciation of their neighbors.

Since it takes a harvest to keep an army going, then if it should be denied them, their aggressiveness would have to cease. When a man faces a future of no bread, the plowshare is more inviting than the sword.

If thou, Lord, shouldest mark iniquities, O Lord, who shall stand? But there is forgiveness with thee, that thou mayest be feared.—130:3,4

If God Marked Iniquities

BUT IF HE DOESN'T MARK THEM, how can He forgive them? How can He erase what He hasn't marked? Obviously, the psalmist means that God does not permanently and irrevocably mark iniquity. Though the iniquity is tallied, He is willing to blot it out and remember it no more. But if our sins were marked against us forever, "O Lord, who shall stand?" Nobody! "For all have sinned, and come short of the glory of God" (Romans 3:23).

What confident hope are these statements in the Psalm:

But there is forgiveness with thee.—VERSE 4

With him is plenteous redemption.—VERSE 7

With the Lord there is forgiveness. For those who care for it, it is available. His merciful forgiveness gives them another chance, and another, and another and another; for the Lord who taught us to forgive one another seventy times seven would not ask of us that which He is not willing to give. Knowing that Jehovah's forgiveness is inexhaustible, we pray:

Dear Lord and Father of mankind,
Forgive our foolish ways!
Reclothe us in our rightful mind,
In purer lives Thy service find,
In deeper reverence, praise.

—JOHN GREENLEAF WHITTIER

I wait for the Lord, my soul doth wait, and in his word do I hope.—130:5

Therein I Hope

IT WASN'T WISHFUL THINKING. It was a solid hope based on the bedrock of God's Word. God had spoken; the poet believed it, and therein was his hope. From God's Word hope springs eternal in the human heart. On this point, Paul says, "that we through patience and comfort of the Scriptures might have hope" (Romans 15:4). So the beacons of hope are the beacons of God's Word.

In all his distress, the psalmist was in a *waiting* posture, hoping, looking to the Lord to take his part. It gave patience and vitality to his endurance. Believers not only wait, they hope because these two qualities are inseparably linked. They are both forms of trust. We can wait because we hope. And our hope is not in vain. Our hope is in our Heavenly Father, who justifies our hopes.

Let us, then, be up and doing,
With a heart for any fate;
Still achieving, still pursuing,
Learn to labor and to wait.
—HENRY WADSWORTH LONGFELLOW

Hope lets us dream. It's no sleeping dream. It's a waking dream. It is real. And in realistic anticipation we wait for it to come to pass.

Lord, my heart is not haughty, nor mine eyes lofty: neither do I exercise myself in great matters, or in things too high for me.—131:1

Not Haughty

IT WASN'T A COUNTERFEIT HUMILITY—a pride that apes humility—but a humility so real that it would not feign a standard so false that would keep it from acknowledging itself.

His heart was not haughty. This gave him a special standing before God. *Haughtiness* God will not tolerate. As we observe in our maturing years the vanity and vexation of the haughty, this trait becomes more and more distasteful.

The composer's eyes were not lofty. Pride in the heart especially manifests itself in the eyes. His eyes were not fixed on the showy, ostentatious things that easily impress those who fall for superficial signs of greatness.

Neither did he exercise himself in things too high for his capacity. Putting a realistic limit on our endeavors is an act of wisdom that saves us from unnecessary frustrations. If we are not driven by pride, nature permits us to drift gradually into the realm where inclination, adaptation and capacity best fit us. The ideal sphere for every person is the place where affinity and ability naturally draw him.

Lord, remember David, and all his afflictions:
How he sware unto the Lord, and vowed
unto the mighty God of Jacob; surely I will not come
into the tabernacle of my house, nor go up into my bed;
I will not give sleep to mine eyes, or slumber
to mine eyelids, until I find out a place for the Lord,
a habitation for the mighty God of Jacob.—132:1-5

A House for God

DAVID MADE AN OATH TO SECURE FOR GOD a special house of worship. He vowed to make the project his first business; not to go to his own house nor sleep until he had found a place for the Lord—a place for the ark of God to remain safely and constantly.

> *See now, I dwell in a house of cedar, but the ark of God dwelleth within curtains.*—II SAMUEL 7:2

The contrast was very inconsistent with true dedication to God. It doesn't add up to true commitment for us to have the finest at home and the cheapest at church. Whatever concerns we have for our own houses are appropriate feelings for God's house—adequacy, beauty, carpets, cushions, new roof and fresh paint. And if our own grounds are well kept while the church grounds grow up in ugliness, how does God see it? This is not pride! This is placing values where they belong!

If thy children will keep my covenant and my testimony that I shall teach them, their children shall also sit upon thy throne for evermore.—132:12

God's Conditional Promises

IN THE FIRST PART OF THE PSALM, David makes a vow to God. In the last part, God makes one to David. However, God's is conditional. "If" is attached: "if thy children will keep my covenant and my testimony." When God issues a conditional promise to bless us, all we have to do to get the blessing is to meet the condition; but to expect the blessing without complying is absurd.

It would be improper for the Just One to unconditionally promise to bless man, who might later turn and misuse the benefaction to harm himself and his Benefactor. God's doing His best for us may dictate that He withhold the blessing and discipline us instead.

That God affixes conditions to His promises is very wise:

- It tests faith and obedience.
- Preserves man's sense of dependence on God's favor.
- Shows our worthiness or unworthiness to receive.

The Divinely stated "if" stands before all of us. If we fail to meet the conditions, we lose all claim to the promises; and it's our fault.

Behold, how good and how pleasant it is for brethren to dwell together in unity! It is like the precious ointment upon the head, that ran down the beard, even Aaron's beard: that went down to the skirts of his garments; as the dew of Hermon, and as the dew that descended upon the mountains of Zion: for there the Lord commanded the blessing, even life for evermore.—133:1-3

Good and Pleasant Unity

THE UNITY OF *BRETHREN*—people with a common Father, a common faith and a common calling—is a state the composer extols as something good and pleasant.

The odor of this oneness is fragrant, he states, like the sacred ointment used in priestly consecration. The anointing oil was composed of several precious ingredients. The author had a vision of its abundance running down from the head of Aaron to his beard and garments. The thought is *unity grants bountiful portions to man.*

And it shines in beauty like the dew on Mount Hermon.

However, to achieve it, we must adhere to a common standard: "walk by the same rule" (Philippians 3:16).

Concerning the necessity of oneness, it is something Paul commanded and something for which Jesus prayed.

When a group has to face the whole world, they had better stand together.

United we stand, divided we fall.
—G. P. MORRIS

Behold, bless ye the Lord, all ye servants of the Lord, which by night stand in the house of the Lord. Lift up your hands in the sanctuary, and bless the Lord. The Lord that made heaven and earth bless thee out of Zion.
—134:1-3

Songs in the Night

IN THIS SHORT PSALM THERE IS A SUMMONS to praise and adoration.

Perhaps it was written to be sung by alternate singers: by the people who approached the temple, calling on the ministers of religion in the sanctuary to lift up their hands and praise God; and then by the ministers who gave the response, pronouncing a blessing on the approaching worshipers.

It is striking that the Psalm speaks of devotion in the night. When the world sleeps and we are alone with God, when noise has ceased and silence refuses to whisper, when nothing stirs except our thoughts of God, it gives us a deeper solemnity and better fits us for holy devotion. Significantly, it was during the night that Nicodemus went to Jesus (John 3:2). Also, even Jesus Himself chose the night to go "out into a mountain to pray," where He continued the whole "night in prayer to God" (Luke 6:12). Sometimes we can see in the night what the day never reveals.

Praise the Lord; for the Lord is good: sing praises unto his name; for it is pleasant.—135:3

Pleasant Worship

OUR HEARTS SHOULD BE SO TUNED to the heart of God that worship strikes a happy note. The house of God should be a joyous place where worship is pleasant. There is nothing to gain in being a church corpse, sitting on coffin-colored pews, surrounded by depressing decoration, wondering if you can endure it until you can get a little fresh air. God is alive. We are alive. And worship to Him should be alive, moving and pleasant—not something dead, rendered by the dead, who dread it.

But for worship to be pleasant, *we* must be pleasant. Resentful, disgruntled, seething-with-anger people are not going to enjoy the worship.

Another thing—worship must come from the spirit or inner nature of man (John 4:24). Praise from the mouth out could hardly expect to satisfy. To the true worshiper, worship is not a hall of politics, not a nest of trifles, not a fair of vanity, not an assembly of babbling voices, nor a circus for misguided people who use it for play acting.

Furthermore, worship must be in truth, according to the truth God has commanded (John 4:24). After all, the God who is being worshiped is the one to be pleased—not the worshiper. And the only way we know to please Him is to offer Him what He has commanded. And this gives peace.

Whatsoever the Lord pleased, that did he in heaven, and in the earth, in the seas, and all deep places.—135:6

God Does as He Pleases

AND WHY SHOULDN'T HE DO AS HE PLEASES?

- Everything He wishes is perfect.
- Everything He does is infallible.
- His every act is merciful.
- Nothing is beyond His power.
- He can do no wrong.

As the absolute sovereign, He has formed a perfect plan and carries it out infallibly.

But with us it is not so. Our weak and vulnerable being errs. It is not within us to direct our own steps. We need guidance. Our will needs to be bent to the will of the Perfect One. So our aim should be to do as God pleases.

What Pleaseth God

What pleaseth God with joy receive;
Though storm-winds rage and billows heave
And earth's foundations all be rent,
Be comforted; to thee is sent
What pleaseth God.

God's will is best; to this resigned,
How sweetly rests the weary mind!
Seek, then, this blessed conformity,
Desiring but to do and be
What pleaseth God.

—PAUL GERHARDT

*O Give thanks unto the Lord; for he is good:
for his mercy endureth for ever.*—136:1

Give Thanks Unto the Lord

GOD, WHO DID MUCH FOR THE ANCIENTS, also does much for us; and our thanks should be every bit as deep and expressive as theirs.

Our Heavenly Father has been good to His offspring. Earth's millions in every land should thank Him. He has given us the earth and the heavenly bodies which operate with unbroken constancy. This makes seed-time and harvest-time dependable, leaving it up to man to apply diligence and enterprise: "...earn his bread by the sweat of his brow."

Truly, a grateful mind is a great mind; and a thankful heart, a thinking heart.

Most of all, let us be thankful for God's mercy. It endures forever. We do not deserve it; but if we deserved such, it would not be mercy. We are the objects of His love and the darlings of His hand. And when the way gets rough, He picks us up and carries us.

Now, let us back up our thanks*giving* with thanks*living.* This shows our words are not just from our lips.

*O Give thanks to the Lord of Lords:
for his mercy endureth for ever.*—136:3

Enduring Mercy

THERE ARE TWENTY-SIX VERSES in this Psalm and all of them end exactly alike, with this note of praise: "for his mercy endureth for ever." Twenty-six times. Repetition. Repetition. But it cannot be said too often. Mercy is one thing everybody needs and something God has plenty of.

When temptation beckons and our weakness succumbs, when our foot stumbles and we fall, when the tide of fortune rolls out and leaves us stranded, when disease strikes and shatters our body like a house torn to shambles, when sorrow pierces our heart and our eyes are turned to tears, when we are shrouded with loneliness because friends forsake, when the job we had counted on folds, when persecution inflicts without cause, when we are bewildered over a problem that seems to have no solution, when the burdens appear too heavy for our frailty, it is then that we can better appreciate the repetitious praise in the Psalm, "his mercy endureth for ever."

Ye fearful saints, fresh courage take:
The clouds ye so much dread
Are big with mercy, and shall break
In blessings on your head.
—WILLIAM COWPER

We must have help, or we shall lose the struggle. Mercy is granted. Help comes, and we become victors. This puts *A Psalm in My Heart.*

By the rivers of Babylon, there we sat down, yea, we wept, when we remembered Zion.—137:1

Memory's Tears

SITTING ON THE BANKS OF THE RIVERS of Babylon (Euphrates and linking canals), the captives wept. Not because their character was weak (no crybaby tears), but because their memory was strong. They remembered who they were and what had happened to them—exiles in a strange land, inflicted with severe suffering.

It was the vivid recollection of the wrongs perpetrated against Jerusalem that sorrowed their hearts and opened wide the valves on their tear ducts. There by the river they sat, they meditated, they remembered, they wept. Their harps hung on the willow trees, and no song graced their lips. Instead, memory touched their heart strings and played the mournful melody of tears. A memory of their land—its former glory; its lost strength; the cruelties inflicted upon it; the devastations; the delightful days spent there in contrast with their Babylonian misery and humiliation; and, no doubt, their sins that had brought them to their low estate. Former privileges versus present privations—this was their changed fortune, and it grieved them. The richer our treasure, the poorer our loss. The fuller our joy, the emptier we are when it is gone.

One priceless power they had left was memory.

For there they that carried us away captive
required of us a song;
and they that wasted us required of us mirth,
saying, Sing us one of the songs of Zion.
How shall we sing the Lord's song in a strange land?
—137:3,4

No Song in Our Heart

THEY DIDN'T FEEL LIKE SINGING. They felt like crying, as mentioned in the previous essay. For they were captives in Babylon, footsore, hand-calloused and heart-wounded. Why the request came we cannot be sure. It may have been a taunt, hateful ridicule, mad derision. However, it could have been no more than curiosity, seeking to hear the songs of foreigners.

Their answer for not complying was, "How shall we sing the Lord's song in a strange land?" It wasn't the place. Nor the time. It was not proper to force from their lips what the heart did not feel.

Remembering Jerusalem and all its joys drove all songs from their hearts. The intensity and pain of Jerusalem's memory was so strong that they would gladly give up the use of their right hand and their tongue if they *ever* forgot Jerusalem.

We all have had the songs driven from our hearts. But why? Was it because of failed greed for greater power or more things? Was it because of unjustified jealousies over another's successes? Or like the Israelites, was it because of our penitence and sorrow for our sins? When no song is in our heart, may it be for a good reason.

If I forget thee, O Jerusalem,
let my right hand forget her cunning.
If I do not remember thee,
let my tongue cleave to the roof of my mouth;
if I prefer not Jerusalem above my chief joy.—137:5,6

Religion Before Pleasure

IF I PREFER NOT *JERUSALEM* (religion*)* above my *chief joy* (pleasure). Here we have the thought of preferring religion before pleasure. Like the man in the parable who searched for the pearl of great price, he thought it wise to give up the appeals of the world for the one great value—his commitment to God.

Unfortunately, too many people have the secondary view of religion. With them, the god of pleasure comes first.

However, the religion of God is one of rightly placed affections and priorities. "Thou shalt love the Lord thy God with all thy heart, and with all thy soul, and with all thy mind. This is…first…" (Matthew 22:37,38). There is one thing sure: it is first in death. And what is first in death ought to be first in life.

Actually, in the pursuit of duty, happiness overtakes us. The sweetest joys spring from higher living—joy of faith, joy of conscience, joy of worship, joy of soul-winning and joy of domestic life.

In the day when I cried thou answeredst me, and strengthenedst me with strength in my soul.—138:3

The Strongest Strength

THE PASSAGE SPEAKS of the strongest strength: soul strength. Indeed, no person is strong unless he is strong on the inside. This is the stamina that comes from God. "Thou didst encourage me with strength in my soul" (*ASV*). God's best blessings come to the inward being, the real *me.* Sometimes He does not change the outward circumstances for us but does strengthen us inwardly to meet them. He did for Paul. He granted him the grace to bear the thorn in his flesh. This made Paul master of his ills and circumstances. Tested by beatings, stonings, shipwrecks, robbers, false brethren, weariness, pain, hunger, thirst, cold and nakedness, he was conqueror.

No person is defeated unless he has lost heart. If God gives fortitude, then a man should ever be triumphant over the opposing circumstances. Truly, "they that wait upon the Lord shall renew their strength…I will strengthen thee…they that war against thee shall be as nothing, and as a thing of nought" (Isaiah 40:31—41:12).

Though I walk in the midst of trouble, thou wilt revive me: thou shalt stretch forth thine hand against the wrath of mine enemies, and thy right hand shall save me.—138:7

Revived to Handle Trouble

THE POET WAS EXPERIENCING some hard blows from trouble's cruel fist. However, he confidently stated that God would revive him with one hand and rebuff his enemies with the other. It's this hope that keeps us going.

Most of our troubles come from people, but their solution comes from God.

The price of living in the world is troubles; but when we think of the alternative, we are glad to have them. However, we do need God's reviving hand to bear them.

No one escapes trouble. Sometimes it closes in from every side. And if it's not handled correctly, anxiety haunts us by day and worry torments us by night. The stomach churns. Our hands tremble. Optimism dies. Pessimism makes a new convert. Now we have the worst troubles—growing, multiplying, self-made troubles—all because we didn't handle the initial problem. But we could have handled it, for "God is...a very present help in trouble." His giving man the power to persevere makes the person a genius.

O Lord, thou hast searched me, and known me.
Thou knowest my downsitting and mine uprising;
thou understandest my thought afar off.
Thou compassest my path and my lying down,
and art acquainted with all my ways.
For there is not a word in my tongue,
but, lo, O Lord, thou knowest it altogether.
Thou hast beset me behind and before,
and laid thine hand upon me.
Such knowledge is too wonderful for me;
it is high, I cannot attain unto it.—139:1-6

The Omniscience of God

GOD HAS "SEARCHED ME, AND KNOWN ME"—all my thoughts and feelings.

He knows "my downsitting and mine uprising"—my every condition, posture, all the day long, even "my thought afar off" when it is just forming.

Jehovah knows (searchest, *ASV*) "my path and my lying down"—when I'm active and when I'm resting, all the time.

"There is not a word in my tongue" He doesn't know—my words, my deeds, even my thoughts, what is said and what is meant.

He is ever close to me, behind me and before me, thus His knowledge of me is complete.

This is wonderful knowledge—too wonderful to comprehend. It is too much for us mere mortals to understand God fully, but we do know enough to follow Him. And on we go.

Whither shall I go from thy Spirit?
or whither shall I flee from thy presence?
If I ascend up into heaven, thou art there:
if I make my bed in hell, behold, thou art there.
If I take the wings of the morning,
and dwell in the uttermost parts of the sea;
even there shall thy hand lead me,
and thy right hand shall hold me.—139:7-10.

The Omnipresence of God

"TELL ME," SAID A PHILOSOPHER, "Where is God?" "First tell me," said the other, "where He is not."

God's presence cannot be escaped, for He is Spirit. This is understandable. For instance, you can be on the road to a cherished gathering when a tire blows. While others are meeting, you are beside the road. But you are at the meeting in spirit. You see them. You shake their hands. You hear their voices. If finite man can be at a place in spirit when his body is absent, think how easy it is for the Eternal Spirit to be everywhere at the same time.

"If I ascend up into heaven," God is there.

"If I make my bed in hell" (*sheol*, the place of departed spirits), God is there.

"If I take the wings of the morning" and fly to the farthest parts of the sea, behold, God is there to lead me and to hold me.

On land or sea, above the earth, below the earth, day or night, God is with me. Anywhere, everywhere, God is there.

I know not where His islands lift
Their fronded palms in air;
I only know I cannot drift
Beyond His love and care.

If I say, Surely the darkness shall cover me;
even the night shall be light about me.
Yea, the darkness hideth not from thee;
but the night shineth as the day: the
darkness and the light are both alike to thee.—139:11,12

The Omnivision of God

IF I SHOULD THINK THAT I MIGHT ESCAPE God's sight by departing into darkness, "even the night shall be light about me." The darkness hides nothing from God. To Him, "the darkness and the light are both alike."

"A land which the Lord thy God careth for: the eyes of the Lord thy God are always upon it, from the beginning of the year even unto the end of the year" (Deuteronomy 11:12).

"The eyes of the Lord are in every place, beholding the evil and the good" (Proverbs 15:3).

The thought that God sees is a terror to the unsaved but a comfort to the redeemed. It is heartening to them to know that "the eyes of the Lord are upon the righteous" (I Peter 3:12). When we are in trouble, His eyes see and His hand stretches out to help.

My soul thou keepest,
Who never sleepest;
'Mid gloom the deepest
There's light above;
Thine eyes behold me,
Thine arms enfold me;
Thy word has told me
That God is love.

For thou hast possessed my reins: thou hast covered me in my mother's womb. I will praise thee; for I am, fearfully and wonderfully made: marvelous are thy works; and that my soul knoweth right well. My substance was not hid from thee when I was made in secret, and curiously wrought in the lowest parts of the earth.— 139: 13-15

The Omnipotence of God

GOD-MADE! The psalmist knew from whence he came, and that gave him peace and comfort. To not know leaves man in a disquieting quandary, robbed of a needed assurance.

Because of God's omnipotence, I can praise Him for my nature; "for I am fearfully and wonderfully made." I say, "Marvelous are thy works."

My substance or frame was not hidden from God when I was secretly made or conceived. Indeed, I was "curiously wrought" in a place beyond human observation.

One thing the Psalms especially emphasizes is that God made man. No matter how much we philosophize and conjecture, we finally have to get back to a First Cause, to the first verse in the Bible: "In the beginning God created the heaven and the earth." Herein is the mystery of creation explained.

One of the most common errors of mankind is a failure to ascribe almighty power to God. Understandably, it is hard for finite minds to fathom His infinite might. This prompted Jesus to say, "Ye do err, not knowing the Scriptures, nor the power of God" (Matthew 22:29). And, wanting us to learn, He included this praiseworthy and transforming thought in the Prayer of Example, Matthew 6:13: "For thine is the kingdom, and the power, and the glory, for ever. Amen."

As for the head of those that compass me about, let the mischief of their own lips cover them.—140:9

Reaping Their Own Mischief

OBVIOUSLY THE THREAT OF THE MISCHIEVOUS was severe; at least, David prayed about it. In the prayer, he requested that God "let the mischief of their own lips cover them." This is in keeping with what God does. He allows us to reap what we sow. He permits a person to fall into the pit he digs for another: "They have digged a pit before me, into the midst whereof they are fallen themselves" (57:6). And the Just One allows the mischief of lips to cover its perpetrator with disarray and defeat. The danger he designs against others becomes his own downfall.

We have seen this happen again and again. It makes us wonder why the mischievous can't see it.

It is the principle of reaping what is sown, a principle ordained of God and confirmed by nature.

The only way to change the reaping is to change the sowing. Now. On harvest day it is too late.

Incline not my heart to any evil thing,
to practice wicked works with men that work iniquity:
and let me not eat of their dainties.—141:4

Keep My Heart From Evil

IT WAS A TIME OF PERIL FOR DAVID. Peril again. Danger and death seemed to stalk David almost daily.

This time he and his men were as good as dead; their bones were at the mouth of the grave. But a plan emerged. By a crafty scheme, evil though it be, they could escape and their enemies would be destroyed. What would they do? Would the rightful end justify the dishonest means?

David would pray about it. Would he pray for forgiveness before committing the act of saving his life by wicked means? Or would he pray for strength to be pure no matter what?

Yes, in a wise perspective, he prayed for strength. He prayed, "Incline not my heart to any evil thing." This did not mean he thought God would push him into sin. But rather he prayed for God to help him stay out of tempting situations. He prayed for God to keep his heart strong and pure and not be drawn into evil.

We face the same dilemma. Our biographies read so much alike. That is because we are all humans. We all have been in a place when a small lie, a little sin would save us or a loved one from "dying" of embarrassment or disgrace. When it happens again, shall we have the courage of David?

Let the righteous smite me; it shall be a kindness:
and let him reprove me; it shall be an excellent oil,
which shall not break my head:
for yet my prayer also shall be in their calamities.—141:5

A Kind Kick

THE SMITING OR LICK SPOKEN OF IS REPROOF. The psalmist welcomed it from the righteous. They would give it in keeping with facts. And in the right spirit.

A person can hardly reject whatever is for his good. To profit from reproach, however, one must be humble and eager to improve. With these attitudes, reprimand is like oil poured on the head of a sufferer; it is a welcome cure.

Indeed, the intended kindness of the righteous reprover should be accepted profitably by the reproved. It should never provoke sullenness, anger and vengeance but rather an appreciation that manifests itself in the appropriation of it. It tells that one is wise.

> *Reprove not a scorner, lest he hate thee; rebuke a wise man, and he will love thee.*—PROVERBS 9:8

But the foolish harden themselves against censure and thereby destroy themselves:

> *He, that being often reproved hardeneth his neck, shall suddenly be destroyed, and that without remedy.*—PROVERBS 29:1

Therefore, let us welcome each reproof.

When their judges are overthrown in stony places, they shall hear my words; for they are sweet.—141:6

Then They Shall Hear

DAVID BELIEVED that when the unjust judges were overthrown, the people would hear his words. For his words would be pleasant, equitable and just, in contrast with the deceit and bitterness of evil men. It was his conviction that when the ringleaders who had been cruel persecutors of the people were hurled down, the rest would listen to godly instruction.

Calamity often opens hearts to receive teaching. In the midst of health and prosperity, there are those who have no disposition to listen. But when the storm strikes and they are left beaten and bruised amid the wreckage, they are more inclined to take heed. Standing there on the rubbish of disappointment and insecurity, stripped of haughtiness, arrogance and self-sufficiency, the aching heart is more receptive.

Joseph's brethren had to be brought low before they were ready to look up (Genesis 44:16).

Jonah had to be swallowed by the big fish before he would listen (Jonah 2,3).

Paul had to be struck blind before he could see (Acts 9:1-6).

Indeed, some people can never sail to a fairer land except on the vessel called *hardship*; for when they board the luxury liner, they head for the opposite port.

*I cried unto the Lord with my voice;
with my voice unto the Lord did I make my
supplication. . . .* —142:1-7

In the Cave He Prayed

THE TITLE OF THE PSALM STATES THIS OF DAVID: "A prayer when he was in the cave." David had fled to escape from Saul. And there he prayed. Feeling that he was forsaken by friends and pursued by enemies, he was left entirely to the mercy of God. It is interesting to note these points in the prayer:

- "I poured out my complaint before him." This is what prayer is. It is individual. Each pours out himself before the throne of God. His real self. There is no point in holding anything back, for God already knows.
- "They privily laid a snare for me." There are snares and entrapments out there. No question about it. This necessitates that we watch and pray lest we be overcome. This enables the victim to become the victor.
- "Refuge failed me." Try every human assurance and every material safety program, and then the weary conclusion is, "Refuge failed me." It is not to be found in materials. There is only one unfailing, protective refuge, and that is God.
- "Deliver me from my persecutors; for they are stronger than I." There are circumstances and people stronger than our bare selves; but with God in our corner, we are stronger than they.

This puts *A Psalm in My Heart.*

I looked on my right hand, and beheld,
but there was no man that would know me:
refuge failed me; no man cared for my soul.—142:4

No One Cares

WHEN DAVID LOOKED ABOUT for human assistance, there was no one to help. No person would even acknowledge knowing him. He was deserted in his trouble. The cave where he had fled was miserable quarters, but there was no other refuge. His sad comment was, "No man cared for my soul."

The word *soul,* used in the text, means *life.* No one sought to save his life. Nobody thought it was worth saving. If David could feel this way, then surely there are legions who feel this way now. No helping hand comes their way. No effort is made to ease their burdens, to enrich their lives.

In all fairness, not every person who thinks no one cares has sized up the matter correctly. Really, there are many who care though they have not been brought face to face with the person who feels otherwise. But each time the church meets, it prays for him. And many workers do go out seeking the lost and the helpless. There are public school teachers, Sunday School teachers, social workers, physicians, dentists, ministers, missionaries—many who care, each anxious to help in his own field.

Many care for you. But if no one on earth should, you can still make it because God cares and provided you care for yourself.

And enter not into judgment with thy servant: for in thy sight shall no man living be justified.—143:2

No One Is Justified

DAVID PRAYS THAT GOD WILL NOT DEAL with him on the basis of strict justice. He stated in another prayer that no one could stand if God marked—never forgave—sin against man:

> *If thou, Lord, shouldest mark iniquities, O Lord, who shall stand?*
> —130:3

Simply, the psalmist understood that he was a sinner; and as such, he would have to rely on the mercy and forgiveness of God. "For in thy sight shall no man living be justified" on his own merit. He is not so sinless as to be totally innocent and fully free of all blame. For one to plead that he is only marks him as being more perverse.

> *If I justify myself, mine own mouth shall condemn me: if I say, I am perfect, it shall also prove me perverse.*—JOB 9:20

However, in David's prayer he does not plead for God's favor on the basis of human perfection, but rather on the grounds of Divine mercy.

David's hope is our hope—the mercy of God. For if we get justice, we shall be forever doomed. But as the objects of Divine grace, we can be forgiven.

Rid me, and deliver me from the hand of strange children, whose mouth speaketh vanity, and their right hand is a right hand of falsehood: That our sons may be as plants grown up in their youth; that our daughters may be as corner stones, polished after the similitude of a palace: That our garners may be full, affording all manner of store; that our sheep may bring forth thousands and ten thousands in our streets. —144:11-14

A Golden Age

WE ALL DREAM OF A GOLDEN AGE of peace and prosperity. David prayed for it:

• That they be delivered from fierce enemies whose word is false and whose covenants are worthless.

• That their sons be permitted to grow up as plants. With nothing between the plant and heaven, it is free to reach toward the sun. Not restricted to the tents of war and the fields of battle, their sons could follow a life of personal freedom and development.

• That their daughters be as polished corner stones. That they be fair and beautiful like the ornaments on a palace.

• That their garners be full. That their fields yield an abundance of every sort of produce and grain.

• That their sheep and oxen multiply, which were essential to their national prosperity.

• That their property be safe and secure. No breaking in of the animals and no escape of them.

• That there be no complaining in the streets. No outcry, no clamor, no strife.

As David did, we should pray for it; and in keeping with our prayers, we should seek it.

Happy is that people, that is in such a case:
yea, happy is that people, whose God is the Lord.—144:15

Happy People

HAPPY OR BLESSED IS THE PEOPLE whose God is JEHOVAH, a people who worship and serve Him. The religion of God is designed to make happy people. It gives peace and quietude. God provides a hope that keeps us persevering. He teaches the principles of prosperity and happiness: work, diligence, thrift, love and goodwill. His way guards us from bitterness and strife, freeing our energies for a more productive life.

The good life is no accident. It is produced by a cause—God's directives.

The best security for any nation is adherence to God's plan. A remembrance of God has always prospered nations. The nations that forget Him are the ones that regress and destroy themselves. "The wicked shall be turned into hell, and all the nations that forget God" (9:17).

To be happy is one of the most prized personal and national goals. We all want to be happy. For some, it is even an obsession. Yet, where do most people and nations look for happiness? To God? Seldom.

Only a few know where real happiness comes from. It is not found in the pleasure palaces of the world. Genuine joy and happiness are found only in Jehovah our God.

One generation shall praise thy works to another, and shall declare thy mighty acts.—145:4

From Generation to Generation

HERE WE HAVE A SACRED CHARGE. This is a Divinely enforced duty: "The father to the children shall make known thy truth" (Isaiah 38:19). "And these words, which I command thee this day, shall be in thine heart: And thou shalt teach them diligently unto thy children" (Deuteronomy 6:6,7).

Handing down the praise of God from generation to generation is a sacred trust. Like a relay race, the torch of truth is given to another. One generation passes to the next one the store of accumulated knowledge and wisdom gathered by succeeding generations. We are the heirs of all the ages. And this makes us debtors to the past and especially to those who walked with God and transferred to us the knowledge of His ways.

As the older men and women declared to us a blessed knowledge of God, so we must do the same for the youngsters who reach out to us as our steps begin to tire.

This service is to be carried out individually by each family. What the home **is** usually determines what the children **become.**

What the parents spin the children must reel.
—GERMAN PROVERB

Parents have been given much, and of them much is required. They must not break the trust.

Happy is he that hath the God of Jacob for his help, whose hope is in the Lord his God.—146:5

God Our Help

IN THIS PSALM, GOD IS PRAISED as our only sure and adequate help.

Our trust in man (even in princes or government, verse 3) is sure to leave us shorthanded, for man's hand is too short to reach our deepest needs.

Oh, how disappointed
Is that poor man who hangs on princes' favors!

God is the only qualified Being, equipped with longevity, power, love and mercy to help us. While measures of trust in men are pleasant and essential, we find in God alone our soul's refuge and our heart's satisfaction.

Help! Help! Help! That's the common cry of man in trying circumstances the world over. It is a word that makes us brothers in adversity and ties us together with sympathy's cord.

As weak mortals we cannot answer all the calls for help, but there are many we can answer where a little assistance will give heart and a renewal of effort to the recipient. This we should do. This has ever been the heartfelt practice: "They helped every one his neighbor" (Isaiah 41:6).

He healeth the broken in heart,
and bindeth up their wounds.—147:3

God Heals Broken Hearts

IN ANOTHER OF THE HALLELUJAH PSALMS that begin and end the same way—"Praise ye the Lord"—the poet mentions a number of reasons for praising God; one of which is, "He healeth the broken in heart." Only those who have languished with broken hearts, eased by God's healing balm, can fully appreciate this as one of the most praiseworthy blessings.

Only the soul that knows the mighty grief
can know the mighty rapture.
—EDWIN MARKHAM

The text refers primarily to the healing God administered to those whose hearts were crushed and broken in their long captivity. He fortified their courage and dried their tears during their stay, and He gave them complete comfort by returning them to their native soil. However, this is a general characteristic of God; it is His nature to heal the brokenhearted among His people.

The Lord is nigh unto them that are of a broken heart.—34:18

When sorrow invades the mind, when trouble vexes the spirit, when the heart is saddened, we may turn to God for the remedy. Read His remedial, therapeutic Scriptures, filled with direction and promise. Trust Him. For there has never been a tear He could not dry nor an aching heart He could not heal.

Praise ye the Lord. Praise ye the Lord from the heavens: praise him in the heights. Praise ye him, all his angels.... Praise the Lord from the earth.... —148:1-14

Let All Creation Praise Him

IN THIS HALLELUJAH PSALM the poet is in a jubilant, exultant mood. The clouds have vanished. Sunshine beams on his path. Joy fills his heart, and praise graces his lips.

He calls for the whole universe to praise God: angels; inanimate objects; beasts, cattle, creeping things and flying fowl; all people: kings, princes, judges, "young men, and maidens; old men and children." All are to praise the Ever-existent First Cause who brought them into creation.

All the hills and mountains, rivers and valleys, trees and plants, beasts and fowl speak His praise. For He made them. Their very existence declares the glory of God. All creation shouts, "Praise ye the Lord."

But man, a creature of intelligence, must do more than breathe to laud God; he must praise his Maker from his heart, out of his own volition. And with a little reflection, this should come easily. So we in our own time and in our own way sing:

Praise the Lord, ye heav'ns adore Him!
Praise Him angels in the height;
Sun and moon rejoice before Him;
Praise Him, all ye stars of light.

—J. KEMPTHORNE

*For the Lord taketh pleasure in his people:
he will beautify the meek with salvation.*—149:4

Beautified With Salvation

IN ANOTHER HALLELUJAH PSALM the writer praised the Lord, among other things, for the beauty of salvation.

This is the beauty that cannot be matched by any outward appearance. It's the heart that makes the person attractive. True beauty is the best of all we know, not the physique or profile we see. And if "pretty is as pretty does," then the lovely spirited person is prepared to win all beauty contests.

The inward beauty is the real person, not the earthly house in which he or she lives a few fleeting years. It's the beauty that never ages but renews with vigor and attraction with the passing of every hour.

This is why outward "beauty is vain" (Proverbs 31:30) and why wise men through the centuries have placed the greatest value on internal appearance.

And if we could wave a wand and make all people beautiful, we would wave it on the inside of man. This is where God's Word works; and for each who receives it, God begins the beauty treatment. That person has no need to fear his or her appearance.

Praise ye the Lord.... Let every thing that hath breath praise the Lord. Praise ye the Lord.—150:1-6

Praise the Lord

THE LAST FIVE PSALMS ALL BEGIN AND END the same way—with praise! Hallelujah! This is a fitting ending to the wondrous, superb, popular book it concludes. With four grand words this book of inspiration and comfort closes: *Praise ye the Lord.*

In view of all the sacred volume discloses about God and man—God's power, man's frailty; God's eagerness to help, man's need of assistance—it is highly appropriate that the Book of Psalms ends with an expressive laudation of the majesty of God. After all it says about man's trials, conflicts, persecutions, bondages, temptations, sicknesses, disappointments, sorrows, sufferings, troubles, tears, defeats, steps of faith, glorious victories, overflowing joys and beckoning hopes—all that accompanied their chequered and eventful lives—it is proper that the Book of Psalms concludes with exuberant praise, rejoicings and hallelujahs.

The closing Psalm grandly rises from verse to verse to end in a grander climax: *Let everything that hath breath praise the Lord.*

Through every period of my life
Thy goodness I'll pursue;
And after death, in distant worlds,
The glorious theme renew.
Through all eternity to Thee
A joyful song I'll raise;
But, oh! eternity's too short
To utter all thy praise.

—JOSEPH ADDISON

Notes

Notes

Notes

Notes

Notes

Notes

Notes

Notes

Notes

Notes

Notes